BROKERED BOUNDARIES

BROKERED BOUNDARIES

CREATING IMMIGRANT IDENTITY IN ANTI-IMMIGRANT TIMES

DOUGLAS S. MASSEY AND MAGALY SÁNCHEZ R.

Russell Sage Foundation • New York

The Russell Sage Foundation

The Russell Sage Foundation, one of the oldest of America's general purpose foundations, was established in 1907 by Mrs. Margaret Olivia Sage for "the improvement of social and living conditions in the United States." The Foundation seeks to fulfill this mandate by fostering the development and dissemination of knowledge about the country's political, social, and economic problems. While the Foundation endeavors to assure the accuracy and objectivity of each book it publishes, the conclusions and interpretations in Russell Sage Foundation publications are those of the authors and not of the Foundation, its Trustees, or its staff. Publication by Russell Sage, therefore, does not imply Foundation endorsement.

Library of Congress Cataloging-in-Publication Data

Massey, Douglas S.
   Brokered boundaries : creating immigrant identity in anti-immigrant times / Douglas S. Massey & Magaly Sánchez R.
      p. cm.
   Includes bibliographical references and index.
   ISBN 978-0-87154-579-4 (alk. paper)
   1. United States—Emigration and immigration. 2. Immigrants—United States. 3. Assimilation (Sociology)—United States. 4. Identity (Psychology)—United States. I. Sánchez, Magaly. II. Title.
   JV6465.B657 2010
   305.9'069120973—dc22   2010004027

Text design by Suzanne Nichols.

RUSSELL SAGE FOUNDATION
112 East 64th Street, New York, New York 10065
10 9 8 7 6 5 4 3 2 1

═ Contents ═

⸺ About the Authors ⸺

Douglas S. Massey is Henry G. Bryant Professor of Sociology and Public Affairs at the Woodrow Wilson School.

Magaly Sánchez R. is senior researcher at the Office of Population Research at Princeton University.

= Preface =

A book of this length and complexity necessarily owes its existence to many people besides the authors. Our first debt of gratitude goes to Eric Wanner, president of the Russell Sage Foundation, whose faith in the project and extension of a presidential award to the investigators made data collection possible in the first place. We also thank our field workers, Karen A. Pren and Gabriela Portas, who collaborated with us in doing much of the interviewing. We likewise owe a debt of thanks to Irena Paola Cubides, who undertook the arduous task of transcribing the interview tapes to create machine-readable text files that could be entered into qualitative databases and subjected to systematic analysis; she also helped us a great deal by later going through the texts to remove identifying information so that the data could be made available to users via the Internet. Chang Chung and Karen Pren worked with us to create the qualitative and quantitative databases and make them publicly available through links to the Immigrant Identity Project on the websites of both the Mexican Migration Project and the Latin American Migration Project (see http://opr.princeton.edu/archive/iip/). Suzanne Nichols, the director of publications at the Russell Sage Foundation, was very helpful and encouraging in all stages of preparation and production, and two external reviewers offered detailed and very helpful comments on two separate drafts of the book. While we owe all of the foregoing people a great debt for making the book possible, we are most indebted to the many migrants we interviewed and interacted with in the course of our fieldwork. All of the textual material reproduced here was translated from the Spanish by Douglas Massey, with assistance from Magaly Sánchez R. on Portuguese texts. Our respondents and informants donated considerable time and effort to the project and freely shared their words and images to help us understand the construction of immigrant identity. It is to them and their future welfare in the United States that we dedicate this book.

═Chapter 1═

Constructing Immigrant Identity

Many Americans view assimilation as a one-way street whereby immigrants arrive in the United States with distinctive languages and cultures and over time steadily adopt American values, acquire American tastes and habits, make American acquaintances, move into American neighborhoods, and eventually come to think and act more like "Americans." Those born and reared abroad, of course, can never entirely shed the markers of a foreign upbringing, but second-generation immigrants born and raised in the United States experience its language, culture, and values firsthand and internalize its sensibilities as they grow up; American customs and values thus become a natural part of their identity. Eventually natives come to perceive the descendants of immigrants as "like us" and allow them to enter the intimate domains of American life, where not only schools and neighborhoods are shared but also friendship and ultimately kinship through marriage and parenthood, thereby creating the proverbial "melting pot."

This is a common idealization of assimilation, at any rate, and one that continues to hold sway among many Americans. According to a 2004 poll, 62 percent of Americans agreed that "the U.S. should be a country with a basic American culture and values that immigrants take on when they come here" (Kennedy School of Government 2009). In their eyes, no one forced immigrants to come to this country. Immigrants decided to come because they saw some benefit to living in the United States. By choosing to emigrate, they necessarily broke with their homeland and entered into an implicit agreement to accept the United States as they found it and to make the best of the life they encountered there. If any adjustments or adaptations were to be made, they were to be made by immigrants, not Americans or their institutions. For many Americans, it is the responsibility of immigrants to adapt to U.S. society as unobtrusively as possible, without imposing costs or inconveniences on

1

natives and without changing American life as it existed before their arrival. In short, immigrants are a "they" who need to become more like "us," not vice versa.

Unfortunately, as we shall see, immigrant assimilation is more complex than many Americans realize, and the process is shaped by the actions of natives as much as by immigrants' own actions. Assimilation is very much a two-way street. Welcoming attitudes and behaviors on the part of natives facilitate integration and serve to blur boundaries between groups, whereas hostile attitudes and actions retard integration and brighten intergroup boundaries. We argue that the emergence of an increasingly harsh context of reception in the United States in recent years has erected needless and counterproductive barriers to immigrant assimilation. Although Latin American immigrants arrive with high aspirations and an abiding faith in the American Dream, the longer they remain the more likely they are to experience exploitation and exclusion on the part of natives and, as a result, the less likely they are to see themselves as Americans. In today's hostile context of reception, in other words, we observe a negative process of assimilation in which the accumulation of discriminatory experiences over time steadily reinforces an emergent pan-ethnic "Latino" identity while promoting the formation of a new, reactive identity that explicitly rejects self-identification as "American."

Assimilation and Its Discontents

The canonical statement of immigration as a one-way street was set forth by Milton Gordon in his classic *Assimilation in American Life* (1964). He argued that assimilation involves an orderly passage through a series of three basic stages: acculturation, in which immigrants adopt the language and values of the host society; structural assimilation, wherein immigrants and their children enter into personal networks and social organizations dominated by natives; and finally marital assimilation, wherein the descendants of immigrants intermarry freely with native-born members of the host society. This scenario sees assimilation as an orderly, linear process, and for this reason it has sometimes been referred to as "straight-line assimilation." The process of assimilation may be faster in some groups than others, but in the end it is inevitable and always follows the same linear progression.

When Gordon was writing in the early 1960s, the United States was not really an immigrant society anymore. Although Americans may have self-consciously described themselves as a "nation of immigrants," by the middle of the twentieth century the United States was more accurately a "nation of the descendants of immigrants." Whereas millions of immigrants arrived in the United States during the late nineteenth and early twentieth centuries, over the next four decades immigration slowed to a comparative trickle, with the inflow dropping from an annual average of around 600,000 between 1880 and 1930 to just 185,000 annually between 1930 and 1970 (Massey 1995). As a result, by the time of the 1960 census, which Gordon used to support his arguments, some 80 percent of all Americans were descended from Europeans and only 5 percent had actually been born abroad, with around 11 percent being black and the remaining 4 percent Hispanic, Asian, or American Indian.

For the vast majority of Americans looking back on the experience of their ancestors from the viewpoint of the 1960s, the canonical expression of assimilation rang true. Their parents and grandparents had moved to the United States and left the "old country" behind. Although they may have encountered barriers, they persevered, moved forward through dint of hard work, and, assisted by a booming postwar economy, earned acceptance as Americans—or so it seemed. Besides adopting this rosy but selective reconstruction of past events, social research on immigration during the 1940s and 1950s was also filtered through a functionalist lens, which viewed assimilation as a logical, adaptive process of social integration inherent to modern industrial societies (Warner and Srole 1945). As a result, contemporary historical accounts read more like a hagiography of immigrants' triumphs than a careful piecing together of what actually happened (see, for example, Handlin 1951).

Even viewed through the selective lens of the 1960s, however, the canonical account of assimilation would have revealed obvious holes to anyone who looked carefully. First, even during the classic era from 1880 to 1930, immigrants did not really make a clean break with the old country and stake their future on America as they stepped off the boat (Nugent 1992; Wyman 1993). Most of the flows from Europe were characterized by extensive circulation back and forth, and as time progressed the circularity only increased (Hatton and Williamson 1994). Estimates suggest that at least one-third of all Polish and Italian immigrants ultimately returned to their home country, and as steamship travel became faster and cheaper, the rate eventually reached 50 percent in the decade before 1914 (Hatton and Williamson 1998). The only real exceptions to the dominant pattern of circularity were the ethnic and religious minorities who were escaping persecution at home—Jews from the Russian Pale, Irish from the Protestant Ascendancy, and Scots and Welsh from the English enclosure movement (Hechter 1975; Wyman 1993).

Second, even a cursory review of American history revealed that assimilation was not as inevitable and inexorable as the canonical account suggested. Indeed, the oldest "immigrant" group with the longest exposure to U.S. society—African Americans—obviously had not made a full transition to complete assimilation in the century and a half since the end of the slave trade. Although black Americans spoke English, many spoke a distinctive version with its own grammar, syntax, and diction (Baugh 1983). Moreover, despite overlap with the rest of American culture, African Americans continued to maintain their own distinct cultural forms (Mintz and Price 1992), and in the absence of social and residential integration, levels of black-white segregation were extreme and social networks isolated (Massey and Denton 1993). Not only was marriage between blacks and whites rare, but the act itself was illegal in many states (Wallenstein 2002). Obviously, then, under certain circumstances the canonical processes of assimilation did not proceed to their inevitable conclusion.

Finally, although their isolation and exclusion was nowhere near as severe as that of African Americans, white ethnic groups in the 1960s also reacted against the dominant ideology of Anglo assimilation, asserting that they had not blended completely into the American melting pot and had no wish to do so. In books such as *Beyond the Melting Pot* (Glazer and Moynihan 1963), *Why Can't They Be Like Us?* (Greeley 1971), and *The Rise of the Unmeltable Ethnics* (Novak 1972), the children and grandchildren of European immigrants began to emphasize the persistence rather than the disappearance of ethnicity in contemporary American society. By the 1970s, social scientists were emphasizing concepts such as emergent ethnicity (Yancey, Ericksen, and Juliani 1976) and reactive ethnicity (Ragin 1977) rather than assimilation, and rather than visualizing U.S. society as a melting pot, observers sought new metaphors to describe immigrant incorporation, such as the ethnic mosaic (Feagin and Feagin 1989), the ethnic salad bowl (D'Innocenzo and Sirefman 1992), and the ethnic quilt (Allen and Turner 1997).

Alternatives to Straight-Line Assimilation

As debates about assimilation swirled among the descendants of immigrants who had arrived before the 1920s, a new era of mass immigration was quietly and quite unexpectedly beginning. As new cohorts of non-European immigrants began to dominate the foreign-born population, doubts about the canonical account of assimilation became more pronounced. Whereas immigrants to the United States before 1930 were seen by people in the 1960s as overwhelmingly "white," after 1965 most Americans perceived the new immigrants as "dark" as source countries shifted to Latin America, Asia, the Caribbean, and sub-Saharan Africa. The fact that the post-1965 immigrants were phenotypically distinct and hence more visible than their predecessors immediately raised the question of whether their descendants would be able to assimilate to the same extent as the Europeans before them. By the 1990s, scholars were speaking not of assimilation, but of the Balkanization of America (Frey 1997) and its ethnic ghettoization (Borjas 1998).

Another important change in the years after the great European migrations was the considerably greater effort by the federal government to manage the size and composition of migratory inflows (Massey 1999). Before 1921, there were few qualitative and no quantitative limits on immigration to the United States (Zolberg 2006), but by the 1970s policies governing the entry of foreigners had become central in determining not only the odds of their coming but also the likely trajectory of their assimilation after arrival. First, legislation defined new criteria for admission that increasingly determined the endowments of human, social, financial, and cultural capital that different immigrant groups possessed. Second, the legal auspices of entry—whether immigrants came in as permanent residents, temporary workers, refugees, or undocumented migrants—determined the rights, privileges, and freedoms they enjoyed or lacked as they made their way forward.

Finally, the official warmth of the welcome varied from group to group depending on a combination of economic, political, and racial criteria. Immigrants from some countries, such as Cuba, were warmly welcomed for ideological reasons as allies in the Cold War. Immigrants from other nations, such as Koreans, were strongly encouraged to come by U.S. policies that favored skills and education. Some refugee populations, such as the Vietnamese, were grudgingly admitted because of perceived moral obligations or political debts, whereas other refugee groups—Salvadorans, for example—were barely tolerated because they had the misfortune of fleeing a right-wing rather than a left-wing regime. The least likely to receive an official welcome were undocumented migrants, who entered the country without authorization or violated the terms of a temporary visa to work or stay without permission—Mexicans were the most prominent example. The welcome was particularly hostile if the undocumented migrants were also black, as with Haitians.

Segmented Assimilation

Given different endowments of financial, social, and human capital among immigrants, as well as different official welcomes, different phenotypes, and different histories of migration and settlement, sociologists began to see the straight-line model of assimilation as a gross oversimplification. Herbert Gans (1992) pointed out that, even in the past, the pathway to assimilation was often "bumpy" rather than smooth. Alejandro Portes and his colleagues (Portes and Zhou 1993; Portes and Rumbaut 2006) went so far as to argue that assimilation was more accurately a "segmented" process in which pathways of adaptation and integration were systematically channeled in different directions depending on the characteristics of the immigrants, their history of immigration and settlement, and the nature of their official and unofficial welcome.

According to segmented assimilation theory, the characteristics of the immigrants themselves place them into one of three groups—workers, entrepreneurs, or professionals. Within each category, immigrants either arrive speaking English or do not, and depending on a group's particular history of migration and settlement, new arrivals either enter an established ethnic community or must somehow establish a beachhead in the receiving country. Upon arrival, moreover, immigrants may concentrate or disperse geographically, whether at the regional or neighborhood level. Finally, new immigrants enter in different legal categories—as legal immigrants, temporary workers, or undocumented migrants—that confer very different rights and privileges. Unofficially they may be perceived as members of the light-skinned majority or as part of the dark-skinned minority.

Depending on its standing with respect to all these variables, an immigrant group's path of assimilation tends to move upward or downward and to proceed rapidly or slowly (Portes and Rumbaut 2001, 2006). In general, those immigrants who are skilled, educated, English-speaking, and present in the country legally experience rapid upward mobility and easy assimilation into the American mainstream. The children of these immigrants enjoy consonant acculturation with their parents, adapting to life in the United States at the same pace as the immigrant generation and generally performing well in school and experiencing significant intergenerational mobility. In contrast, immigrants who are unskilled, poorly educated, and non-English-speaking are expected to experience significant barriers to upward mobility. They are more likely to follow a relatively slow path of assimilation and their children are at heightened risk of dissonant acculturation.

Dissonant acculturation occurs when immigrant children learn English and master American culture faster than their parents, thereby weakening parental authority. If the immigrant children are dark-skinned, lack documentation, and inhabit poor, minority neighborhoods, this loss of parental control through dissonant acculturation significantly increases their odds of downward mobility. Rather than assimilating into the middle, upper-middle, or even working class, dissonantly acculturated children may adopt a cultural stance in opposition to the mainstream—detaching from school, withdrawing from work, and integrating into the informal economy—essentially becoming part of the domestic urban underclass.

Segmented Labor Markets

The idea of segmentation is not new, of course, and the idea did not originate in studies of immigrants but in research on the structure and organization of labor markets (see Piore and Doeringer 1976; Tolbert, Horan, and Beck 1980). After much theoretical debate and empirical research, a consensus has emerged among social scientists that contemporary labor markets are not homogeneous but structured (for a review, see Massey et al. 1998). That is, labor markets do not comprise equivalent workers competing uniformly for similar jobs offered by identical employers. Instead, they are structured according to the characteristics of both the jobs and the workers. Rather than representing a single, homogeneous competitive arena, labor markets in advanced industrial societies are segmented into distinct sectors with very different patterns of organization and divergent opportunities (Dickens and Lang 1988).

The most fundamental segmentation is between primary and secondary labor markets; this bifurcation is intrinsic to the structure of advanced industrial societies and stems from the powerful consequences of economic dualism, hierarchical social organization, and contemporary demography (Piore 1979). Economic dualism refers to the fact that capital is a fixed factor of production that can be idled but not laid off, meaning that owners bear the costs of its unemployment. In contrast, labor is a variable factor of production that can be released by employers when demand falls, forcing workers to bear the costs of their own unemployment. To the extent possible, therefore, firm owners seek to identify the stable, permanent portion of demand and reserve it for the deployment of capital and attempt to meet the variable portion of demand by adding or subtracting labor.

Because capital-intensive methods are used to meet constant demand and labor-intensive methods are reserved for variable, fluctuating components of demand, a fundamental distinction arises between workers in the two sectors. Those in the capital-intensive primary sector enjoy access to stable, skilled jobs and work with advanced equipment. Because the jobs are often complicated and require considerable knowledge and experience to perform, a premium is placed on education and firm-specific human capital. Primary-sector workers tend to be unionized or highly professionalized and to work under contracts that require employers to bear a substantial share of the costs of their idling (in the form of severance pay and unemployment benefits). Because of these costs and obligations, workers in the primary sector become expensive to let go; they become more like capital. In the labor-intensive secondary sector, however, workers hold unstable, unskilled jobs from which they may be laid off at any time at little or no cost to the employer. They are a variable factor of production and thus expendable. There are few ladders of mobility and little long-term growth in earnings or occupational status. In this way, the inherent dualism between labor and capital yields a segmented labor market structure.

The effects of dualism are reinforced by structural inflation, which occurs because wages are determined not only by labor supply and demand but also by the hierarchies of status and prestige that characterize socially embedded labor markets. If employers seek to attract workers for unskilled jobs at the bottom of the occupational hierarchy, they cannot simply raise entry-level wages, because doing so would violate socially defined relationships between status and remuneration. As a result, if wages are increased at the bottom, strong social pressures arise to raise wages by corresponding amounts at other levels of the hierarchy, leading to structural inflation that greatly increases costs and threatens profitability.

Occupational hierarchies also have important implications for worker motivation since, as social beings, people work not only for income but also for the accumulation and maintenance of social status. Acute motivational problems arise at the bottom of any hierarchy because there is no status to be maintained at the bottom and there are few avenues for upward mobility. The problem is inescapable and structural because the bottom cannot be eliminated. There is always a bottom. Mechanization to eliminate the least desirable and lowest-skill jobs simply creates a new bottom tier.

The problems of motivation and structural inflation are inherent in modern occupational hierarchies, and together with economic dualism, they create a steady demand for workers who are willing to labor long hours under unpleasant conditions, at low wages, with great instability, and with little chance for advancement. The workers who fit this bill are those who view the job simply as a means to an economic end, not as a source of status, prestige, or personal satisfaction. In the past, this demand was met by three sets of people who are now in scarce supply in developed nations because of demographic trends: women, teenagers, and rural-to-urban migrants.

Historically, women worked up to the time of marriage or first birth, and to a lesser extent after their children left home, seeking to earn supplemental income for themselves and their families. Women endured low wages and instability not only because of patriarchal constraints but also because they viewed their work as transient and their earnings as supplemental and therefore not threatening to their main social status, which was grounded in the family. Likewise, teenagers historically worked to earn extra money, to gain experience, and to try out different occupational roles. With the expectation of getting better jobs in the future, teens did not view dead-end jobs as problematic and worked primarily to earn spending money that could provide them with clothes, cars, and consumer goods that enhanced their status among same-aged peers. Rural areas also used to provide industrial cities with a steady supply of low-wage workers. Movement from social and economic backwaters to the excitement of the city created a sense of upward mobility and personal improvement. Menial urban jobs provided in-migrants with access to housing, food, goods, and services that often constituted a real improvement compared with what was available in the impoverished countryside.

In contemporary developed societies, however, these historical sources of workers have disappeared because of powerful demographic shifts. Female labor force participation and the feminist revolution have transformed women's jobs into careers pursued for social status, and the rise in divorce rates has changed female jobs into a source of primary income support for women rather than a mere supplement to a husband's earnings. The decline in fertility rates associated with rising female education and labor force participation now produces small cohorts of teenagers who remain in school longer rather than enter the labor force. Finally, the full urbanization of society eliminated rural migrants as a source of unskilled workers.

It is the imbalance between the structural demand for entry-level workers and domestic supplies that generates the long-term demand for immigrants in developed societies. As a result, every developed country has now become a nation of immigration (Massey and Taylor 2004). Immigrants satisfy this structural demand because they typically begin as target earners—that is, they seek to earn money for a specific goal that will improve their status or well-being *at home*, such as building a house, paying for school, buying land, or acquiring consumer goods. Moreover, the contrast in living standards between developed and developing societies makes even low wages abroad appear generous by the standards of the home country. Although immigrants realize that a foreign job caries low status in the host society, at least initially they do not view themselves as being part of that society.

The problem for employers, of course, is that the longer their immigrant employees spend in the host country, the more they come to see themselves as members of the receiving society and participants in its system of status and prestige (Piore 1979). The longer they stay abroad, the more likely they are to shift their aspirations and goals from the home country to the United States and to seek a way out of the secondary labor market for themselves and especially their children. Meanwhile, the children of immigrants, having grown up in the United States and been socialized into its values, are just as put off as natives are by the low status and lousy working conditions of the secondary labor market, and so they are much more reluctant to take the dead-end jobs that were acceptable to their parents. Thus, the structural demand for unskilled labor persists over time despite immigration.

Immigrant Enclaves

Shifting from a job in the secondary sector to one in the primary sector is a difficult and daunting prospect for unskilled immigrants with limited English proficiency and low levels of education, and for those without legal documents it is virtually impossible. For unskilled or undocumented immigrants, such barriers to economic advancement yield feelings of frustration and exclusion. Whereas segmented assimilation into the underclass is one possible response to limited mobility prospects in the United States, another is the immigrant enclave. In their analysis of the process by which Cuban immigrants have been incorporated into the United States, Alejandro Portes and Robert Bach (1985) uncovered a third labor market sector that blends features of primary and secondary labor markets; they labeled this third sector the "ethnic enclave."

Like the secondary labor market, ethnic enclaves contain mostly low-status jobs that are routinely shunned by natives and characterized by low pay, instability, and unpleasant working conditions. Unlike the secondary labor market, however, the enclave provides immigrants, even those without documents, with significant economic opportunities and real returns to experience. Immigrant enclaves arise when mass immigration produces a geographically concentrated ethnic community that in-group entrepreneurs can exploit, either by catering to specialized ethnic tastes or by drawing on cultural and social capital within the enclave to gain privileged access to low-cost labor to produce goods and services for the wider market (Wilson and Martin 1982; Portes and Stepick 1993).

In the latter case, immigrants working in the enclave trade low wages and harsh conditions upon arrival for the chance of advancement and independence later on (Portes and Bach 1985). The implicit contract between employers and workers stems from the norms of ethnic solidarity (cultural capital) that suffuse the immigrant community (Portes and Manning 1986; Portes and Rumbaut 2006), while personal linkages to other entrepreneurs (social capital) are mobilized to launch new immigrants on independent careers in small business. Once established, new entrepreneurs are expected to promote other immigrants in return, creating an economic mobility ladder that would otherwise be lacking in the receiving society and providing a viable alternative to segmented assimilation.

Transnationalism

Another potential escape from the poverty trap of the secondary labor market is transnationalism—the channeling of one's hopes, dreams, efforts, and earnings into projects in the sending country. Whereas upward mobility may be blocked in the United States, the dollars earned there, although meager by American standards, still count for something at home and can be invested and spent in ways that bring real improvements in status and material well-being to migrants and their families. By financing mobility at home, menial wage labor offers immigrants the possibility of maintaining a positive identity and self-respect in the face of a U.S. experience characterized by grueling conditions, low status, and a constant threat of arrest and deportation.

Although by the 1980s circularity was visible in a variety of immigrant flows around the world, it was particularly salient among immigrants from the Americas, and nowhere was it more prominent than among Mexicans. The obvious circularity that characterizes much of the new immigration prompted theorists to hypothesize a new, transnational option for migrants seeking to construct identity and broker hard boundaries. This option reflects the reality of life in a globalizing market economy (Sassen 2007) and represents an example of "globalization from below"—ordinary people responding to profound structural shifts in the political economy by migrating internationally (Smith and Guarnizo 1998; Portes 1999). Over time, extensive movement back and forth across international boundaries produces a set of "transnational villages" (Kyle 2000; Levitt 2001) in which communities of origin and destination are linked together to form regular "transnational circuits" (Mahler 1995; Smith 2006) within which people move to create "transnational social spaces" (Pries 1999; Faist and Özveren 2004) and "transnational social fields" (Basch, Glick-Schiller, and Blanc-Szanton 1994; Levitt and Glick-Schiller 2004).

The processes that unfold within transnational social fields combine elements from both origin and destination areas but are not fully a part of either context. Instead, they constitute a hybrid and yield a social reality that is sui generis—meaningful and fully comprehensible only to the migrants themselves (Glick-Schiller, Basch, and Blanc-Szanton 1992). Some theorists posit that the resulting hybridization of cultures and identities (Ong 1999; Faist 2000) will ultimately challenge the monopoly of the nation-state on cultural production and identity formation (Basch, Glick-Schiller, and Blanc-Szanton 1994; Sassen 1996). Transnationalism thus offers another alternative to straight-line assimilation—a new kind of selective assimilation in which migrants do not abandon the language and culture of their homeland, but pick and choose strategically from sending and receiving societies in ways that advance their interests in both, often creating and sustaining new transnational identities and multinational cultures that incorporate disparate elements (Lie 1995; Smith 1997; Portes 1999; Kivisto 2002; Guarnizo, Portes, and Haller 2003; Portes and Rumbaut 2001, 2006; Kasinitz et al. 2008).

The interpersonal social structures that migrants create to overcome distance and facilitate circulation are generally labeled "transnational networks" (McKeown 2001; DiCarlo 2008), whereas the social organizations they construct are "transnational institutions" (Portes, Escobar, and Radford 2007). Together networks and institutions support the circulation not only of people but of money, ideas, and values, giving rise to financial remittances (Massey and Parrado 1994), social remittances (Levitt 1998), and cultural remittances (Flores 2008). Together, the arrival of financial, social, and cultural remittances systematically changes people and institutions, creating a "culture of migration" that supports international migration normatively (Massey and Kandel 2002).

The current wave of globalization and the accompanying rise of transnationalism are still relatively new, and many questions remain unanswered. Although the circulation of migrants and their social and financial remittances have been well documented in a variety of migratory systems (see Levitt and Jaworsky 2007), the long-term viability of transnationalism as a way of life remains an open question. It remains unclear, for example, whether current circulations of people, ideas, and funds will continue at the same rate as migrants accumulate time at places of destination, or whether they will persist at the same level into the second generation, or whether circulation by people of unauthorized status can survive internal arrests and tightened enforcement at the borders.

Assimilation as Boundary-Brokering

Despite discontent with assimilation theory, the proliferation of revisionist theories, and the recognition that assimilation can proceed faster or slower and go upward or downward, by the 1990s a scholarly consensus had emerged that the descendants of the European immigrants who arrived between 1880 and 1930 had in fact substantially integrated into American society (Alba and Nee 2003). As a result of widespread socioeconomic mobility and intermarriage, once-distinct European origins had blended together to form a single Euro-American "white" population within which ethnic identification was an "option" that was voluntary and contingent rather than involuntary and invariant (Waters 1990). Even religion had ceased to be a significant marker, since the increase in generations and the rise of education led to extensive intermarriage between Jews, Catholics, and Protestants (Sherkat 2003). For Richard Alba (1985, 1990), these trends were moving descendants of earlier generations of European immigrants into "the twilight of ethnicity."

Given this evidence of massive assimilation among Euro-Americans by the 1990s, but also evidence of segmentation and transnationalism among new immigrant arrivals, social scientists began to shift their focus to view assimilation not as a one-way process of immigrant accommodation, but as a two-way process of boundary negotiation carried out by immigrants and natives (Alba and Nee 2003). Assimilation occurred as group boundaries were crossed in a growing number of ways by a growing number of people moving in both directions. By sharing ties of friendship, kinship, and intermarriage as well as social and residential spaces, formerly "bright" dividing lines between immigrants and natives become "blurred," and social categories were reconfigured.

In this conceptualization of assimilation as boundary-blurring, the central theoretical task is specifying the conditions under which formerly impermeable boundaries come to be crossed with increasing frequency and ultimately blur to eliminate categorical divisions (Lamont 2000; Lamont and Molnar 2002; Tilly 2005; Zelizer and Tilly 2006). The associated empirical task is to model the process by which boundary-blurring occurs and to determine how various independent variables influence its frequency and pace (Alba and Nee 2003). Since power and resources tend to be skewed toward natives, another way of approaching the issue is to ask under what conditions natives do or do not take steps to maintain intergroup boundaries and enforce mechanisms of exclusion directed at immigrants and their descendants.

According to Alba (2009), the remarkable assimilation of European-origin groups in postwar American society was facilitated by a variety of factors, including the forty-year suspension of immigration from 1930 to 1970, the relative "whiteness" of Europeans despite their diverse national origins, and of course, the strong motivation of immigrants and their descendants to advance economically. By far the most important enabling factor identified by Alba, however, was the structural transformation of the American economy during the New Deal and the remarkable economic boom that unfolded after the Second World War, which together brought steadily rising incomes, declining inequality, and massive occupational mobility (Hout 1988; Danziger and Gottschalk 1995; Levy 1998).

Postwar economic growth was such that upward social mobility by second- and third-generation immigrants was "non-zero sum," in the sense that their progress did not come at the expense of existing white elites (Alba 2009). With the economic pie growing for all, the descendants of earlier northern and western European immigrants felt comfortable in relaxing the mechanisms of exclusion and exploitation directed at the descendants of more recently arrived southern and eastern Europeans. Barriers to the entry of Italians, Jews, and Poles into elite domains were gradually lowered, and discrimination in labor and housing markets waned, enabling these immigrant groups to achieve social contact, spatial proximity, and ultimately biological melding with people of British, German, and Scandinavian extraction, who in turn reconfigured their cognitive maps to identify the descendants of southern and eastern Europeans as true "Americans" who were de facto and de jure equals (Alba 2009).

Ultimately, then, assimilation is about the restructuring of group identities and the redefinition of social boundaries so that immigrants and their descendants are perceived and treated by natives as "us" rather than "them." From the perspective of natives, boundaries are blurred or brightened through psychological processes of *framing*, by which social actors in the host society attach positive or negative meanings to immigrants and their descendants and emphasize group differences (Kahneman and Tversky 2000), and socially through processes of *boundary work*, by which natives create mechanisms that either facilitate or inhibit interactions with persons of foreign origin and thus serve to incorporate or exclude them (see Gieryn 1983; Lamont and Molnar 2002).

In general, social actors who control more resources in society—those positioned at the top of the stratification system—have the upper hand in framing and boundary work. Whites, for example, have historically perpetuated negative stereotypes of African Americans as unintelligent, violent, and shiftless (Schuman et al. 1998) and devised a host of anti-black mechanisms of exclusion and discrimination to maintain social boundaries (Foner 1988; Massey and Denton 1993; Katznelson 2005). Within any system of stratification, people with power and authority are prone to undertake boundary work to define one or more out-groups and then frame them as lacking basic human attributes of warmth and competence, thus justifying their ongoing exploitation and exclusion (Tilly 1998; Massey 2007).

Throughout American history, a succession of immigrant groups have been subject to framing and boundary work done by natives to define them as undeserving and hence excludable (Higham 1955). In their time, the Irish, Chinese, Japanese, Italians, Poles, and eastern European Jews were all subject to harsh anti-immigrant campaigns that framed them as threats to American society and thus meriting the discrimination and exclusion inflicted on them. Immigrants naturally resisted these actions and engaged in their own framing and boundary work to position themselves favorably in the eyes of natives and ultimately to gain access to material resources, such as wealth and income, as well as to emotional resources, such as respect and esteem.

Fredrik Barth (1969) argues that ethnic identities are thus formed through a complex interaction between processes of ascription (negative framing and boundary work undertaken by natives) and processes of self-definition (positive framing and boundary work done by immigrants). Foreigners arrive with their own aspirations, motivations, and expectations about what the host society will be like. Over time, they learn about the stereotypes that natives have about their group. They embrace those that advance their interests in the host society and resist those that serve to justify their exploitation and exclusion. Through this two-way encounter, immigrants actively participate in the construction of their identity: they broker the boundaries to help define the content of their ethnicity in the host society, embracing some elements ascribed to them and rejecting others, while simultaneously experiencing the constraints and opportunities associated with their social status.

Through daily interactions with native citizens and host-country institutions, immigrants construct an understanding of the host country's identity system, gradually piecing together mental constructs of meaning and content for themselves (Barth 1981). Like all human beings, immigrants and natives have both group and individual identities, and membership in social categories plays a critical role in how people develop a sense of themselves as social beings (Tajfel and Turner 1979, 1986; Capozza and Brown 2000). Whenever two people interact, they engage one another not only as individuals but as representatives of the social groups to which they belong. In their interaction, they broker intergroup boundaries and through this process of brokering extract meaning to construct and modify identity on an ongoing basis.

Sociologists have theorized two basic processes of identify formation. *Emergent ethnicity* views ethnic identity as developing out of the "structural conditions characterizing American cities and the position of groups in American social structure"; the role of the analyst is to determine "under what conditions ethnic culture emerges" and "what social forces promote the crystallization and development of ethnic solidarity and identification" (Yancey, Ericksen, and Juliani 1976, 391). *Reactive ethnicity*, in contrast, views identity as "the product of confrontation with an adverse native mainstream and the rise of defensive identities and solidarities to counter it" in which "the discourses and self-images that it creates develop as a situational response to present realities" (Portes and Rumbaut 2001, 284). Reactive identities are rooted in shared perceptions of exclusion and exploitation that are spread through social networks extending transnationally through postmodern means of telecommunication such as the Internet, cell phones, and calling cards to create, under certain circumstances, powerful "resistance identities" that may become associated with specific political projects (Castells 2004).

In a sense, emergent ethnicity views identity formation as the cultivation of in-group solidarity, whereas reactive ethnicity sees identity as arising in opposition to rejection and exclusion by members of the host society. In this book, we focus on the expression of "American" and "Latino" identities among Latin American immigrants and draw on their words and images to discern the meanings and content ascribed to each category and to learn about the nature of the boundary between them. The key issue for us is determining whether the intergroup boundary is brightening or blurring and, relatedly, whether self-identification as Latino versus American is occurring emergently or reactively.

Bright Boundaries and Reactive Identities

Whatever labels a society imposes on immigrants, whatever boundaries natives erect to exclude them, and whatever meanings natives attach to people from different lands, immigrants nonetheless are always active agents in negotiating, constructing, and elaborating their own identities (Barth 1969). As they encounter actors and institutions in the receiving society and learn about the categorical boundaries maintained by natives, they *broker* those boundaries and try to influence the meaning and content of the social categories defined by those boundaries. We thus conceptualize immigrant assimilation as a process of boundary-brokering in which immigrants, encountering categorical boundaries that separate them from natives, do whatever they can to challenge, circumvent, or accommodate those divisions to advance their interests. We see three basic inputs into the process of boundary-brokering and identity formation.

First are the characteristics and motivations of the immigrants themselves—who they are, what they look like, the language they speak, their cultural beliefs, and most particularly what they are trying to achieve by migrating to the United States. Second are the characteristics and motivations of natives, with respect to both themselves and the newcomers—how secure they feel socially and economically, how they define themselves as an in-group, and the frames and boundaries they deploy to define and characterize immigrants as an out-group. Finally, the third input into boundary-brokering and identity formation is the daily encounter in a real-world setting—workplaces, schools, offices, stores, parks, and streets; both immigrants and natives broker these everyday interactions by means of competing frames and motivations from which both parties extract meaning.

In this book, we approach the construction of immigrant identity using this tripartite conceptualization and begin by outlining the characteristics, traits, motivations, and aspirations of the immigrants themselves. At present, Latin Americans constitute 35 percent of all legal immigrants to the United States and 80 percent of those present in the country without authorization (Passel and Cohn 2009). Given that Latin Americans constitute the largest single bloc of immigrants to the United States, are the principal target of contemporary anti-immigrant rhetoric, and not coincidentally are the group for which the authors have the greatest cultural knowledge and expertise, this book focuses on them.

In appendix A, we outline the strategy we used to compile a sample of 159 first- and second-generation Latin American immigrants living in the urban corridor running from New York through New Jersey to Philadelphia. We specified a quota design that called for recruiting roughly equal numbers of Mexicans, Central Americans, South Americans, and Caribbeans living in New York, New Jersey, and Philadelphia, divided evenly between males and females and first- and second-generation migrants. We then recruited respondents to fill these quotas by visiting streets, shops, restaurants, businesses, schools, and other settings that outwardly suggested the presence of Latin American immigrants. We spoke to those we recruited at considerable length, following a semistructured schedule that reviewed different facets of the immigrant experience and focused on issues related to identity.

These interviews were taped, transcribed, and coded to produce the data analyzed here. Those interested in the methodological details of data collection, coding, and analysis are invited to consult the appendices, but those who are more interested in the findings themselves can simply read the ensuing chapters with no loss. As described in appendix A, all information used in this book—both the transcribed qualitative interviews and the coded quantitative data—is publicly available to users for download from the website of the Latin American Migration Project (http://opr.princeton.edu/archive/iip).

In chapter 2, we introduce our informants to readers, describing their social, economic, and physical characteristics, their motives for migrating to the United States, and their long-term intentions with respect to settlement versus return. Our informants originated in fifteen countries from throughout Latin America. Most come from the middle strata of their home countries, and many, though not all, have access to significant human and social capital. Although the immigrants we interviewed are concentrated in the labor force ages (eighteen to sixty-four), the sample also includes younger and older immigrants. We spoke to males and females, people with and without documents, and members of the first, second, and "1.5" generations (those who were born abroad and arrived in the United States as children). Our respondents include persons of mixed European and indigenous ancestry, but also people with antecedents originating in Africa and Asia, yielding a diversity of phenotypes and skin tones ranging from very light to very dark.

Although the large majority of our respondents were gainfully employed at the time of the interview, not everyone had come to the United States for economic reasons. Indeed, some did not want to come at all and were compelled to leave their home country for family reasons. Others had had no plans to emigrate until people in their social network induced them to go; a few people left to escape domestic or civil violence. Even those who had left for economic reasons offered a diversity of rationales for their departure. Some came to achieve economic mobility in the United States; others sought to finance economic mobility at home;

and still others left home because an unanticipated event had created an urgent need for income. Relatively few first-generation respondents were fully committed to life and mobility in the United States, and a majority expressed a desire ultimately to return home.

Having considered what our respondents bring to the brokering of boundaries in the United States, in chapter 3 we consider the reception they faced upon arrival. Because a critical determinant of natives' willingness to abandon mechanisms of exclusion and allow boundaries to blur is the health of the U.S. economy, we begin by considering economic trends. As of 2009, the U.S. economy is far removed from the non-zero-sum configuration that is most conducive to boundary-blurring and assimilation. Between 1968 and 2008, income inequality rose and the economic fortunes of the lower, middle, and upper classes diverged. In response, most American households put themselves at serious risk of insolvency in the event of a loss of income by taking on debt, drawing down savings, and accumulating rising interest payments. The illness or injury of a breadwinner became a particular threat as the rate of health insurance coverage eroded. These trends came to a head in the economic meltdown of 2008 through 2009, when the economy shrank, joblessness surged, and bankruptcies rose to record levels despite congressional efforts to tighten bankruptcy law. In response, during 2009 consumer confidence dipped to record low levels.

The deterioration of economic conditions in the United States was accompanied by a new framing of Latino immigrants as a threat to American society. After 1965, avenues for legal immigration from Latin America were progressively closed off, leading to a rise in unauthorized migration that enabled a framing of Latino immigrants as "illegal" and thus threatening. Martial metaphors were increasingly used to depict Latino immigration as a hostile "invasion" of "aliens" that threatened to "overrun" the "defenses" at the border and achieve the "conquest" of the United States. The events of September 11, 2001, only exacerbated the negative framing of immigrants, enabling propagandists to portray them not just as criminals or hostile invaders but as dangerous terrorists. The deteriorating economy and rise in anti-immigrant rhetoric combined to create a climate of public opinion in which politicians felt compelled to implement harsh, restrictive, and increasingly repressive policies against foreigners, legal as well as illegal.

In the remainder of the book, we consider how the emergence of such a hostile context of reception affects our first- and second-generation Latino respondents as they navigate daily life in the urban Northeast. Given that the initial point of contact between immigrants and natives occurs in the labor market, in chapter 4 we begin our substantive analysis of boundary-brokering by considering the comments of respondents about their U.S. work experiences. What they describe is a world of unstable jobs that offer low wages for hard work under stressful conditions and exploitive terms of employment, with employers taking advantage of their status as stigmatized, undocumented minorities without legal rights. Labor subcontracting arrangements, which open the door to numerous violations of tax, labor, safety, and health regulations, are common. Most respondents are paid in cash with no benefits and in those few instances where taxes are deducted, the respondents have no idea how much money has been withheld or for what purposes. They receive no formal accounting of either pay or deductions, and most do not expect to see the money again or to receive any concrete benefits in return.

A few respondents with significant educational achievements, strong English-language skills, and, perhaps most importantly, legal documentation were able to attain stable, well-paying jobs in the primary labor market. A few undocumented migrants reported decent treatment and mobility in the secondary sector, and a few others were able to advance economically through individual entrepreneurship. The large majority of undocumented workers, however, have simply cycled through an endless series of dead-end jobs with little hope of improving their status or income over time. The only practical way to raise income for most respondents is to increase their hours of work, but in many cases hours can grow so long that workers literally wear themselves out. Although respondents were proud of being hard workers and dedicated employees and rarely volunteered complaints about their circumstances, they did perceive rampant inequalities in the world of work around them and had few illusions about getting very far ahead in American society. These narrative reports are confirmed by quantitative analyses of coded interview data.

In chapter 5, we show how these negative experiences primed respondents for disillusionment and disappointment in the United States. They arrived holding fast to the dream of America as a land of opportunity and equality that would offer abundant opportunities for work at wages that would be high by the standards of their own countries. Although our respondents initially viewed opportunities as open and accessible, over time they came to appreciate and, more importantly, experience significant barriers to advancement. A majority of respondents said that inequality in the United States is the same or worse than in their home country, and 60 percent said that they had personally experienced or witnessed discrimination in the United States. Thus, over time, they increasingly came to see the United States as a place riven with categorical inequalities on the basis of race, gender, and legal status, and most told horror stories about their negative experiences in brokering the categorical boundaries they had encountered as they moved through American society. Statistical models once again confirm these qualitative reports.

As noted earlier, one potential escape from the poverty trap of the secondary labor market is transnationalism—the channeling of migrants' hopes, dreams, efforts, and earnings into projects in the sending country. In chapter 6, we confirm the existence of a vibrant transnationalism among our respondents—both the documented and the undocumented—that shows little sign of dissipating across the generations. Virtually all respondents (92 percent) communicated with friends and relatives in the sending country and regularly sent back "social remittances" by calling home to exchange ideas, information, concepts, and perceptions. Respondents found telephone conversations to be essential for maintaining emotional bonds to their friends and relatives abroad. The Internet, by enabling the rapid transmission of photographs and other mementos of family life, generally served as a complement to rather than a substitute for phone calls. Virtually no one relied on regular postal mail as a means of communication.

Although not quite as universal as social remittances, financial remittances were sent abroad by the large majority of migrants, with nearly 80 percent regularly remitting cash and 54 percent sending gifts and presents. Among those making such remittances, a majority sent funds at least once a month, and most sent a steady amount; one-quarter said that they regularly remitted between one-fifth and one-half of their earnings. The remittances, which were mainly sent via money orders, were generally viewed as a moral obligation; this social debt was usually not suspended until relatives at home no longer needed support or they had all died or moved to the United States. The bulk of the funds went to family maintenance, but some money was usually also directed to productive investments in order to advance the family's economic interests at home.

Transnational practices are thus an essential part of life for our respondents and a fundamental component of their identities. Detailed multivariate analyses suggest, moreover, that transnational practices are intrinsic to the immigrant experience itself, not a reaction to circumstances in the United States. We found no evidence that migrants respond to negative experiences or blocked mobility in the United States by intensifying contacts with friends and relatives abroad, increasing the frequency or amount of their remittances, or channeling funds toward more productive ends; nor do these transnational behaviors weaken appreciably with time spent in the United States or across the generations. The most we can say is that, as people become more socially integrated in the United States—acquiring documents and becoming fluent in English—they shift their remittances more toward consumption than investment, but even those who say they no longer plan to return home do not cease remitting, though the frequency and amount of the remittances do decline. In general, both social and financial remittances continue as long as there are close friends or relatives at home to receive them.

Both qualitative and quantitative data thus paint a decidedly mixed picture of boundary-brokering for Latin American immigrants in the United States. Most arrive with dreams of social or material advancement and initially perceive the United States as a land of opportunity. Over time, they encounter a harsh world of work and experience the indignities of prejudice, discrimination, and blocked opportunities, and most eventually come to see the United States as a place of inequality and racism. They experience the categorical boundaries imposed on them by the framing and boundary work undertaken by American natives. The dual reality of ongoing engagement and disillusion with the United States suggests a fundamental tension between American and Latino identities and yields a bright categorical boundary that Latin American immigrants must broker in their daily lives.

We explore this tension in chapter 7 by analyzing answers to questions we posed about the meaning and content assigned to the labels "Latino" and "American," which we discovered were expressed in emergent and reactive ways, respectively. Interview data revealed widespread adherence to a common Latino identity among our respondents, even those from Brazil. More than 80 percent perceived the existence of such an identity, and around three-quarters personally identified themselves as Latinos. As with transnationalism, a Latino identification appeared to be a fundamental and intrinsic component of immigrant identity that was relatively constant in its expression and did not depend on circumstances. Among our respondents, the perception of an emergent Latino identity seemed to be a global reality that is unrelated to individual perceptions, motivations, characteristics, or experiences. It unfolds automatically after arrival in the United States.

In contrast to the near-universal embrace of Latino identity, two-thirds of the immigrants in our sample explicitly rejected an American identity. Moreover, among the one-third who did report the adoption of an American identity, their adherence to it was contingent and highly selective. Contrary to the predictions of classical assimilation theory, adopting an American identity grew progressively *less likely* the more time a migrant had spent in the United States. The likelihood of adopting an American identity was also negatively related to experiencing discrimination in the United States and to hours of labor. Thus, the more time migrants spent in the workplace—that is, the more knowledge they gained about exploitive conditions in the secondary labor market and the more they came to know and experience discrimination—the more likely they were explicitly to dis-identify as American.

The brightness of the categorical boundary between Latino and American identity came through clearly in the words of respondents.

When asked what made them feel Latino, respondents mentioned a strong attachment to the Spanish language, pride in being mestizo and having mixed racial roots, appreciation of Latin American food and music, self-reliance and hard work, and the willingness to persevere without complaints. They also reported a strong and palpable sense of solidarity among Latinos, one characterized by intense devotion to family, loyalty to friends, interest in helping others, and commitment to mutual support to achieve common goals. In terms of personality, respondents spoke of the warmth, spontaneity, joy, and passion expressed by Latinos, as evidenced by their love of banter and lively conversation, strong sense of humor, appreciation of colorful clothes and lively styles—as exemplified in salsa dancing and Latin music—and frequent expression of physical affection.

American identity, in contrast, was defined in polar opposite terms. Americans were seen as judgmental and rejecting, concerned with racial purity and suspicious of racial mixture, and cold, calculating, and hypercompetitive. American food was seen as bland and American music as uninspiring, and respondents mentioned a tendency of Americans to complain while making others do all the work. Americans were seen as excessively individualistic—always looking out for themselves and not devoting enough time and energy to friends or family. Respondents perceived them as having little respect for other people, especially members of the older generation and other authority figures, and lacking a sense of humor and playfulness. Americans were perceived as distant and dry in their interpersonal relations and hesitant to engage in playful banter, to touch one another, or to display physical affection in the form of kisses, hugs, and embraces.

These contrasting verbal descriptions of Latino and American identity were confirmed by an experiment in visual sociology in which we gave two disposable cameras to a subsample of respondents, labeling one "American" and the other "Latino." As explained in chapter 8, we then asked respondents to take pictures of things, people, or situations in their daily lives that, to them, seemed American or Latino. After developing the resulting photographs, we subjected them to a content analysis, which yielded a rather stark contrast in the themes and imagery associated with the two identities.

To depict American identity, respondents took pictures of skyscrapers and monumental buildings, public spaces devoid of people, cars and traffic, commercial symbols, signs announcing discounts and sales, discarded consumer goods stacked on sidewalks, and crumbling apartment houses. To a remarkable degree, the "American" photos focused on places and things rather than people, and there was a notable absence of facial close-ups among the photos. Judging from the photos, our respondents apparently viewed American identity as being about size and power, motion and haste, competition and individualism, impersonality and alienation, and barrenness and waste. The imagery seemed to convey the underlying moral that power, motion, commerce, and competition have produced a wealthy, monumental society, but have also squandered resources and dehumanized interpersonal relations.

In contrast, respondents portrayed Latino identity by taking pictures of people in different social settings, with many facial close-ups and many smiles. Common settings for these person-oriented pictures were work, home, and Hispanic businesses such as restaurants and shops. When not focused on people, the pictures tended to concentrate on Latin American cultural products and symbols. A few pictures depicted gang-related graffiti and displayed gang hand signals, suggesting the possibility of dissonant acculturation and its sequela of downward assimilation and oppositional identity. There were few of these photos, however, and on the whole the pictures suggested that the building blocks of Latino identity are work, home, family, friends, Hispanic business enterprises, and emblematic cultural products and symbols. In general, the photographic images offered by our respondents suggest the construction of Latino identity through social links and interpersonal networks experienced predominantly through face-to-face interactions with other immigrants.

In Chapter 9 we close by returning to our conceptualization of assimilation as a two-way street, on which integration is contingent on the actions and beliefs of both immigrants and natives, although natives do have greater power in determining the context of reception and the structural conditions that channel immigrant identification in reactive or integrative directions. We argue that public discourse and political actions in recent years have been counterproductive, serving to brighten intergroup boundaries, heighten categorical divisions, and discourage the crossing of social and psychological boundaries. Rather than facilitating assimilation, anti-immigrant rhetoric and boundary work have brought about a rejection of American identity by immigrants who otherwise are disposed to believe and follow the American dream. Although immigrants inevitably bear the lion's share of the burden in brokering categorical boundaries within the United States, we don't have to make it so difficult for them.

Immigrant Identity in Anti-Immigrant Times

In this chapter, we have argued that immigrant identity is not a primordial sentiment passed down through the ages or inherited from a "pure" national culture abroad, but a dynamic repertoire of practices, beliefs, and behaviors that are subject to constant readjustment and reorganization in response to changing circumstances. Immigrants do not arrive with a static identity and progressively shed it to adopt a new American identity over time. Instead, they arrive with their own dynamic tool kit of practices and beliefs, learn about the prevailing practices and beliefs in the host country, and then select those cultural elements from each repertoire that work best in trying to survive and prosper in the host society, often creating new beliefs and practices in the process. Natives respond either by accepting the immigrants and their innovations, and thus making it easy for them to cross boundaries and gain access to societal resources, or by rejecting them and making it hard for immigrants to accumulate resources and cross boundaries. Over time, this negotiation between immigrants and natives leads to boundaries that are either blurred or brightened.

For Latin American immigrants in the United States today, the processes of assimilation and identity formation are unfolding within a context characterized by an exceptional degree of anti-immigrant framing and immigrant-isolating boundary work. The tail wagging the dog is undocumented migration. Within the media and in political discourse, the line between legal and illegal immigrants is elided and foreigners are increasingly portrayed as criminals, invaders, and terrorists who threaten American society. As a result, the more time immigrants spend in the United States, the more they come to perceive themselves as subject to discrimination and exclusion. In this hostile context, immigrants from Latin America quickly embrace a Latino identity that emphasizes their common linguistic and cultural roots, but over time they increasingly adopt a reactive identity that explicitly rejects American identity.

At this point, of course, no one knows exactly how the assimilation of Latin American immigrants will unfold or what configuration their identities will ultimately take. Nonetheless, the boundaries between immigrants and mainstream American society are presently harder than they have been in generations. Whether in the coming years those boundaries are blurred or brightened remains to be seen, but from the immigrants' point of view the bright lines of today must still be brokered on a daily basis.

There are two schools of thought about where today's brokering will lead. A pessimistic school sees considerable potential for underclass formation owing to the rising prevalence of undocumented status, the ongoing racialization and demonization of Latinos in the media, and an increasingly hostile context of reception directed toward foreigners (Portes and Rumbaut 2001, 2006; Massey 2007; Telles and Ortiz 2008). By contrast, an optimistic school sees today's immigrants following the path of earlier generations of foreigners, who, despite experiencing prejudice, discrimination, and racialization, nonetheless managed to become incorporated into the American mainstream (Foner 2000; Alba and Nee

2003; Perlman 2005). Some of the optimists see particular potential in the impending retirement of baby boomers, which they hope will open up new positions throughout the occupational hierarchy and create a new round of non-zero-sum mobility for second- and third-generation immigrants (Myers 2007; Alba 2009). Although it is impossible to say with certainty which scenario will prevail in the future, perhaps the best place to begin an assessment is by listening to what the immigrants themselves have to say.

=Chapter 2=

Roots and Motivations

As argued in the last chapter, immigrants play an active role in constructing their own identities by brokering the social and psychological boundaries they encounter in the host society. A key input into the process of identity formation is what the immigrants bring with them to the United States—their traits and characteristics, their socioeconomic resources, and their motivations and aspirations. As described in appendix A, to learn about the process of identity construction we conducted in-depth interviews with Latin American immigrants living in the dense urban corridor that stretches south from New York through New Jersey and into Philadelphia. Here we describe the social and racial background of our respondents and describe their reasons for migrating to the United States.

Social Origins

We begin by considering the social, demographic, and economic characteristics of our respondents, which are presented by gender in table 2.1. As can be seen, the immigrants we spoke to were relatively evenly distributed by place of interview, with 36 percent each in Philadelphia and New Jersey and 28 percent in New York, a geographic distribution that did not vary much by gender. In terms of place of origin, the largest share of respondents, 25 percent, were of Mexican origin, compared with 27 percent from South America, 28 percent from the Caribbean, and 13 percent from Central America. South Americans were people from Argentina, Bolivia, Brazil, Colombia, Ecuador, Peru, and Venezuela. Central Americans were from El Salvador, Guatemala, Honduras, Nicaragua, and Panama, and Caribbeans were Dominicans and Puerto Ricans.

Respondents from Brazil were included because that country is a growing source of immigration to the Northeast, and it offers a diversity of racial and ethnic origins to shed light on the expression of race in the United States (see Margolis 1993; Goza 2004; Jouët-Pastré and Braga

2008). Puerto Ricans, though U.S. citizens by birth, were included because they were the first Latin American population to enter the region and are still among the largest origin groups. After they arrived in the northeastern United States during the late 1940s and 1950s, their migration slowly tapered off during the 1960s (Rivera-Batiz and Santiago 1996). They were followed by the Dominicans, whose migration began in the mid-1960s and peaked in the 1970s (Grasmuck and Pessar 1991). Mexican migration began in the late 1970s and grew rapidly in the 1980s and 1990s (Smith 2006), and Central and South Americans emigrated at roughly the same time (Cordero-Guzman, Smith, and Grosfoguel 2001).

At the time of our study, some 4.4 million Latinos lived in New York, New Jersey, and Pennsylvania; their origins were around 10 percent Mexican, 54 percent Caribbean, 6 percent Central American, and 10 percent South American (U.S. Bureau of the Census 2009). This tabulation overstates the share of Caribbeans in our target population, however, because a large share of Dominicans, and especially Puerto Ricans, were in the third generation. Among the 1.8 million foreign-born persons in the tri-state area, only 34 percent were Caribbean, compared with 15 percent Mexican, 17 percent Central American, and 34 percent South American.

Our sample clearly overrepresented Mexicans in the region, underrepresented South Americans and Caribbeans, and roughly approximated the relative share of Central Americans. Our goal, however, was not to create a representative sample but to capture the views of different national-origin groups. We focus particularly on Mexicans because they are the largest immigrant group in the United States, a rapidly growing population in the Northeast, and the most salient target of recent anti-immigrant propaganda.

Table 2.1 reveals notable differences in the distribution of national origins by gender, reflecting the varying propensity of men and women from different countries and regions to migrate internationally. Although overall the sample was 57 percent male and 43 percent female, Mexican origin was more heavily represented among males, whereas Caribbean origin predominated among females. As Marcela Cerrutti and I (Cerrutti and Massey 2001) have shown, Mexico is a patriarchal culture, and emigration from there is overwhelmingly led by males, principally adult household heads and older adolescents moving in search of work. In contrast, family patterns in the Caribbean are matrifocal, and women play more autonomous roles, both socially and economically (Massey, Fischer, and Capoferro 2006) . As a result, migration to the United States from Puerto Rico and the Dominican Republic is often led by females, who, like their male counterparts, move in search of work rather than to accompany male family members. Among males, 41 percent were from Mexico and just 19 percent were from the Caribbean, whereas among

Table 2.1   Characteristics of the Ethnographic Sample of First- and Second-Generation Latin American Immigrants in the New York–to–Philadelphia Urban Corridor

Characteristic	Females	Males	Total
Region of origin			
Mexico	26.5%	40.7%	34.6%
Central America	16.2	11.0	13.2
South America	23.5	29.7	27.1
Caribbean	33.8	18.7	25.2
Place of interview			
New York	26.5%	29.7%	28.3%
New Jersey	36.8	35.2	35.9
Philadelphia	36.8	35.2	35.9
Generation			
First	54.4%	81.3%	69.8%
Second	45.6	18.7	30.2
Legal status			
Documented	42.7%	30.8%	35.9%
Undocumented	36.8	55.0	47.2
Suspicious documents	17.7	12.1	14.5
Age			
Fourteen or younger	4.4%	2.2%	3.1%
Fifteen to nineteen	26.5	9.9	17.0
Twenty to thirty-nine	64.8	84.7	76.1
Forty or older	4.4	3.3	3.8
Average (years)	24.4	26.8	25.7
Years of schooling			
Zero to eleven	26.5%	27.5%	27.0%
Twelve	33.8	38.5	36.5
Thirteen to fifteen	25.0	18.7	21.4
Sixteen or more	13.2	11.0	11.9
Average (years)	11.6	11.8	11.7
U.S. occupation			
Not working	30.8%	17.5%	23.3%
Unskilled laborer	1.5	6.6	4.4
Unskilled services	35.3	33.0	34.0
Small business owner	8.8	5.5	6.9
Skilled services	11.8	29.7	22.0
Professional	11.8	7.7	9.4
Sample size (N)	68	91	159

Source: Immigrant Identity Project (Office of Population Research 2009).

females, 34 percent were from the Caribbean and 27 percent were from Mexico.

Males were more heavily concentrated in the peak labor force ages, with 85 percent reporting ages between twenty and thirty-nine. Women were also concentrated in the working ages, but not nearly to the same extent. Whereas 65 percent of our female respondents were age twenty to thirty-nine, 27 percent fell into the late teen years from fifteen to nineteen. As a result, males had a slightly older average age, 26.8 years, compared with 24.4 years for females.

Consistent with the preponderance of Mexican origin among men in the sample, males were also overwhelmingly in the first generation, and most lacked legal status. Some 81 percent of men were in the first generation, 55 percent had no documents, and 12 percent had documents of questionable validity. The last category included people who said that they possessed a legal document but could not clearly describe which document they held, or who reported having entered the country with a visa that did not allow work or long-term residence. In contrast, women were more evenly balanced between the first and second generations, as well as with respect to documentation. Among females in the sample, 54 percent were first-generation, and 46 percent were second-generation; just 37 percent lacked documents, and 18 percent reported suspicious documents. Across the entire sample, 70 percent of respondents were first-generation, and only 36 percent had valid documents.

The bottom two panels of table 2.1 summarize the human capital resources that our respondents had at their disposal to broker the categorical boundaries they encountered in American society. Educational levels were quite similar for males and females and ran the gamut from primary school to postgraduate studies. On average, both males and females had roughly twelve years of education each, meaning that the typical respondent was a high school graduate, but this average conceals substantial underlying variation. More than one-quarter of all respondents had not completed high school, whereas 34 percent of women and 39 percent of men were high school graduates, and some 25 percent of women and 19 percent of men had taken college courses. At the top end of the educational distribution, 13 percent of females and 11 percent of males had finished college or done postgraduate work.

A majority of both males and females were working at the time of the interview, but the share of females not working (31 percent) was almost double that of males (17.5 percent), mainly because of the larger share of females who were fifteen to nineteen years old and still in school. Among workers, both men and women were concentrated in unskilled services, with about one-third of each group falling into this category. Males were more likely to work as unskilled laborers (7 percent) or in skilled services (30 percent) compared with their female counterparts (with respective figures of 1.5 and 12 percent). Around 12 percent of females and 8 percent of males held professional-level occupations in the United States.

In summary, our respondents were by no means the most marginal or dispossessed, whether compared to American natives or to the inhabitants of their home countries. In general, our respondents came from the middle ranges of the class hierarchy, with a few from the lower reaches and a few from the upper reaches. The large majority had completed high school, many had some college under their belt, and a few had completed college. They were concentrated in the younger labor force ages, and most were productively engaged in work or attending school.

In meeting the challenge of creating and defending an identity in the United States, therefore, our respondents had significant class and human capital resources. The principal detriment to their brokering of categorical boundaries was their irregular legal status: a large majority of males and a clear majority of females were undocumented or had suspicious documents. For immigrants during a time when undocumented status is increasingly penalized by public policy, to lack bonafide documents is to be extremely vulnerable.

Racial Roots

Beyond class resources and legal status, the encounter between immigrants and U.S. natives is complicated by the contrasting conceptualizations of race north and south of the border. Within the United States, race historically has been defined by a rule of hypodescent: *one drop* of African blood defines one socially and legally as black (Higginbotham 1996; Fredrickson 2002; Packard 2002). In contrast, race in Latin America is generally conceived as a continuum that includes a range of different mixtures and categorical labels, each of which connotes subtle variations in color, class, and racial-ethnic origins (Wade 1997; Whitten and Torres 1998; Andrews 2004; Appelbaum, Macpherson, and Rosemblatt 2007). Although racial distinctions clearly exist in Latin America and race is an important stratifying variable there, the racial categories are multiple and the boundaries between them are typically blurred rather than bright (Telles 2004).

Rather than a one-drop rule, the prevailing ideology in Latin America is one of mestizaje, or mixture, and what differs from place to place is the nature of that mixture. For this reason, in our ethnographic sample we sought to compile information about the racial and ethnic origins of respondents. Given the racial-ethnic heterogeneity of the population, the likely selectivity of migration to the United States, and the continuing salience of race in American society, we developed two measures of racial-ethnic origins.

The first is skin tone, which, according to numerous studies, continues to influence the success and well-being of people in the United States, stratifying them socioeconomically (Herring, Keith, and Horton 2003; Telles and Murguia 1990), differentiating them residentially (Denton and Massey 1989; Massey and Denton 1992), and determining the likelihood that they will experience discrimination in various markets (Darity and Mason 1998; Ondrich, Stricker, and Yinger 1998). Early in our fieldwork, therefore, we worked to develop an interviewer-assessed skin tone scale.

In the absence of a spectrophotometer, the assessment of skin tone is necessarily an exercise in subjectivity. It was therefore critically important for field-workers to develop a common understanding of what is implied by labels such as "light" and "dark." Our initial attempts to categorize respondents used a tripartite division of complexion into a light-medium-dark continuum, but it quickly became apparent that this approach was analytically useless, since most interviewees were placed in the "medium" category. We considered borrowing the skin tone instrument developed by the New Immigrant Survey, which contains pictures of ten human hands with skin colors ranging from very dark to very light and asks interviewers to assign the number of the hand closest to the skin tone evinced by the respondent (see Massey and Martin 2003). A ten-category scale, however, proved too cumbersome: interviewers reported frustration at splitting hairs to adjudicate between scores of, say, 6 and 7, and often could not agree on the right classification.

After some trial and error, we settled on a categorical designation of five ordinal labels: light, medium light, medium, medium dark, and dark. In test classifications over a range of people, we found a high degree of consensus among field-workers about the meaning of these labels, and so we applied this scheme to all interviews in the survey. As shown in the top panel of table 2.2, the majority of our respondents fell into the segment of the continuum going from light to medium, as we might expect in a mestizo society. Across all immigrants, 32 percent were classified as light and 53 percent as medium, with 8 percent rated in between as medium light. Only 5 percent were rated as medium dark, and just 2 percent as dark.

There are, however, significant differences in the distribution of skin tone by region. At one end of the continuum are South Americans, who generally display the lightest complexions, and at the other end are Caribbeans, who are generally darkest. The Caribbean islands, of course, were originally colonized as plantations for the production of export commodities destined for European markets, yielding a mercantilist economic system that relied on massive inputs of slave labor imported from Africa (Fredrickson 2002). As a result, African roots are especially prominent in the Caribbean, both culturally and biologically. In our sample, 5 percent of Caribbean respondents were judged to be dark, and 13 per-

Table 2.2   Skin Tone and Racial-Ethnic Roots Exhibited by Latin American Immigrants from Different Regions

Characteristic	Mexicans	Caribbeans	Central Americans	South Americans	Total
Skin tone					
Light	23.6%	25.0%	19.1%	55.8%	32.1%
Medium light	7.3	7.5	19.1	4.7	8.2
Medium	65.5	50.0	57.1	37.2	52.8
Medium dark	1.8	12.5	4.8	2.3	5.0
Dark	1.8	5.0	0.0	0.0	1.9
Racial-ethnic roots					
African	7.2	92.5	52.4	30.2	40.9
European	81.8	97.5	95.2	93.0	90.6
Indigenous	98.2	90.0	100.0	93.0	95.0
Asian	9.1	2.5	9.5	7.0	6.9
Total (N)	55	40	21	43	159

Source: Immigrant Identity Project (Office of Population Research 2009).

cent were classified medium dark, compared with only 25 percent rated as light. This distribution probably understates the actual distribution of African origins in the region, however, since migration to the United States tends to be selective of lighter-skinned inhabitants, who are more likely to possess the class resources to effect an international move. Nonetheless, the distribution of skin tone among Caribbean respondents stands in stark contrast to that among immigrants from other regions.

Among South Americans, for example, *not a single respondent* was rated as dark, and only 2 percent were seen as medium dark, compared with 56 percent rated as light and 5 percent as medium light. Although Brazil has a very large Afro-origin population (Telles 2004), U.S. emigration is concentrated in the Southeast, a region of the country settled by Europeans that is still quite white (Goza 2004; Jouët-Pastré and Braga 2008). Similarly, although Venezuela, Colombia, Ecuador, and Peru have isolated populations of African slave descendants, immigrants generally do not come from these areas. Argentina is perhaps the most European of all nations in South America, having exterminated most of its indigenous inhabitants in the early nineteenth century and experienced little mestizaje; the country then actively sponsored European immigration during the late nineteenth and early twentieth centuries in a deliberate national program of "whitening." These factors combine to yield a decided skew in skin tone toward the lighter end of the color spectrum among Argentineans.

In general, Mexicans and Central Americans lie between the two extremes marked by South Americans and Caribbeans. Both areas experienced some importation of African slaves during the colonial era, and during the early twentieth century some Central America nations experienced black Caribbean migration to their eastern shores; in most nations, however, the African influence remains small and the prevailing mixture is between Europeans and American Indians. As a result, medium is the modal skin tone in both regions, accounting for 66 percent of all Mexicans and 57 percent of Central Americans. When this category is combined with medium light, the grouping encompasses around three-quarters of respondents in both cases.

Not only did Latin America experience extensive mixing among Indians, Africans, and Europeans, but several countries had significant immigration from Asia as well. Moreover, the arriving colonists from Spain were themselves of mixed origins, being the product of intermingling between Moors, Jews, and Christians. As a result, categorical distinctions in Latin America are based not only on skin tone but also on other phenotypical features such as hair texture, facial structure, eye shape, lip configuration, and other subtle markers.

A person's actual racial and ethnic origins, of course, are not always expressed outwardly. Indeed, a person's racial and ethnic roots may not be expressed in any obvious physical way. For example, one of our interviewees, a first-generation Peruvian male, was initially perceived as mestizo by the interviewer and rated with a skin tone of medium based on what was perceived to be a blend of European and indigenous features. In the course of the conversation, however, it emerged that the respondent had Chinese ancestry on his father's side and Japanese ancestry on his mother's, in addition to European and indigenous roots. Another respondent, a Colombian female, had light skin and features that appeared indigenous because of her high cheekbones, but it turned out that these could just as easily have come from her Lithuanian father as from her mestizo mother.

Thus, in addition to measuring skin tone, we also sought to discern the specific racial and ethnic roots of each respondent. In consultation with the respondents themselves, we identified their ancestral roots in Europe, Africa, pre-Columbian America, or Asia. Given the legacy of mestizaje in Latin America, these classifications are not, of course, mutually exclusive. Indeed, most respondents reported at least two and often three or four racial-ethnic origins, with the average number being 2.3. The distribution of respondents by ancestral roots is shown in the second panel of table 2.2. Owing to a common history of European colonization, there is very little variance in European origin by region. Across all origins, between 82 and 98 percent report at least some European roots. Likewise, given that colonization in Latin America everywhere involved miscegenation with indigenous peoples, 90 to 100 percent of all respondents claimed indigenous roots as well.

Relatively few respondents of any origin reported Asian roots—the proportion was always under 10 percent and ranged from 2.5 percent in the Caribbean to 9.5 percent in Central America. The greatest heterogeneity across regions occurred with respect to African origins. As expected, the prevalence of African roots was greatest in the Caribbean, at 93 percent. African ancestry was least frequent among Mexicans, only 7 percent of whom reported African roots. In between were South Americans at 30 percent and Central Americans at 52 percent. Thus, African origin is a critical variable that differentiates Latin Americans from one another.

To assess how racial and ethnic roots varied by region of origin and other background characteristics, we estimated a series of logit models that regressed dichotomous indicators of African roots, European roots, and indigenous roots on region of origin along with age, gender, generation, legal status, and social class as measured by education and parental occupation. To derive a continuous measure of occupational status and conserve degrees of freedom, we matched each of the occupational groups shown in table 2.1 with its associated international socioeconomic status index (from Ganzeboom and Treiman 1996). If the father's occupation was missing, we substituted the mother's index, but if that value was missing, the case was dropped from analysis.

In preliminary work we found that neither region nor any of the background characteristics significantly predicted having European or indigenous roots; this is not a surprising finding considering that the vast majority of all Latin Americans claim these origins. Asian roots also were not related to region of origin or background characteristics. What did vary substantially by region was the relative importance of African origins, as shown in the left-hand columns of table 2.3, which presents the model predicting the odds of having African roots. Our sample is not random, of course, so tests of significance do not indicate the likelihood that a coefficient is a result of sampling error. Nonetheless, here and elsewhere we report significance tests to provide a rough guide to the substantive importance of relevant variables.

As already noted, the roots that truly differentiate Latin Americans from one another are those leading to Africa. Compared with Mexicans, immigrants from the Caribbean are far more likely to report African roots, followed by Central Americans and then South Americans. As the model indicates, the significant concentration of African roots in the Caribbean cannot be attributed to cross-regional differences in age, gender, generation, or socioeconomic status, since these variables are held constant in the model.

Table 2.3   Logit Regression Predicting African Roots from the Region of Origin, Controlling for Demographic Background and Social-Class Origins

Predictors	African Roots		Darkness of Skin Tone	
	Regression Coefficient	Standard Error	Regression Coefficient	Standard Error
Racial-ethnic roots				
African	—	—	1.709***	0.484
European	—	—	−2.378***	0.654
Indigenous	—	—	2.807*	1.294
Region of origin				
Mexico	—	—	—	—
Caribbean	5.000***	0.937	−1.215+	0.665
Central America	2.674***	0.736	−0.669	0.554
South America	1.587**	0.661	−1.819***	0.498
Demographics				
Age	0.097*	0.043	0.022	0.033
Male	−0.267	0.495	0.234	0.383
Generation				
First generation	—	—	—	—
Second generation	0.713	0.683	−0.539	0.498
Legal status				
Documented	−0.176	0.610	1.095*	0.472
Class origins				
Years of schooling	−0.003	0.021	−0.020	0.014
Parental International Socioeconomic Index	−0.011	0.016	−0.001	0.012
Intercepts	−4.527***	1.674	0.054	1.860
			0.529	1.864
			4.213*	1.878
			5.693**	1.940
Log-likelihood	−60.334***		−143.080***	
Pseudo-R-squared	0.397***		0.151	
Sample size (N)	147		147	

Source: Immigrant Identity Project (Office of Population Research 2009).
+p < .10; *p < .05; **p < .01; ***p < .001

In the right-hand columns of table 2.3, we estimate an ordered logit model of the association between region and skin tone, controlling for racial and ethnic roots, demographic background, generation, legal status, and class origins. As can be seen, once a person's roots are held constant, interregional differences in skin tone are muted. Indeed, the strong association between darker skin tone and Caribbean origins not only goes away but is reversed and almost achieves significance. As we have argued, therefore, it is the prevalence of people with African roots in the region that explains the darker complexion of Caribbean immigrants. Holding constant a person's roots, only South America stands out from other regions in terms of skin tone. Irrespective of the specific roots of South American immigrants, their skin tone tends to be much lighter than that of immigrants from other regions. Although indigenous origins also predict darker skin tone, the effect is not as strong or as significant as that of African roots.

In sum, simple categorizations and multivariate analyses both confirm the diversity of racial and ethnic roots, skin tone, and phenotype among immigrants from Mexico, Central America, South America, and the Caribbean. Among our respondents, skin tone runs the gamut from light to dark and varies systematically by region, with immigrants from South America displaying the lightest complexions, those from the Caribbean the darkest, and those from Mexico and Central America the tones in between. If we assign ordinal values to the five skin tone categories, such that 1 corresponds to light and 5 to dark, then Mexicans and Central Americans both have an average of 2.5, compared with 1.9 for South Americans and 2.7 for Caribbeans. This variation is explained mostly by the relative prevalence of African roots in different regions. Although having European roots is strongly associated with lighter skin tone, European origins are so common across all regions that they do not account for cross-national variation in skin tone.

Classifying Immigrant Motivations

The foregoing results suggest that many Latino immigrants have to deal somehow with the framing and boundary work by natives who seek to position them in the nonwhite realm of American social space. To the extent that racial formation occurs along a black-white divide in the United States, skin tone carries obvious consequences within the American stratification system (Omi and Winant 1986; Winant 2002; Massey 2007). As we have argued, however, whatever their apparent skin tone and phenotype, immigrants are still active agents in brokering the boundaries they encounter, and the content of their identity also depends greatly on their motivations for coming to the United States.

If the ultimate goal of immigrants is to settle permanently and advance socioeconomically in the United States, then they have a strong incentive to challenge racist frames and exclusionary practices and to engage in boundary work to overcome categorical barriers to achieving acceptance and mobility. If, on the other hand, they seek only to work in the United States temporarily in order to earn money in anticipation of an eventual return home, then the path of least resistance may be to tolerate exploitation and marginalization in the short run in return for the opportunity to accumulate savings and repatriate earnings in the longer term.

Our interview schedule asked immigrants what made them want to come to the United States in the first place. This open-ended question yielded a wide variety of responses and extended reflections about the motivation to pull up stakes and strike out northward. Many factors bear upon the decision to come to the United States. Obviously, average incomes and wages are lower in Latin America than in the United States, and rates of unemployment and underemployment are higher, yielding significantly lower expected wages and significantly lower lifetime earnings in every Latin American nation compared with the United States. Such a persistent earnings gap would predict sustained south-north migration under neoclassical economic assumptions (Todaro and Maruszko 1987).

Although the size of this gap has fluctuated historically, at any given time it is large enough to be almost a constant from the perspective of individual decisionmakers. No matter what epoch we consider, expected lifetime earnings are always much greater in the United States than south of the border, yet movement between Latin America and the United States has varied dramatically over time and with markedly different trajectories in different countries (Durand and Massey, forthcoming). Moreover, historical variation in the size of the earnings gap is not strongly associated with fluctuations in the rate of migration northward, suggesting the need to move beyond simple wage differentials to account for the dynamics of international movement (Massey, Arango, et al. 1994).

What has changed markedly over time in Latin America is the structure of its political economy (Massey, Sánchez, and Behrman 2006). Up through the 1980s, economies in the region were guided by the philosophy of import substitution industrialization (ISI), which held that economic development is best achieved through a set of deliberate government interventions to create internal markets. These interventions included tariffs, import quotas, and restrictions on capital mobility as well as the targeted investment of public funds through government financial agencies, state-owned firms, and special subsidies to private producers (Bharat-Ram 1994). After 1982, however, a series of economic crises swept through the region, bringing about conditions of hyperinflation, falling employment, declining production, and stagnating wages and living standards; for people throughout the region the 1980s became known as "the lost decade" (Fiscia and Kovacs 1994).

The failure of ISI to sustain growth and prosperity cleared the way for the imposition of an alternative, "neoliberal" model of economic development based on a strategy of export industrialization. The neoliberal approach lowered tariffs, eliminated quotas, ended restrictions on capital mobility, privatized state-owned firms, downsized government, and generally opened nations to global trade and investment, a package of policies that came to be known as "the Washington Consensus" (Williamson 1990, 2000). The structural shift from ISI to neoliberalism proved to be a wrenching adjustment for most Latin Americans, bringing about additional job displacement, further declines in real wages, and costlier commodities that led to rising income inequality, declining living standards, and increasingly bleak prospects for socioeconomic mobility (Portes 1997; Portes and Hoffman 2003; Cohen and Centeno 2006). The structural shift has been linked to the onset of mass international migration in some nations (Massey and Capoferro 2006) and regions (Massey, Kalter, and Pren 2008). As economic conditions deteriorated, levels of crime and violence also rose in many quarters, and that trend, in turn, increased the propensity for out-migration, at least in some countries (Lundquist and Massey 2005; Sánchez 2006; Alvarado and Massey, forthcoming).

The consolidation of neoliberal reforms throughout Latin America in the 1990s coincided with a sustained economic boom in the United States that produced record low levels of unemployment, tight labor markets, and rising wages throughout the country. Although the United States tightened immigration policies and accelerated border enforcement—especially after 1993—American authorities suspended internal enforcement during the late 1990s in response to complaints from employers (Massey, Durand, and Malone 2002). As a result, undocumented immigrants flooded into the country, not just to traditional receiving areas but to a plethora of new destinations as well (Hernández León and Zúñiga 2005; Massey 2008). At the same time, the increased costs and risks of undocumented border crossing promoted longer trips, lower rates of return migration, and higher probabilities of settlement (Durand and Massey 2004).

Falling wages, rising unemployment, and dimming mobility in Latin America (Cohen and Centeno 2006) coincided with a surge in labor demand and rising productivity in the United States, yielding an economic boom known as "the roaring nineties" (Krueger and Solow 2002; Stiglitz 2003), and new links arose to connect regions of labor supply and demand (Massey et al. 1998). Globalization itself produced new transportation and communication links that made movement between periphery and core cheaper, faster, and more reliable (Sassen 1988, 1991), and once people began moving in significant numbers, interpersonal networks formed to provide an expanding social infrastructure that encouraged additional migration (Massey 1990), yielding a positive feedback loop wherein international migration expanded migratory networks that, in turn, facilitated additional migration (Massey et al. 1987; Massey, Goldring, and Durand 1994; Massey and Zenteno 1999).

Thus, the coincidence of structural adjustment in the south, an unprecedented economic boom in the north, and proliferating networks in between yielded a "perfect storm" for migration between Latin America and the United States during the 1990s. Not all people moving internationally during this period, however, used networks instrumentally as a way of adapting to displacements at home. Some of those who departed for the United States—spouses, younger children, and older dependents—simply tagged along with migrating workers, moving for reasons of family reunification or to end a period of enforced separation (see, for example, Aysa and Massey 2004; Cerrutti and Massey 2001).

A review of the literature thus suggests five basic categories of motivation for international migration: economic conditions at origin, economic conditions at destination, network connections, violence at origin, and family reunification. We carefully read through the answers to our general query ("What made you want to come to the United States?") and classified the motivations for migration into one of six mutually exclusive categories, five pertaining to the five categories of motivation plus a sixth residual "other" category. Although respondents could and did mention multiple factors in describing their decision to leave, we coded responses according to what we perceived to be the dominant motivation as indicated by the frequency of mentions or the relative emphasis given by the respondent.

The results of this coding exercise appear in the top panel of table 2.4, which reveals the motivations for migration expressed by those in our sample who were born abroad. The last column shows the distribution for the sample as a whole and shows a fairly even distribution of motivations across four of the six categories. Violence in the country of origin—both in and outside of the home—figured prominently in just 3 percent of the cases, though it was more commonly expressed by women (6 percent) than by men (1 percent). Likewise, the mobilization of network ties either by the migrants themselves (Massey et al. 1987) or by friends and relatives in the United States (Bashi 2007) provided the motivation in just 13 percent of the cases, but more commonly among men (19 percent) than among women (4 percent). All of the other categories—origin economic conditions, destination economic circumstances, family reasons, and other reasons—varied quite narrowly in the frequency range of 20 to 22 percent. Across these categories, the main difference between men and women was that females were slightly more likely to give family reasons (25 percent) as a motivation compared with origin or destination circumstances (17 percent each).

Table 2.4   Motivations for Migration, by Gender, Among Latin American Immigrants to the United States

Variable	Females	Males	Total
Motivation for migration			
Economic conditions at origin	17.0%	22.5%	20.3%
Opportunities at destination	17.0	22.5	20.3
Network links	3.8	18.8	12.8
Violence at origin	5.7	1.3	3.0
Family reasons	24.5	20.0	21.8
Other	32.1	15.0	21.8
Settlement intentions			
Intends to return	47.2	42.5	44.4
Intends to stay	34.4	27.5	32.1
Doesn't know	18.9	30.2	25.6
Total born abroad (N)	53	80	133

Source: Immigrant Identity Project (Office of Population Research 2009).

Expressing Immigrant Motivations

In describing conditions in their countries and communities of origin, respondents were often quite blunt about the economic problems they faced. One male respondent, for example, when queried about his reasons for coming to the United States, said flatly that "the Mexican economy does nothing." When asked to elaborate, he said that in Mexico "one earns little and cannot seem to give oneself the pleasure of doing well, with nice clothes, clean pants—not only clean but brand-new pants—like that, you know? Because there isn't any money."

Another Mexican who headed north with a friend said, "We were both flat broke economically, really, so we had to come here," and a Guatemalan female attributed her departure simply to "the economic situation in my country," citing the need "to have a little more money to help my family." A Honduran male candidly opined that "the truth is that in my country I work, but there are hardly any jobs, and those that exist are very badly paid. There one does not earn enough to get ahead—just enough to get by if nothing bad happens—barely enough for food. These are the things there that motivate one to come, to migrate here, to the United States." A Honduran woman noted that poverty was a motivator for action: "My parents were always very poor, and for me poverty was good up to a certain point, as poverty made me long for not suffering hunger."

Generalizing from his own experiences and those of his friends, one undocumented male migrant from Guatemala went on at some length about his poor economic prospects at home, telling us that

I consider that this is a very special topic in which I not only speak for myself but also for all the other immigrants who come here to this country for economic reasons: economic scarcity, lack of jobs, the devaluation of the currency in different parts of the world. Then we look at the situation and consider it and see the dollar not as a god but as a source of energy to support our communities, our people, and our families more than anything, and also for personal ends.

Another respondent, a Dominican male from New York, agreed, saying that at home "I had little more than a position and an income. I can still have the position and income, but I don't see anything from them, or rather nothing is left to me."

Often it was a misfortune of some kind that pushed people over the edge financially and made their material needs so acute that they turned to international migration as a solution to the economic pressures they faced. One of the most common misfortunes was a medical emergency. As one Mexican woman said, "Because down there . . . the children get sick and there is no money to take care of them, or rather the little girls I have got sick, and we did not have the money to bring them to a doctor. It is very difficult there—to have a family is very difficult. So my husband decided to come here, and later on he brought me." Another Mexican woman described a similar experience, saying that she migrated

> because one of my sisters got sick. She was very ill and spent, like, two months in the hospital, and they charged my mom fifteen thousand pesos, and she did not have the money to pay the bill to get herself out, so she took out a loan to obtain her release and ended up owing a lot of money. So I said to my sister [in the United States] that she should help me come up, and so we set to work and paid off the loan that my sister extended to get us here, and now we are sending Mom the money to pay off the loan she has there.

As these narratives indicate, it is usually not a total lack of employment or income that underlies a move northward, but the insufficiency of the jobs and earnings that people do have. Some people, frustrated with the lack of opportunity at home, leave to earn higher incomes and enjoy greater mobility abroad; for those with this motivation, improved wages and more jobs at home might be important in forestalling additional moves. Others, however, see themselves as getting along fine until a shock comes along and they are compelled to migrate in order to finance a large and unexpected expense, in which case better access to social insurance might be more important in lowering the pressures for migration. Still others aspire to homeownership and in the absence of access to credit markets migrate to finance home construction or acquisition; in this situation, government mortgage programs might reduce the incentives for international migration. As one man from El Salvador told us, his decision was motivated mainly by his desire "to someday have my own home."

Even among those migrants who face serious economic difficulties at home, departure for the United States is usually not undertaken without ambivalence. In the words of one undocumented man from Ecuador, "It's not that I just up and left. I left because I had to. Out of necessity." In this sense, economic conditions in Latin America do not have to be equal to those in the United States to end migration—just improved enough so that life is manageable without resorting to extraordinary actions. Modest investments in social insurance and micro-credit programs could make a considerably greater difference than much larger investments in job creation and infrastructure.

In their answers to our question, other respondents emphasized the lure of opportunities in the United States more than economic insufficiencies at home. Although labor supply and demand are always jointly implicated in international migration, in the minds of migrants opportunities often loom larger, and the forces of attraction have more psychological power than those of expulsion. Rather than turning to international migration as a means of survival or a temporary coping strategy, many use it strategically as part of a broader project of socioeconomic mobility. Thus, one young Colombian male attributed his move to "my interest in educating myself. Basically to obtain a doctorate." Likewise, a Venezuelan male said that, although he had family in the area, he moved northward because "I wanted to study at the University of Pennsylvania at the Wharton School of Business. It has been my dream all my life, which so far hasn't happened, but maybe someday."

Rather than seeking to gain education, another migrant took advantage of an international exchange program to teach in the United States. When asked what brought her to the United States, a Venezuelan female said,

> Well, first because I applied for an international program, and this program was focused strictly on the United States. It is an international program for teachers to come here to offer classes in Spanish in schools, primary and secondary schools, although that is not what I dream, because my dream is to be able to give classes at a university, at a more advanced level, understand? But once again I, as I was saying to myself, it is better to have something sure than not to have anything, or to have something that makes you feel, or feeds your sense of frustration.

Business opportunities also bring people to the United States. One young Brazilian man said that he had reached what seemed like a dead end in his career at home, and "either I was going to stay where I was or I was going to try some other line of work." About this time he "had the opportunity to work for another company. Then they said to me, 'Look, do you want to come to work in another firm here?' And at the same time they offered me the possibility of coming here to the United States. At the time I judged it better to come here because I was going to have an international experience for my résumé and it was going to be a good, very good thing to improve my English."

Several respondents referred to the "dream" of coming to America. One Mexican man in Philadelphia said, "I always thought, always dreamed of being here in the United States." A Dominican woman referred explicitly to the American Dream. In answer to our question about what made her want to come to the United States, she said, "Ah, it is a dream that everyone has, to know what is here, because [at home] everyone speaks a lot about the American Dream, so one wants to know what it's all about, and for this reason I first came." Another respondent, a young Mexican man, compared the desire to migrate to an emotion: "Well, the desire to come is like an emotion, right? Because at home they say that in the United States life is very different than in Mexico—that here it is nicer, that there are more opportunities to get ahead. That is the source of the emotion to come here."

A Mexican respondent eloquently addressed the trade-off between money and social status in moving from Mexico to the United States, coming down firmly on the side of money as the most efficacious mobility strategy for someone in his position:

> I said to myself, what do I have here in Mexico? I live with two uncles in Mexico City, right? I saw that my uncle was a full-time secondary school teacher in physical education, and he worked part-time at another school, and even though his wife had a business selling chickens and chiles and things like that in the same neighborhood—they had their money separated, so at times he asked her for a loan. So I said to the uncle who was a secondary school teacher, "Listen, when are they going to call you to be a professor? You don't have any money, and so what am I doing here?" And my father, who has no education, I call him, and I even get money to loan my uncle at times. So I said to myself, I am not putting up with this. It does not work for me, for in the United States it is easy to earn good money.

As noted earlier, having a social connection to someone who has worked or lived in the United States, or is currently residing there, can play a pivotal role in determining whether a potential migrant stays or goes. People in origin communities are embedded within social network, and when these networks contain current or former U.S. migrants, the tie yields a valuable source of social capital. By drawing on that connection, they can gain access to a high-wage job in the United States. A Bolivian man, for example, although he mentioned his "unstable economic situation" as one motivation, emphasized that it was his friendship with successful migrants who had already gone to the United States and then returned to his home community that made the difference. "Because I have various friends who came here to work and told me good things about the United States, that you could earn a lot—well, I decided to come."

This migrant went on to describe how his friends served as role models who inspired him to test his own fortune because "they were very well set up in my country. They had houses, cars, and a business." Similarly, a young man from Puerto Rico was inspired by the example of his older brother. When asked what had prompted his journey to the United States, he quickly answered, "What made me want to come to the United States was to see the success that my brother had here . . . he had graduated from Drexel University after two years and now works for the Federal Office of Puerto Rico here in Philadelphia. It's part of the government of Puerto Rico, and you know, things are going real well for him. He bought his house and his car, and that made me think this is where I should be."

One Honduran male who had steady work and was earning fairly good money as a truck driver admitted that "I never wanted to be here [in the United States]." Although he was getting tired of the long hours and low wages, remaining in the United States was the way, he said, to realize his dream of having his own truck. "This is the only way to make it happen because here, unlike in my country, where I could never buy a truck—with the money one earns there one barely has enough to eat and buy clothes but nothing more—I had never dreamed of being here, but when the opportunity presented itself, I took it."

In these cases, an economic desire for social mobility was already growing or present, and access to a network tie tipped the balance in favor of migration; the migrants made strategic use of the social capital at their disposal to gain access to higher wages abroad. In other cases, the social tie is mobilized, not by potential migrants for their own instrumental purposes, but by friends and relatives in the United States, who have their own purposes or reasons (Bashi 2007). As one Mexican male noted with some wonderment about his coming to the United States, "Well, I never really wanted to leave, but the desire came about very rapidly, faster than I thought possible. They invited me, and then I came here. I denied it to myself two times, but finally I just said, well, okay, let's strike out on an adventure and see what happens." Another Mexican man put it more simply: "A friend who lived here went and told me how things were here, and from there came the desire to come to know the United States."

Sometimes the call to migrate to the United States comes from unexpected and unanticipated sources. The Internet has opened new possibilities for cultivating and accessing social capital that did not exist before. As one Brazilian university student who had never really contemplated migration to the United States told us:

RESPONDENT: I really didn't have much desire to come here. I really wanted to get to know China and Spain, but my interest came from the Internet.

INTERVIEWER: How did this happen? Tell me.

RESPONDENT: Knowing some people online.

INTERVIEWER: Really?

RESPONDENT: Yes, and they said I could come here and live, and well, here I came.

INTERVIEWER: How did this happen? Describe it to me, because it is important.

RESPONDENT: In the university I was checking my e-mails, and I went to a chat room.

INTERVIEWER: Of your Brazilian friends there?

RESPONDENT: No, I didn't know who. I looked in the Internet and began: Hi. How are you? Very well. What's your name and everything, and, oh, you live in the United States? Yes! Well, he told me a little about the United States, and I told him a little about Brazil. And so here my U.S. friends began to tell me, come there. Okay, I'll go.

INTERVIEWER: Didn't you reach any sudden agreement to bring things up from Brazil?

RESPONDENT: No, no. It was just an Internet friendship.

INTERVIEWER: Ah, okay. And was a girl involved?

RESPONDENT: It was a bunch of people—a guy, a girl, and another two people. It was a house with five people, and I was chatting with all of them.

INTERVIEWER: So then you decided to come to the United States, to Philadelphia, or were they in another city?

RESPONDENT: No, they were in Philadelphia.

INTERVIEWER: So did you come directly to Philadelphia?

RESPONDENT: Directly to Philadelphia.

In this case, a new technology, the Internet, facilitated the formation and elaboration of social connections that turned into a migrant network. In other cases, particularly where out-migration from a community has been massive, young people may pack up and leave simply because all their friends have gone and no one is left at home to socialize with. In this case, their motivation for migration (loneliness or envy) and the solution to their dilemma (migration) are one and the same (friends living abroad). In the words of one young Ecuadoran man who felt abandoned by his peers, "All my friends had come here, so I didn't have anyone left at home and I was just passing the time. So then I came here, where I have plenty of friends, and it has turned out better."

Violence, civil as well as domestic, also figures into mobility decisions, though evidence suggests that most people who directly flee civil violence simply go to adjacent countries or regions (Zolberg, Suhrke, and Aguayo 1989; Schmeidl 1997, 2001). Those who move internationally in response to violence do so indirectly: civil conflict has depressed local economic conditions, undermining their ability to earn a suitable living (Jones 1989; Funkhouser 1992). Nonetheless, civil violence itself seemed to play the key role in one family's decision to emigrate. An undocumented Salvadoran male migrant reported that his mother had come to the United States because of "the same old situation down there." When pressed to clarify, he admitted that the move was

> more because of the war. There were reasons that she, you know, the, the, the country was going, going, as we say, downhill in 1978 when she came. It was when there were demonstrations by university students, you know, protests against the government, you know, because the government, the government, you know, did not respect human rights, understand? Because of this, because of the other thing that then happened, she came in 1978, and when she came down in 1982, she was ready for us, ready to leave El Salvador and take us here.

Violence was more common as a motivation for women than for men, and for some women the violence was domestic in nature, as they were fleeing abusive or threatening husbands. Such was the case of a twenty-eight-year-old Puerto Rican woman who fled with her children to Philadelphia because she found herself "running from gunshots." As she saw it, "I have two choices: I stay and he kills us all, or I go and leave him for a while, because I first came for fifteen days, and then a month, and here I have remained because of the fear of returning to the same problems."

Instances of domestic violence in some sense constitute a "family reason" for migration, but we instead gave precedence to violence in our coding. Most family reasons had to do with family reunification or dependent migration: someone moved either to end a separation or to avoid one. This motivation was far more common among women than men, but not exclusive to them. Many women originally had no intention of leaving the country and manifestly did not want to come to the United States. One Ecuadoran woman was particularly adamant in her answer:

> Well, in all honesty my desire wasn't to come to the United States. Never. Not even when my parents went and asked that my brothers and sisters be sent. Even when they all went, I was opposed to leaving, and they could not make me go. I was against it and never wanted to come here to the United States. I told myself I could get ahead down there just the same . . . because we all had, well, a university education, we were all studying, but my idea was to stay there and make my dreams come true there. But then, when I met my husband, he had lived in the United States. So hardly had I married when the first thing that happened was that he told me that we had to come here.

Another such "tied mover" who came because of her husband's decision to move was a young undocumented Ecuadoran woman living in New Jersey who pointedly contrasted her outlook on life before and after marriage, stating that, "before I married I was still a little girl, and the only thing that I thought about was studying and enjoying life and going out with my girlfriends to have fun. Well, then, when I got married . . . things changed, and what I thought was one thing before marriage became a different reality afterward. My ideals were to continue studying before marrying, to continue studying and finish my training, but I did think about coming here."

In another case it was a mother's remarriage to the respondent's stepfather that ultimately led to U.S. emigration. The daughter, a twenty-year-old from the Dominican Republic, reported that she had been very content living with her family in Santo Domingo, where "all our families lived in the same place side by side, with my grandparents, my aunts and uncles, and all of us depending on each other." But then, after her mother's remarriage, her stepfather included the entire family in his visa application, and they all ended up emigrating: "We all went together— they gave us all visas at the same time."

Sometimes migration came about less because of a "tied move" with a specific person than because of the general attraction of family abroad.

One Ecuadoran male in New York stated that, "in reality, well, for me it was that I came to be with my family. I have a lot of family here, a ton of family members." One young Mexican man had so many relatives living in the United States that immigration seemed almost inevitable to him, and in fact he had no trouble securing a green card. He had so many relatives north of the border that he could not even keep track of them: "They are cousins, uncles, aunts . . . [in] Sacramento, Los Angeles, Chicago. Like, when I think about it, like, large populated areas is where I would find them. I still need to find them all. I just don't know where they are."

The attractive power of families was such that many people ended up overriding their own preferences to make the move northward. Despite her access to legal documents, a young Dominican woman said that "at first I didn't want to go because I did not want to leave my grandmother alone, but then my grandmother died. But it was *really* my mom who made the effort. She lived here alone, so I decided to come to be with her." In one case, parents pushed a rebellious son to join his even more rebellious "hippie" brother in the United States, who had "lived a long time in New York and said that one could do many things there, and it was like a lever that gave my parents a reason to say, well, I think that over there you both can grow and develop in a different way."

In another case, the grandmother of a young Mexican man pushed him to take advantage of an uncle's presence in the United States to advance the family's interests. He insisted that

> the truth is that I had no desire to come here to this country, but suddenly my . . . uncle with whom I came arrived here. He came and said to me that if I did not want to go or did not wish to come and that was the decision, then I would not go. I did not want to because I did not want to leave my mom all alone, but my grandmother said to her, "Tell him to go, because over there he will have something that can allow the purchase of land.". . . But no, I had this anxiety about coming here, understand?

Settlement Versus Return

Both the words of the immigrants and our classification of their reasons for moving indicate a diversity of motivations for international migration that often work interactively to bear on the migration decision. Whereas some people are eager to migrate, others are reluctant and have to be persuaded by family members or forced into it by circumstances. Irrespective of the reasons for departure, however, most people are at least ambivalent about leaving, and most are employed at the time of departure. Even the young Brazilian man who eagerly jumped at the chance to be transferred to the United States by his company because it was "good for his résumé" later expressed considerable ambivalence about his decision, admitting that "naturally at times I miss the country, the people, because I have, yes, I have many friends there in Brazil."

Thus, even for this eager immigrant, the attraction of return migration remained palpable because "before I left I lived with family, but now I live alone here. I have my independence, but I also had it in Brazil in a certain way." Although this respondent viewed work in the United States as part of a career strategy, a more common motivation is to see U.S. labor simply as a means to achieving a goal at home—building a house, purchasing land, starting a business, investing in education, or preserving health. For those with goals such as these, success is not defined by settlement and socioeconomic progress in the United States, but by successfully accumulating enough funds to achieve their goal at home and then going back to enjoy the fruits of their foreign labor. For those who did not want to migrate in the first place, the dream of returning home is an ever-present longing that never disappears.

Although it is difficult for many American natives to comprehend, the United States, whatever its advantages as a source of income and employment, is not all that attractive a place to live for many Latin Americans, particularly those who have just arrived and who lack legal documents. Although migrants may be strongly motivated to enter the country for reasons of work and resource accumulation, most are also strongly motivated to return home once they have achieved their economic goals. Audrey Singer and I (Massey and Singer 1995) found that 85 percent of annual undocumented entries from Mexico were offset by departures, and Guillermina Jasso and Mark Rosenzweig (1982) estimated that each year at least one-third of legal Mexican immigrants return home. Paradoxically, heightened border enforcement has reduced the rate of return migration by raising the costs and risks of border crossing. Once they make it across, migrants increasingly tend to hunker down and stay (Massey, Durand, and Malone 2002).

The mixed motivations and feelings about the United States are reflected in the answers we got when we asked respondents whether they would like to return to their country of origin or remain in the United States. The bottom panel of table 2.4 summarizes the answers to this question. The ambivalence that immigrants feel is indicated by the relatively large share who could not answer or who said that they did not know whether they would stay or return—about 26 percent overall. The modal response was an expressed intention to return home rather than remain in the United States, comprising 44 percent of the answers. The main difference between women and men was the relative certitude of females compared with the greater ambivalence of males. Whereas 30 percent of males said that they did not know about returning, with 43 percent expressing the intention to return and 28 percent the intention to stay, only 19 percent of females said that they did not know, with 47 percent expressing a firm commitment to return and 34 percent firmly saying that they wished to remain in the United States.

Thus, migration to the United States is fraught with ambivalence for Latin Americans, and even a U.S. presence of long duration with strong attachments and multiple connections cannot be assumed to constitute "permanent" settlement. Among Latin Americans in the United States, the probability of return migration never really drops to zero. Indeed, the migrant whom my colleagues and I profiled in *Return to Aztlan* (Massey et al. 1987) as an exemplar of permanent settlement returned to Mexico the year after the book's publication.

The ambivalence that pervades the decision to remain in the United States is well illustrated by selected quotes from the answers to our questions. A common response to the question of whether a person preferred to return or stay was, "It depends." One thirty-three-year-old Dominican male with legal documents answered: "It could be, though it depends on how it goes. One always yearns to go to one's country, but it's like the old adage says, to get ahead you have to leave home, and I think that one can create a home wherever one is." He concluded: "I don't know if I will return, because now I am settled here, but if I were to go back, it would be because I wanted to."

A similar response came from a twenty-seven-year-old documented Venezuelan student in New Jersey, who based her choice on a variety of contingencies. She did not see the choice as black-and-white because

> it's all relative, right? Because, if the situation continues as it is in Venezuela, well, then naturally I am not going to want to go back. If it changes and if I can finish my preparation . . . well, I love my country and its people, and I identify a lot with Venezuelans. You see how we're very open, warm people. I am generalizing, of course. There are all kinds, and you can bump into whatever kind of person there. But in general, I don't know, I don't know whether I am idealizing, but I really like our way of being.

For some immigrants, family ties and connections in the United States arise to block the way home even though economic goals have been met, as reported by one thirty-two-year-old undocumented Ecuadoran woman in New Jersey: "I would like to have stable financial capital, and naturally I would like to go back to my country to establish a good company and make my dream a reality, right? To be the executive of my own business, yes, naturally." When probed further on this point, she became more realistic, however, admitting, "That's a decision I will have to make and take with my husband, because now I am not single, and he is not Ecuadoran but from India, so we would have to make the decision together and perhaps find a neutral country so that we can both be satisfied with the decision."

Not too long ago the issue of staying versus returning was not terribly serious for most Mexican migrants, even those who lacked documents. Coming and going across the two-thousand-mile land border was easy and inexpensive and not terribly risky. On average the odds of getting caught were only around one in three, and they were even lower for those who used border crossing guides or who had prior border-crossing experience (Singer and Massey 1998). Most of the crossings were in urban areas, and the costs and risks were quite low, so that circulation back and forth on an annual basis was the norm.

However, since the passage of the Immigration Reform and Control Act (IRCA) in 1986 and the launching of Operation Blockade in El Paso in 1993, its expansion to Operation Gatekeeper in San Diego in 1994, and the huge increase in border enforcement since 9/11, the costs and risks of clandestine border crossing have risen sharply, rates of return migration have plummeted as a consequence, and circulation back and forth has substantially decreased (Massey, Durand, and Malone 2002). One thirty-three-year-old undocumented migrant, remembering the old days, reported that he would return if only there were a different policy at the Mexico-U.S. border. When asked if he wished to return, he answered:

RESPONDENT: Oh, yes, if I had the option, yes, I would do it.

INTERVIEWER: So then, you would prefer to go back.

RESPONDENT: Perhaps yes, but maybe in another way.

INTERVIEWER: If you could do it, or if you didn't have to worry about borders and papers, would you bring them home?

RESPONDENT: Oh, well, if I could come and go freely, yes.

INTERVIEWER: Really?

RESPONDENT: Sure.

Even those with professional training and possibilities in the United States often express a desire to return, like a twenty-one-year-old Mexican woman who was in the United States for practical training in architecture. We asked her, "[Do] you aspire, then, to get your training maybe as an architect and then return home to Mexico?" Her answer was immediate and unconditional: "Of course." When the interviewer probed further and asked, "Wouldn't you like to live and work here?" she admitted the attractions of America but nonetheless came down firmly on the side of return migration: "Yes, but for me I would rather return to Mexico." A twenty-three-year-old undocumented Guatemalan woman expressed a similarly unequivocal view, saying simply, "I would not like to stay very long here." When asked how long, she replied, "A year and a half," and in response to the interviewer's further probing, she cut short the discussion by saying, "Yes, I prefer to return."

Even those who have experienced considerable economic success often see a downside in terms of the personal and social sacrifices they had to make. A thirty-year-old Brazilian male in Philadelphia was quite conflicted. Although he appreciated the financial opportunities offered by life in the United States, he was not so keen on its rampant individualism:

INTERVIEWER: Would you like to return to your country?

RESPONDENT: Yes, I like Brazil a lot—the place, the people, the way of life, the way of seeing life, how the people are. I like it a lot. But it was a great change of life that I had—my life turned 180 degrees. Before I left . . . I lived with family, but now I live alone here. I have my independence, but I also had it in Brazil in a certain way. But I accommodated peacefully to living with my aunt here, didn't I? Here I live alone, I have my things, total independence, so that little remains. You grow a lot as a person, and when people engage in personal growth, it's good.

INTERVIEWER: Did you mature then?

RESPONDENT: Yes, I matured. Adeptness and dexterity improved. Naturally at times I miss the country, the people, because I have, yes, I have many friends there in Brazil. They're people of ten or fifteen years' friendship, because I like to maintain my friendships. So it is a good thing to miss them, but for the opportunity, the opportunity, I couldn't say no.

INTERVIEWER: So do you want to stay here to live and work forever?

RESPONDENT: I don't know. It's difficult because I've not been here very long, no more than eight months. So one definite idea about the future of life, if the situation here with us goes on, it remains a little indefinite because I don't know if I am going to stay here. If my company wants me to stay here for a longer time. I don't know—it is a process of learning and other things.

Although many Americans today believe the historical fiction that their immigrant ancestors pulled up stakes in Europe, struck out for the United States, found opportunity here, and never looked back, in most cases this was not what happened. Except for those suffering persecution at home, the flows were never one-way, and during the late nineteenth and early twentieth centuries circulation back and forth was extensive. Settlement has always been more of a process than an event, as indicated by the last respondent's comment: "I don't know—it is a process of learning and other things." For most Latino immigrants, the shift of perspective from solving problems at home to getting ahead in the United States is an uncertain path with many detours and ambiguities, owing both to an ongoing attachment to Latin American culture and its mores and to uncertainties about their position the United States.

To sum up what we know about motivations and intentions and their relation to various background characteristics, table 2.5 presents the results of a multinomial logistic regression equation that we estimated to predict which class of motivation an immigrant emphasized from a set of independent variables that included racial and ethnic roots, region of origin, demographic background, immigrant status, and socioeconomic origins. To simplify the analysis and derive stable estimates, we collapsed the motivations into four basic categories: origin conditions (including violence at origin), destination conditions, and a combined category of family reunification and network connections, and "other" motivations served as the reference category. Only those born aboard are included in the model.

These estimates show clearly that motivations for migration do not differ by racial-ethnic roots or region of origin. (Skin tone was also insignificant but is too collinear with African and indigenous roots to include in the equation at the same time.) For the most part, class origins also do not play much of a role, though greater education does seem to be negatively associated with migration for family or network reasons and to a lesser extent for reasons of economic conditions at origin. The two variables that principally determine the motivation for migration to the United States are age and time since arrival. As age rises, immigrants grow more likely to express a motivation that falls under one of the three principal categories—origin conditions, destination conditions, or family-network connections—than the diverse "other" category. Moreover, as one might expect, the longer immigrants have been in the United States, the less likely they are to say that they moved because of conditions at home or because of family or network conditions.

As a final exercise, we used a logistic regression model to predict the desire to return as a function of the motivation for migration, controlling for different background characteristics. As the results in table 2.6 show,

Table 2.5 Multinomial Logit Regression Predicting Motivation for Migration from Selected Variables

Predictors	Origin Conditions		Destination Conditions		Family and Network	
	Regression Coefficient	Standard Error	Regression Coefficient	Standard Error	Regression Coefficient	Standard Error
Racial-ethnic roots						
African	1.029	0.947	1.264	1.009	1.401	0.917
Indigenous	0.140	1.625	1.465	1.751	2.319	1.581
Region of origin						
Mexico	—	—	—	—	—	—
Caribbean	0.312	1.343	0.654	1.456	0.205	1.211
Central America	0.471	1.042	-1.058	1.283	-1.410	1.102
South America	0.211	0.903	0.829	0.923	0.143	0.811
Demographics						
Age	0.181**	0.065	0.280***	0.073	0.185**	0.061
Male	1.035	0.725	0.443	0.770	0.893	0.665
Immigrant status						
Documented	-0.617	1.120	0.386	1.072	1.455+	0.906
Years in the United States	-0.080	0.065	-0.263**	0.083	-0.190**	0.067
Class origins						
Years of schooling	-0.186+	0.111	-0.011	0.049	-0.197*	0.101
Parental International Socioeconomic Index	-0.037	0.026	-0.035	0.026	-0.009	0.024
Intercept	-1.246	2.537	-6.255*	2.769	-3.816+	2.051
Log-likelihood	-128.553***					
Pseudo-R-squared	0.239					
Sample size (N)	124					

Source: Immigrant Identity Project (Office of Population Research 2009).
Note: The reference category is "other."
+p < .10; *p < .05; **p < .01; ***p < .001

Table 2.6   Logit Regression Predicting Intention to Return Home from Selected Independent Variables

Predictors	Regression Coefficient	Standard Error	P-Value
Motivation for migration			
Conditions at origin	1.482*	0.726	0.041
Conditions at destination	1.413+	0.781	0.071
Family-network	1.244+	0.677	0.066
Other	—	—	—
Racial-ethnic roots			
African	−0.052	0.528	0.921
Indigenous	−0.963	1.053	0.361
Region of origin			
Mexico	—	—	—
Caribbean	−1.616+	0.879	0.066
Central America	−0.865	0.697	0.215
South America	−1.484**	0.579	0.010
Demographics			
Age	−0.023	0.041	0.580
Male	−0.757	0.481	0.116
Immigrant status			
Documented	0.732	0.627	0.464
Years in United States	−0.102*	0.050	0.042
Class origins			
Years of schooling	−0.011	0.027	0.693
Father's International Socioeconomic Index	0.025+	0.015	0.090
Intercept	1.190	1.586	0.453
Log-likelihood	−72.446***		
Pseudo-R-squared	0.149***		
Sample size (N)	124		

Source: Immigrant Identity Project (Office of Population Research 2009).
+p < .10; *p < .05; **p < .01; ***p < .001

the desire to return cuts across all major motivational categories. Compared with the "other" motivation category, those migrating because of origin conditions, destination conditions, and family considerations are all more likely to express a desire to return, and this desire is equally powerful across the three categories. The desire to return is unrelated to racial and ethnic roots, but is less strong among South Americans and Caribbeans compared with Mexicans and Central Americans, who enjoy greater access to a land border. The background characteristic most strongly associated with the desire to return is, unsurprisingly, time spent in the United States. The longer people have been here, the less desire they feel to return home, illustrating once again that settlement is more of a process than an event.

Our Slice of Immigrant Reality

Obviously with a selectively chosen sample of 159 ethnographic respondents, we cannot readily make broad generalizations to entire population of immigrants to the United States. What we get is a window on the perceptions of a specific set of first- and second-generation Latino immigrants living in the urban Northeast. All of the immigrants in our sample were from Latin America, and among them, Mexicans were overrepresented. Although our respondents were positively selected with respect to socioeconomic status and many had significant resources of skill and education to draw upon in brokering boundaries within the United States, most were undocumented. Even among those we classified as second-generation, around 40 percent were undocumented, having come to the United States as children but in irregular status. They had grown up in the United States and spoke English fluently, but they entered the negotiation of boundaries in the United States from a fundamentally weak position. In addition, most of our respondents would probably be perceived and classified as nonwhite by the typical white American, and a number of them would be perceived as black given prevailing notions of race in the United States.

Our sample is thus quite different from others that have been used to study patterns and processes of assimilation, such as the Children of Immigrants Longitudinal Survey (Portes and Rumbaut 2001, 2006), the Immigrant Second Generation Study of Metropolitan New York (Kasinitz et al. 2008), and Immigration and Intergenerational Mobility in Metropolitan Los Angeles (Rumbaut 2008). It contains none of the advantaged Asian or European groups characterized by high levels of professionalization; it is weighted toward the first generation; it is concentrated in the lower echelons of the urban economy; it is dominated by undocumented migrants; and most of our sample would be considered by most Americans to be of nonwhite racial origins.

In short, our sample represents an immigrant population that is particularly vulnerable to exclusion, discrimination, and exploitation, and this point should be borne in mind when reading the ensuing chapters. Nonetheless, vulnerability is the condition of a large and growing fraction of Latin American immigrants. According to estimates by the Office of Immigration Statistics of the U.S. Department of Homeland Security (Hoefer, Rytina, and Baker 2008), 40 percent of all Latin Americans present in the United States lack documents, with notably high percentages observed among Hondurans (67 percent), Guatemalans (66 percent), Mexicans (60 percent), Brazilians (54 percent), and Salvadorans (50 percent). By underrepresenting the experience of undocumented migrants in their surveys, prior studies have missed an important slice of immigrant reality.

=Chapter 3=

The Rise of Anti-Immigrant Times

Whatever goals and motivations immigrants may have in migrating, their brokering of boundaries and construction of identities depend strongly on the context of reception they encounter in the United States (Portes and Rumbaut 2001, 2006). In this chapter, we argue that circumstances in the United States have *not* evolved in ways that favor a blurring of boundaries between immigrants and natives. On the contrary, economic, social, and political conditions have shifted so as to harden categorical divisions between immigrants and natives.

Economically, the long postwar boom came to an end in the 1970s and gave way to an era of rising inequality that ended with economic collapse in 2008, leaving the United States far removed from the non-zero-sum economy that Alba (2009) posits as a critical precursor to widespread assimilation and boundary-blurring. Socially, in recent years immigrants have been framed in public rhetoric and media coverage as a threat to American culture and society, and as a result the salience of the line between natives and foreigners has increased rather than decreased. Politically, a series of harsh anti-immigrant policies, unusual in their scale and severity, have been implemented to promote systematic discrimination not only against unauthorized migrants but against legal permanent residents as well. Ironically, however, these repressive policies did not reduce undocumented migration but led to an accumulation of undocumented migrants living north of the border. The end result is a context of reception that is more hostile to immigrants than any time since the Great Depression.

The Zero-Sum Economy

An important determinant of natives' openness to immigrants' assimilation and boundary crossing is their own sense of economic security.

Figure 3.1   Household Income Inequality in the United States

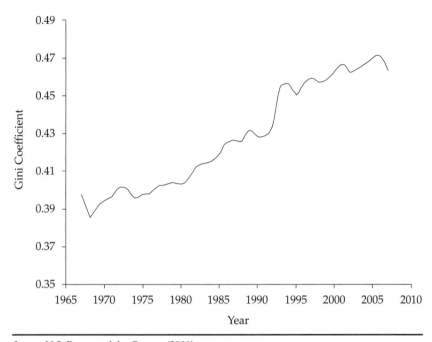

Source: U.S. Bureau of the Census (2009).

When people feel confident about their prospects for continued employment and ample earnings, they naturally tend to feel less threatened by potential competitors and are less likely to impose mechanisms of exclusion or discrimination on foreigners or other socially defined out-groups. Unfortunately, over the past several decades the prospects for employment and earnings have been anything but sanguine for most Americans. Although a minority of households did extremely well up at least until the economic collapse of 2008, the vast majority saw their economic circumstances steadily deteriorate.

Figure 3.1 begins our consideration of economic trends by documenting the singular rise in income inequality in the United States since the late 1960s (using data from U.S. Bureau of the Census 2009). Whereas in 1968 the Gini coefficient for income inequality stood at a record low level of 0.386, thereafter it steadily rose to peak at 0.470 in 2006, a remarkable increase of 22 percent over three decades. By 2006 it was as if the equalizing gains of the New Deal had been wiped out. Indeed, by then the distribution of U.S. income was more unequal than at any time since 1929.

Figure 3.2   Share of Income Earned by Top Quintile and Next Two Quintiles

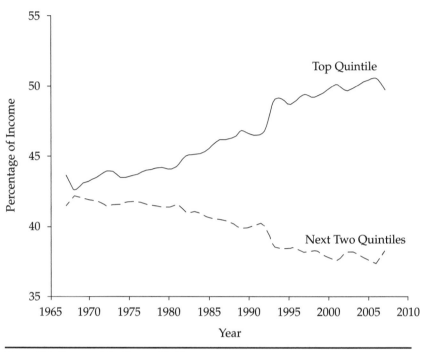

Source: U.S. Bureau of the Census (2009).

What this increase in inequality meant for American households in practical terms is suggested by figure 3.2, which shows the share of income earned by the top quintile compared with the share earned by the next two quintiles combined (U.S. Bureau of the Census 2009). If positions in the socioeconomic hierarchy are to open up for immigrants with the retirement of the baby boom generation, as Richard Alba (2009) and Dowell Myers (2007) suggest, then most of the openings are likely to occur in these two middle segments of the income distribution. As can be seen, however, the earnings of these two classes have not fared well in recent decades. Whereas the top and the next two quintiles accounted for about the same fraction of total U.S. income in 1970, 42 to 43 percent, their fortunes steadily diverged over the ensuing decades. By 2006 the top quintile was earning 51 percent of total income, whereas the next two quintiles together earned just 37 percent. Under these circumstances, it is hard to imagine those living in the middle two fifths of the income distribution feeling secure enough to perceive a non-zero-sum economy with respect to immigrants.

Figure 3.3   Average Consumer Debt per U.S. Household

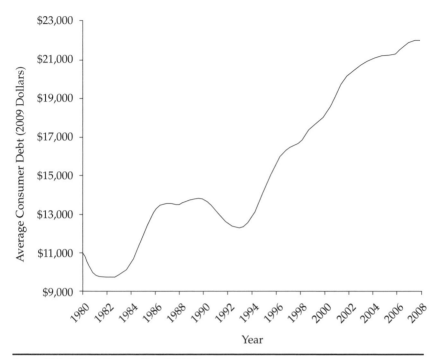

Source: U.S. Federal Reserve Board (2009).

On the contrary, beyond the simple rise in inequality and stagnating earnings, the economic fortunes of most Americans have grown steadily more precarious in other ways. As wages fell in real terms for most American workers, households reacted by sending more family members into the labor force to bolster total income, a trend that was expressed most clearly as a rise in female labor force participation. Even with multiple earners, however, many households were still unable to maintain desired levels of consumption and covered the shortfall in funds by borrowing, leading to an explosion of household debt. Figure 3.3 shows average consumer debt per household in recent decades, using constant 2009 dollars (U.S. Federal Reserve Board 2009). Whereas in 1980 the average household owed around $10,000, this figure rose steadily to reach $22,000 in 2008. Over the past twenty-eight years, in other words, the indebtedness of the typical American household more than doubled.

In a context of stagnating earnings, rising debt sharply and necessarily increased the debt service ratio faced by American households—the money they must pay as interest on consumer loans divided by total in-

Figure 3.4   Debt Service Ratio for U.S. Household

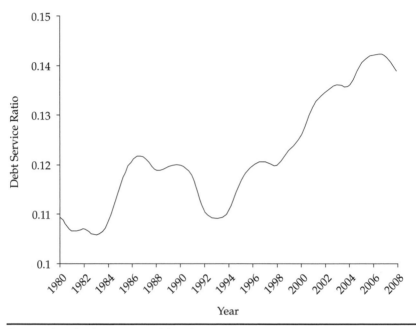

Year

Source: U.S. Federal Reserve Board (2009).

come. As can be seen in figure 3.4, the average household devoted around 11 percent of its income to debt service in 1980, but by 2006 the figure had climbed to 14 percent (U.S. Federal Reserve Board 2009). Ironically, as households borrowed more to maintain current consumption, they had less disposable income for future consumption.

In addition to borrowing, households also dipped increasingly into savings, and over the same period the savings rate dwindled. Figure 3.5 shows the personal savings rate among American income earners from 1980 to the present (U.S. Bureau of Economic Analysis 2009). In the early 1980s, Americans were saving around 10 to 11 percent of income, but by 2005 the savings rate had reached a record low of just 1.4 percent. As they went further into debt, therefore, Americans also whittled down their cash assets. Taking debt and money devoted to debt service into account, Americans actually had a negative savings rate by 2005.

With no savings to fall back on, a rising mountain of debt, and more intense pressure on earnings to service that debt, American households drew closer and closer to the financial edge and increasingly courted economic disaster when unanticipated but costly needs arose. This risk was exacerbated by the steady fraying of the U.S. social safety net; one of

Figure 3.5   Personal Savings Rate in the United States

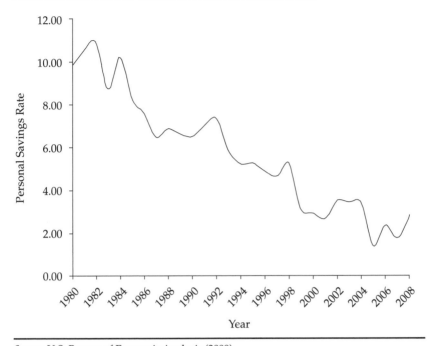

Source: U.S. Bureau of Economic Analysis (2009).

the most serious risks faced by American households was the illness or injury of a breadwinner, which did not simply reduce earnings but often brought serious costs. Figure 3.6 shows the percentage of Americans without health insurance, which rose from 12 percent in 1980 to peak at over 16 percent in the late 1990s (Levit, Olin, and Letsch 1992; Cohen et al. 2009). The lack of insurance coverage is greatest for young workers. Around 30 percent of nineteen- to twenty-four-year-olds and 26 percent of fifteen- to thirty-four-year-olds lacked health insurance in 2009 (see Andrea Fuller, "Young Adults Swelling Ranks of Uninsured," *New York Times*, September 5, 2009).

With so many households living so close to the edge with so little protection, it is inevitable that many are pushed into insolvency. A recent study in California found that 14 percent of working-age people had accumulated medical debt by 2009 and that, among those with medical debt, 35 percent responded by taking out loans or drawing on savings, 32 percent took on additional credit card debt, and 20 percent stopped buying basics (cited by Reed Abelson, "Insured but Bankrupted by Health Crises," *New York Times*, July 1, 2009). For many people, these

Figure 3.6   Share of Americans Without Health Insurance

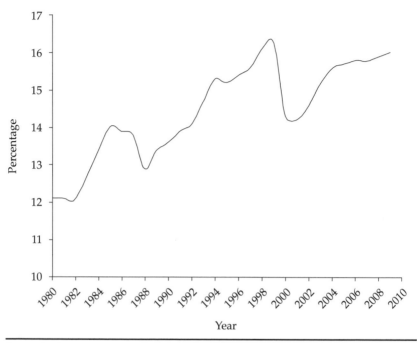

Year

Source: Authors' compilation based on Levit, Olin, and Letsch (1992) and U.S. Bureau of the Census (2009).

defensive measures proved insufficient: as figure 3.7 shows, bankruptcy filings in the United States climbed from just 330,000 in 1980 to reach 2.1 million in 2005 (Administrative Office of the U.S. Courts 2009).

With so many households filing for protection to escape accumulated debts, the banking industry struck back in 2005 by prevailing upon Congress to pass the Bankruptcy Abuse Prevention and Consumer Protection Act. Bankruptcy laws in the United States historically had been forgiving of overstretched borrowers, allowing them to go to court to wipe out a significant share of their debt and start over. After 2005, however, declaring bankruptcy was made more difficult. Under the new law, debtors were required to undergo "credit counseling" in a government-approved program before filing for bankruptcy, and they were forced to pay back taxes before being allowed to proceed in court. Moreover, debtors whose monthly income fell above the state median were compelled to continue making payments to creditors based on a strict expense-to-income formula (Henry 2006). As a result of these legislative changes, bankruptcy

Figure 3.7   Bankruptcy Filings in the United States

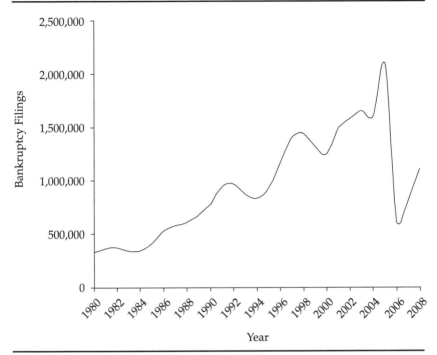

Source: Administrative Office of the U.S. Courts (2009).

filings plummeted between 2005 and 2006, going from 2.1 million to 618,000 within twelve months. The decline, however, proved to be temporary: by 2008 the number of filings was back over 1 million and rapidly rising. By February 2009, Americans were filing for bankruptcy at the rate of 5,400 per day, yielding an annualized rate of 2 million.

The new surge in bankruptcies was heightened by a major financial collapse that unfolded in the latter half of 2008, an economic tsunami that not only put many consumers underwater but wiped out a number of major financial institutions as well. Overnight, credit markets froze, home foreclosures skyrocketed, and for a time economic activity came to a virtual standstill. The acuteness of the crisis is illustrated in figure 3.8, which shows the sharp turnaround in the U.S. gross domestic product between 2006 and 2009 (U.S. Bureau of Economic Analysis 2009). In the first quarter of 2006, GDP stood at $12,916 billion, and by the fourth quarter of 2007 it had reached $13,391 billion. Growth then stalled, and GDP inched slightly upward to reach $13,415 billion in the second quarter of 2008, but then plummeted to $12,893 billion in the second quarter

Figure 3.8   Trend in U.S. Gross Domestic Product

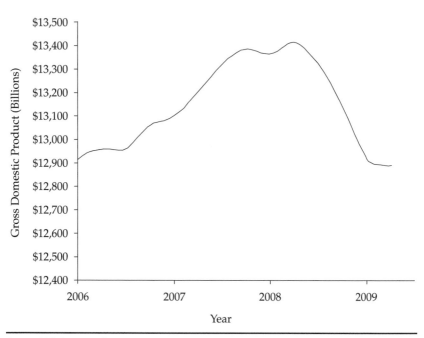

Source: U.S. Bureau of Economic Analysis (2009).

of 2009. Billions of dollars in equity were wiped out as GDP contracted by 3.9 percent in twelve months, the largest yearly decline in production since the end of the Second World War.

Inevitably such a sharp contraction was accompanied by rising joblessness, as indicated in figure 3.9, which shows trends in unemployment and underemployment since 1980 (U.S. Bureau of Labor Statistics 2009). As can be seen, the unemployment rate bottomed out at just 4 percent in early 2000 and then, after oscillating from 2002 through 2007, surged to reach 9.7 percent by August 2009. The increase in underemployment was even greater. The underemployment rate takes into account those who are working part-time involuntarily as well as those who have given up looking for work, in addition to those searching for work. From 2007 to 2009, the rate of underemployment more than doubled, going from 8 percent to 18.1 percent (Haugan 2009). A recent survey of the unemployed by the Center for Workforce Development at Rutgers University found that 84 percent received no severance pay, 63 percent were drawing down their savings or retirement accounts, 56 percent had borrowed from friends or family, and 34 percent were incurring

Figure 3.9   Rates of U.S. Unemployment and Underemployment

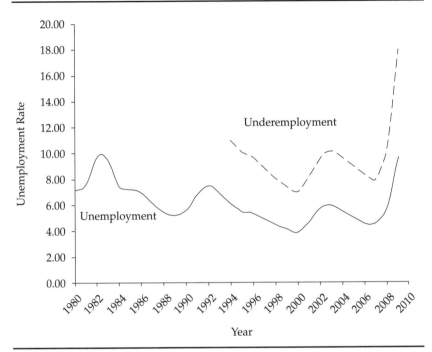

Source: U.S. Bureau of Labor Statistics (2009).

greater credit card debt (cited in Bill Marsh, "Jobless, Sleepless, Hope-less," *New York Times*, September 5, 2009).

Needless to say, the sharp rise in joblessness, the rapid contraction of the economy, and the surge in bankruptcies took a toll on consumer confidence. As shown in figure 3.10, the consumer confidence index peaked at 145 in January 2000, fell to 95 in February 2002, then rose back to 112 in July 2007 before collapsing to a record low value of just 27 in March 2009 (Consumer Confidence Board 2009). Since the Consumer Confidence Board began taking its measurements back in the 1960s, the American confidence index had never been shaken so badly.

In sum, at the end of the first decade of the twenty-first century, the U.S. economy finds itself in worse shape than at any time since the Great Depression, with rising joblessness, declining production, cascading bankruptcies, mounting debt, and record low levels of consumer confidence, and these dire trends come at the end of a remarkable period during which, even before the crash, most Americans had found themselves working more, earning less, and taking on additional debt simply to stay afloat. For the past two decades, economic growth has been fueled by

Figure 3.10   Monthly Consumer Confidence Index (1984 = 100)

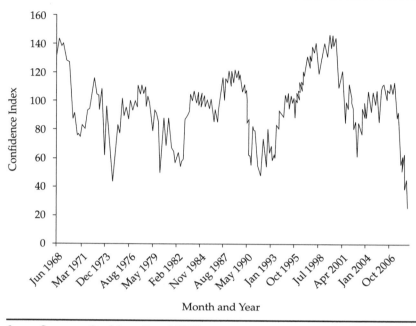

Source: Consumer Confidence Board (2009).

easy credit, surging stocks, and rising real estate values, but these bub-
bles have all burst. American households must now live on reduced incomes while paying down huge debts on devalued assets in the face of
rising unemployment. Most baby boomers do not have the assets to retire anytime soon, and neither young nor old workers have the income
to support the kind of broad-based demand that might fuel a full and
speedy recovery. For the foreseeable future, we appear to be mired in a
zero-sum economy in which the economic progress of immigrants is
likely to be perceived as coming at the expense of deserving natives.

The Latino Threat

The increase in income inequality and the deterioration of economic
circumstances for most American households over the past several decades have been accompanied, probably not coincidentally, by a new
framing of immigrants in the public media. Increasingly, Latin American and particularly Mexican immigrants have been portrayed as dangerous to America's culture, society, and economy, a trope that Leo
Chavez (2008) calls the "Latino threat narrative." Among the national
magazine covers on immigration between 1965 and 2000 that he examined, two-thirds portrayed immigration as threatening or alarming,

and the frequency of these depictions steadily rose over time, going from a relative share of just 18 percent in the 1970s to 45 percent in the 1990s (Chavez 2001).

At first the most popular framing metaphors were marine: they pictured immigration as a "tidal wave" that was "flooding" the United States and "drowning" its culture. During the 1980s, however, marine imagery gave way increasingly to martial metaphors (Chavez 2001): the Mexico-U.S. border was framed as a "battleground" that was "under attack" from "alien invaders," and Border Patrol officers were "defenders" who, though "outgunned," valiantly labored to "hold the line" against the attacking "hordes" that launched "Banzai charges" along a beleaguered "front." Latino immigrants living in the United States became a "ticking time bomb" waiting to "explode" and destroy American values and prosperity (Dunn 1996; Rotella 1998; Andreas 2000). In its coverage of immigration during the early 1990s, for example, the *Los Angeles Times* made use of war metaphors in 23 percent of its stories about immigration and in 20 percent of its stories about immigrants (Santa Ana 2002).

The Latino threat narrative began to gain particular traction in the 1980s when President Ronald Reagan framed immigration as a question of "national security," stating that terrorists and subversives were just "two days' driving time from the nearest border crossing" and referring to foreigners as a "fifth column" of subversives who would "feed on the anger and frustration of recent Central and South American immigrants" (Massey, Durand, and Malone 2002). During the 1990s, the negative portrayal of immigrants grew increasingly strident (Newton 2008). Whereas in the congressional debates of 1985 and 1986 the need for immigration reform was justified by facts and analysis and immigrants were portrayed as entering to find jobs, by the period 1994 to 1996, facts and analysis had disappeared from the debate and immigrants were portrayed as criminals coming to the United States not to find jobs but to avail themselves of generous welfare benefits, thus burdening U.S. taxpayers.

Based on her careful content analysis of statements made by legislators on the floor of Congress and recorded in the *Congressional Record* between 1994 and 1996, Lina Newton (2008, 164) concluded:

The language officials employed to justify [the legislation] combined the contemporary ideology of balanced budget conservatism and the divisions forged between deserving and undeserving members with ascriptive traditions that linked Mexicans to undesirable attributes. Not only did deviant constructions of the unauthorized correspond with punitive policy measures, but these constructions also accentuated a list of qualities and behaviors that marked immigrants more broadly as unworthy of consideration for social membership. The immigrant family was portrayed as another invasion of the nation, as individuals brought their unproductive dependents into the nation: pregnant wives, children, and elder family members would end up on welfare or take up space in schools, hospitals, and communities.

By the late 1990s, not only were undocumented migrants framed as undeserving and undesirable, but legal immigrants increasingly were being tarred with the same brush: "This image of the immigrant free-loader obscured the various legal statuses of the subject population. . . . From 1994 to 1996 both congressional rhetoric and policy promoted a construction of legal immigrants that looked much like that of the un-documented" (Newton 2008, 164).

Thus, the events of September 11, 2001, occurred against a backdrop of growing anti-immigrant hysteria directed at all foreigners, docu-mented or undocumented. The attacks only heightened the tide of suspi-cion, prejudice, and xenophobia that was already rising in the country. Thereafter, war metaphors exploded in the media and became the stan-dard trope used by social conservatives to describe immigration from Latin America. Indeed, Lou Dobbs (2006) referred to undocumented mi-gration explicitly as "an invasion of illegal aliens" and framed it as part of a broader "war on the middle class."

For his part, Patrick Buchanan (2006) alleged that immigration was part of an "Aztlan Plot" organized by Mexican elites to recapture lands lost in the Mexican-American War of 1848. In an August 28, 2006, inter-view with *Time* magazine, he said that immigration constituted a "state of emergency," and he warned: "If we do not get control of our borders and stop this greatest invasion in history, I see the dissolution of the U.S. and the loss of the American southwest—culturally and linguistically, if not politically—to Mexico."

In 2004, Chris Simcox and Jim Gilchrist took this framing beyond words and joined together to found the Minutemen Civil Defense Corps to "do the job the government won't do . . . defend the U.S. border," and they deployed vigilante volunteer "border agents" to prevent the entry of "drug dealers, gang bangers and way too many criminal foreign na-tionals [who] are creating havoc in our communities and threatening our public safety" (quoted in Massey 2007, 147). The project quickly became a media sensation, with 1,725 news and magazine articles on the Min-utemen appearing in 2005 and 1,182 in 2006 (Chavez 2008).

Within academia, the Harvard political scientist Samuel P. Hunting-ton (2004, 30) provided a veneer of respectability to the cresting wave of xenophobia by issuing his own dire warning:

The persistent inflow of Hispanic immigrants threatens to divide the United States into two peoples, two cultures, and two languages. Unlike past immigrant groups, Mexicans and other Latinos have not assimilated into mainstream U.S. culture, forming instead their own political and linguistic enclaves—from Los Angeles to Miami—and rejecting the Anglo-Protestant values that built the American dream. The United States ignores this challenge at its peril.

All this boundary work and conceptual framing done by politicians, academicians, and pundits to portray Latin American immigrants as a threat made considerable headway with the public. According to polls conducted by the Pew Charitable Trusts, as late as 2000 just 38 percent of Americans agreed that "immigrants today are a burden on our country because they take our jobs, housing, and health care." Five years later, the percentage had risen to 44 percent, and as the drumbeat of anti-immigrant rhetoric reached a crescendo in 2006 it became a majority viewpoint at 52 percent. In keeping with this shift, the percentage of Americans who rated immigration as a moderately big or very large national problem rose from 69 percent in 2002 to 74 percent in 2006 (Kohut and Suro 2006). At the same time, around half of all Americans (48 percent) believed that "newcomers from other countries threaten traditional American values and customs," 54 percent said that Americans needed to be "protected against foreign influence," and 60 percent of those who had heard of the Minutemen approved of their activities (Kohut and Suro 2006).

As attitudes toward immigrants hardened, physical attacks on them also increased. In the words of Renato Rosaldo (1997, 33): "The U.S.-Mexico border has become theater, and border theater has become social violence. Actual violence has become inseparable from symbolic ritual on the border—crossings, invasions, lines of defense, high-tech surveillance, and more." Indeed, according to U.S. Justice Department statistics, the number of anti-Hispanic hate crimes increased 24 percent from 2002 to 2007, and the number of victims rose by 30 percent (Federal Bureau of Investigation 2009). By 2008, random killings of Latinos had become common in headlines throughout the country; according to one news story, attacks on immigrants had become "such an established pastime that the youths . . . had a casual and derogatory term for it, 'beaner hopping.' One of the youths blithely told the authorities, 'I don't go out doing this very often, maybe once a week'" (Anne Barnard, "Seeing a Pattern of Hate in Attacks on Immigrants on Long Island," *New York Times*, January 8, 2009).

The War On Immigrants

It is well established in the research literature that immigration policy responds to broader social and economic currents within society. Specifically, during periods of economic distress and social conservatism, policymakers tend to enact more restrictive immigration legislation and to undertake more repressive anti-immigrant actions (Lowell, Bean, and de la Garza 1986; Shughart, Tollison, and Kimenyi 1986; Goldin 1994; Timmer and Williamson 1998; Massey 1999; Meyers 2004). Given the economic trends and rhetorical shifts observed in the United States over the past three decades, it is hardly surprising that U.S. immigration policies have grown steadily more restrictive and enforcement actions more and more repressive, especially with respect to those born in Latin America.

Although the wave of anti-immigrant hysteria crested after 9/11, the shift toward more restrictive immigration policies can be traced back to 1965. The immigration legislation enacted in that year is usually portrayed as liberalizing, and for Asians and Africans it was. For Latin Americans, however, immigration became more difficult because Congress terminated a large, twenty-two-year-old guest worker treaty with Mexico and imposed a new quota on legal entry from the Western Hemisphere (Zolberg 2006). After 1976 Latin American immigration was limited to twenty thousand persons per country per year, and in 1978 separate quotas for the Eastern and Western Hemispheres were abandoned. As a result, legal movement into the United States from Latin America became increasingly difficult.

The immediate result was a sharp increase in undocumented migration from Latin America, most notably from Mexico. Figure 3.11 shows Mexican migration into the United States in three categories: temporary legal workers, legal permanent residents, and undocumented migrants. Data on legal immigrants and temporary migrant workers come from official U.S. immigration statistics (U.S. Office of Immigration Statistics 2009), whereas data on undocumented migration comes from the Mexican Migration Project (MMP). The net annual inflow of unauthorized migrants from Mexico was estimated by computing annual probabilities of undocumented entry and exit from MMP data and then applying these to annual population counts obtained from the Mexican census (see Massey, Durand, and Pren 2009).

As can be seen, from 1940 through 1965 Mexicans entered the United States in very large numbers, but mostly through legal channels, with nearly 450,000 per year coming as temporary workers and 55,000 entering as permanent legal residents. With the restrictions implemented in 1965, legal entry became much more difficult, and undocumented migration rose steadily until the late 1980s, when annual flows included around 300,000 undocumented migrants. Legal immigration rose to around 100,000 per year, despite the restrictions, as Mexicans increasingly naturalized to U.S. citizenship, which exempted their immediate family members from the restrictive quotas, but this increase was insufficient to counterbalance the loss of guest worker visas.

Figure 3.11   Mexican Migration to the United States in Three Legal Categories

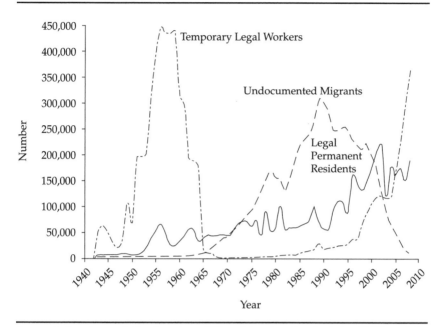

Source: Authors' compilation based on Office of Immigration Statistics (2009), and the Mexican Migration Project (2009).

In the end, the *number* of annual migrants did not change very much between the 1960s and the 1980s, but the legal auspices of entry shifted dramatically, and this made a huge difference in how immigrants were framed in the American mind. Whereas before 1965 undocumented migration was virtually nonexistent and the overwhelming majority of Mexicans entered as legal guest workers or permanent immigrants, by the late 1980s three-quarters of all Mexican entries were unauthorized. This shift gave ivory tower intellectuals, media pundits, and enterprising political entrepreneurs new opportunities to portray Mexican immigrants as lawbreakers and criminals and thus people deserving of exclusion from and discrimination within the United States.

In response to the rising tide of demonization, in 1986 Congress passed the Immigration Reform and Control Act (IRCA), which launched a new militarization of the Mexico-U.S. border and criminalized the hiring of undocumented migrants. Although the legislation also established two legalization programs that ultimately provided residence documents to 3.1 million immigrants, these programs required that adjusting migrants take English and civics classes to prove their worth before they could be granted permanent residence, something not normally required until immigrants apply for U.S. citizenship. Ironically, this facilitated a surge in naturalizations during the late 1990s that prompted a subsequent surge in legal immigration outside the restrictive quotas.

With the end of the Cold War in the early 1990s, cutbacks in defense spending sparked an economic recession that was particularly deep and bitter in California, and in this state Latino immigrants quickly became scapegoats for native economic anxieties. During 1993, petitioners launched Proposition 187, the Save Our State Initiative—which framed immigrants as criminals, freeloaders, and potential predators—and sought to force local government officials and law enforcement agencies into active anti-immigrant enforcement. It also sought to ban undocumented migrants from receiving all public services except emergency medical care, including education (Jacobson 2008).

The initiative passed with overwhelming voter support in 1994, and in that same year the U.S. Border Patrol launched Operation Gatekeeper in San Diego—an all-out militarization of the border between San Diego and Tijuana designed to stop the flow of undocumented migrants through what had been the busiest sector of the two-thousand-mile frontier (Rotella 1998; Andreas 2000). In response to the rising wave of anti-immigrant hysteria, Latin American migrants began to mobilize politically and to naturalize in large numbers. Mexicans historically had exhibited the lowest rate of naturalization of any major immigrant group, but in the early 1990s they began applying for citizenship en masse, aided, ironically, by IRCA's requirement that legalizing immigrants take English and civics courses. Whereas the number of Mexican naturalizations averaged just 18,000 per year between 1980 and 1993, the annual average rose to 123,000 per year afterward.

Not only did these newly minted citizens acquire the right to vote, of course—and thereby the ability to fight back electorally against the anti-immigrant mobilization—but, as noted earlier, they also have the right as citizens to sponsor the immigration of their spouses, minor children, and parents without numerical limitation. As a result, as can be seen in figure 3.11, the number of legal entries from Mexico began to rise sharply after 1990, an eventuality that Congress tried fruitlessly to prevent by capping family immigration. Unable politically to limit the entry of relatives of U.S. citizens, in 1990 it reduced the quota for immediate relatives of legal resident aliens, which only pushed more legal immigrants toward citizenship. By 2008 the annual number of naturalizations was running at 231,000 per year for Mexicans.

In 1996, Congress responded to continued documented and undocumented migration by passing three major pieces of restrictive legislation. The Illegal Immigration Reform and Immigrant Responsibility Act authorized the hiring of thousands of additional Border Patrol agents and the construction of more walls and fences to bring the militarization of the border to new heights (Massey, Durand, and Malone 2002). It also permitted the removal of aliens from ports of entry without a judicial hearing; declared undocumented migrants ineligible for all public benefits; and, in an effort to restrict family migration still further, required sponsors of legal immigrants to provide affidavits of support that demonstrated a household income of at least 125 percent of the federal poverty line. The new law also contained a provision known as 287(g) that authorized local agencies to assist in federal immigration enforcement (Newton 2008).

The Personal Responsibility and Work Opportunity Reconciliation Act (PRWORA) of 1996 extended the portrayal of undocumented migrants as greedy freeloaders to legal immigrants and placed new restrictions on the access of legal permanent residents to public services, barring them from receiving food stamps, Supplemental Security Income (SSI), and other means-tested benefits for five years after admission. Finally, the Anti-Terrorism and Effective Death Penalty Act of 1996 formalized the equation of immigrants with terrorists and lawbreakers by declaring that any alien who had ever committed a crime, no matter how long ago, was immediately deportable.

The Anti-Terrorism Act also gave the federal government broad new police powers to effect the "expedited exclusion" of any alien who had *ever* crossed the border without documents, no matter what his or her current legal status (Legomsky 2000, 1616). Given that the majority of legal immigrants to the United States from Latin America have prior experience as undocumented migrants (Massey and Malone 2003), this new provision instantly rendered millions of legal immigrants—and the vast majority of Mexican resident aliens—as deportable for past infractions.

Finally, the Anti-Terrorism Act granted the State Department authority to designate any organization as "terrorist," thereby making all members of groups so designated immediately excludable. It also narrowed the grounds for asylum and added alien smuggling to the list of crimes covered by the RICO (Racketeer Influenced Corrupt Organizations) statute, while severely limiting the possibilities for judicial review of deportations. According to Stephen Legomsky (2000, 1616), the 1996 legislation constituted "the most ferocious assault on the judicial review of immigration decisions" ever launched "by creating new removal courts that allow secret procedures to be used to remove suspected alien terrorists; by shifting the authority to make 'expedited removals' to immigration inspectors at ports of entry; and by setting unprecedented limits on judicial review of immigration decisions."

The most recent surge in anti-immigrant legislation came in response to the 9/11 terrorist attacks when, on October 26, 2001, Congress passed, without significant debate, the USA PATRIOT Act, which granted executive authorities even more powers to deport, without hearings or any presentation of evidence, all aliens—legal or illegal, temporary or permanent—whom the attorney general had "reason to believe" might commit, further, or facilitate acts of terrorism. For the first time since the Alien and Sedition Act of 1798, Congress authorized the arrest, imprisonment, and deportation of noncitizens upon the orders of the attorney general, without judicial review.

These repressive federal laws were not enough to placate the hysteria cultivated by the Latino threat narrative, however, and recent years have witnessed an unprecedented surge in anti-immigrant measures enacted at the state and local levels (Hopkins 2008). According to the National Council of State Legislatures, state laws related to immigration increased dramatically after 9/11. Although some 200 bills on immigration had been introduced and 38 laws enacted by 2005, this proved to be just the tip of the iceberg: by 2007, immigration-related legislation had tripled to 1,562 bills introduced and 240 laws passed. By 2009, twenty-three states had signed cooperative agreements with federal authorities to assist in arresting and detaining undocumented migrants under the 287 (g) program.

Although the 1990s brought a great geographic diversification of Latino immigrants to new destination areas throughout the United States, a recent analysis by Daniel Hopkins (2008) found that changing demographics by itself was not enough to incite anti-immigrant mobilization in a particular state or local area. Specifically, his results showed that

> those who live near larger proportions of immigrants do not consistently exhibit more negative attitudes. Instead, at least as far as immigrants are concerned, people respond to the demographics of their communities only under specific circumstances. When faced with a sudden, destabilizing change in local demographics, *and when a salient national rhetoric politicizes that demographic change*, people's views turn anti-immigrant. (Hopkins 2008, 34, emphasis added)

In sum, over the past several decades the repressive power of the state has increasingly been directed against immigrants, documented as well as undocumented. Although the escalation of anti-immigrant repression is apparent at the state and local levels, it is most clearly reflected in federal statistics. Figure 3.12 shows trends in the budget of the U.S. Border Patrol, the number of Border Patrol agents, and the number of line-watch hours spent by agents guarding the Mexico-U.S. border (U.S. Office of Immigration Statistics 2009). Each series has been divided by its value in 1986 to indicate the factor by which enforcement has increased since that date.

Figure 3.12   Indicators of Immigration Enforcement (1986 = 1)

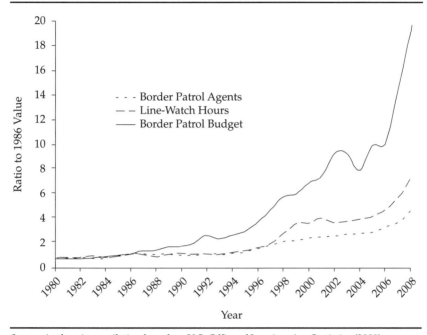

Source: Authors' compilation based on U.S. Office of Immigration Statistics (2009).

As can be seen, U.S. enforcement actions began to rise somewhat in the mid-1980s and then increased more rapidly in the 1990s, but the acceleration during the last decade of the twentieth century proved to be nothing compared with what happened after 9/11, when all three series grew exponentially. By 2008, line-watch hours stood at nearly eight times the 1986 level, the number of Border Patrol agents had increased by a factor of 4.7, and the Border Patrol's budget was twenty times its 1986 level. In terms of size, the Border Patrol went from around 3,700 officers in 1986 to 18,000 in 2008.

The massive increase in immigration enforcement occurred despite the steady decline in the rate of undocumented migration since 1990, and in fact the rate plummeted after 2001 to reach levels near zero by 2008 (see figure 3.11). Despite the decline in traffic, apprehensions of undocumented migrants at the border nonetheless continue apace, while internal arrests and deportations of undocumented migrants from within the United States have risen to unprecedented heights. As figure 3.13 shows, since 1980 border apprehensions have fluctuated between 800,000 and 1.2 million per year, but what is truly remarkable is the steady rise in deportations. Whereas in 1986 only 25,000 immigrants

Figure 3.13   Border Apprehensions and Deportations from the United States

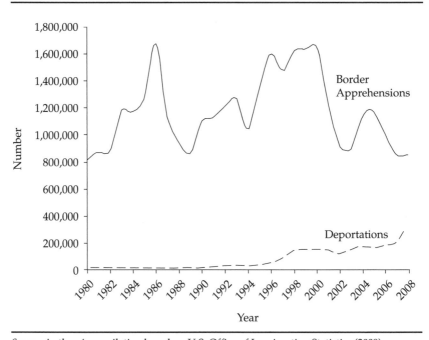

Source: Authors' compilation based on U.S. Office of Immigration Statistics (2009).

were arrested and deported from the United States, by 1996 the figure had climbed to 160,000, and by 2001 to 189,000. Thereafter, deportations surged to reach a record 359,000 in 2008; this level has never been seen before in U.S. history and outdoes the mass deportation campaigns of the 1930s by a factor of three.

In a very real way, then, the United States now increasingly looks like a police state to immigrants, whatever their documentation. Under current conditions, it is as if the militarized border program of 1953 and 1954 (Operation Wetback) has been made permanent and the mass deportation campaigns of 1929 to 1934 have been institutionalized at three times their earlier size. As a result, the number of immigrants under detention has exploded, increasing by 50 percent since 2001. In 2008, the most recent fiscal year for which data are available, some 320,000 immigrants were incarcerated and awaiting trial or deportation, 350,000 more were expelled from the United States, and 860,000 persons were apprehended at the southern border and summarily returned to Mexico.

Life During Wartime

Not surprisingly, the collapse of the U.S. economy, the surge in anti-immigrant enforcement at the national, state, and local levels, and the ongoing demonization of Latinos in the media have taken their toll on immigrants. New undocumented migration has effectively ceased (see figure 3.11), but undocumented migrants already present in the United States are not returning home. Indeed, rates of return migration have dropped to near zero, and the undocumented population has stabilized at just under 12 million (Hoefer, Rytina, and Baker 2009; Passel and Cohn 2009). At the same time, Congress has quietly increased the number of temporary worker visas to levels not seen since the late 1950s. As figure 3.11 shows, the number of Mexican guest workers reached 361,000 in 2008, a level last seen in 1959.

With 12 million people out of status and temporary worker migration now pushing toward 400,000 per year and constituting the bulk of new entrants, the share of migrants who lack full legal rights in the United States has never been greater. Undocumented migrants alone now constitute one-third of all immigrants in the United States, but as noted in the last chapter, the share is much greater among Latin Americans. The large share of respondents in our sample who lack documents (62 percent) thus reflects a fundamental facet of contemporary Latino immigration to the United States. Latin Americans living in the United States are probably more vulnerable and exploitable than at any point in American history. Even documented and native-born Latinos are typically connected to people who lack documentation and thus share their vulnerability and exploitability. According to estimates by Jeffrey Passel (2005), about one-quarter of all persons living in households that contain an undocumented migrant are U.S. citizens.

Recent survey data illustrate the degree to which immigrant and native Latinos perceive their fates to be interconnected. In 2008, 72 percent of Latino immigrants surveyed by the Pew Hispanic Center said that they worried about deportation some or a lot, and the figure was still quite high at 35 percent among native-born Latinos, who were presumably not vulnerable to deportation themselves but worried about the deportation of friends or relatives (Lopez and Minushkin 2008). As of 2007, some 72 percent of foreign-born Latinos agreed that the immigration debate has made life difficult for Hispanics, compared with 53 percent among the native-born (Pew Hispanic Center 2007).

By 2008, Latinos had become much more pessimistic about life in the United States, with 63 percent of foreign-born Hispanics and 30 percent of natives saying that the situation for Hispanics had deteriorated compared with a year earlier. Irrespective of birthplace, the vast majority of Hispanics disapproved of workplace raids (76 percent) and opposed the criminal prosecution of employers who hired undocumented migrants (70 percent), as well as the arrest and deportation of the migrants themselves (73 percent). Only 46 percent of all Hispanics were confident that the police would treat them fairly, and just 49 percent said that they expected fair treatment in the courts (Lopez and Livingston 2009).

Thus, both objective conditions in American society and the subjective perceptions of immigrants suggest that we are indeed in the midst of harsh anti-immigrant times. The economic outlook for most Americans is as bleak as it has been at any time since the Great Depression, and there are few prospects that most baby boomers will be able to retire anytime soon and thereby generate job openings to fuel immigrants' mobility (DeVaney and Chiremba 2005). Anti-immigrant rhetoric in the public sphere has reached a crescendo, public opinion against foreigners has hardened, and enforcement budgets and deportations are at record levels. Most immigrants fear deportation and do not trust the police or the courts to defend their rights in the United States. In the next chapter, we explore the process of labor market integration under these repressive circumstances.

=Chapter 4=

Worlds of Work

The primary point of contact between immigrants and U.S. society is usually the labor market. As we have seen, one of the most prominent reasons immigrants give for coming to the United States is economic conditions, and even those who were motivated by the pull of family ties, the fear of violence at home, or some other reason usually end up in the workforce. What happens to immigrants as they make their way through the world of work can thus be expected to play a disproportionate role in determining their perceptions of life in the United States and in shaping their construction of identity.

Chapter 3 described what is a particularly difficult and hostile context of reception for immigrants in the United States today, one typified by anti-foreign hostility in the media, high levels of repression in public policy, and an increasingly precarious economy; all of these conditions put immigrants in a very vulnerable position. It would be surprising if this vulnerability were not expressed somehow in U.S. labor markets, and indeed, a recent survey conducted by the Pew Hispanic Center found that discrimination against Latinos has been rising. Whereas 44 percent of respondents viewed discrimination as a major problem in 2002, 51 percent said so in 2004, and 58 percent in 2006, with an additional 18 percent in 2006 seeing discrimination at least as a minor problem (Kohut and Suro 2006). Thus, a large majority of Hispanics have come to perceive discrimination as a problem in the United States.

This subjective perception is borne out by objective data on conditions in America's low-wage labor markets. A 2008 survey of low-wage workers in Chicago, Los Angeles, and New York by Annette Bernhardt and her colleagues (2009) revealed that two-thirds were immigrants and that 56 percent of these were undocumented. Their finding that only 6 percent were white whereas 63 percent were Latino, 14 percent were black, and 17 percent were Asian confirms that low-wage workers in the United States are now predominantly immigrant, minority, undocumented, and Latino. Among them, 26 percent earned less than the legal minimum wage, 70 percent were not paid for work done beyond their regular shift, and 76 percent were not paid extra for overtime work.

Without exception, these violations occurred at higher rates for undocumented migrants, among whom 38 percent earned less than the legal minimum, 76 percent were not paid for extra work, and 85 percent were not paid required overtime (Bernhardt et al. 2009). These findings from representative urban labor market surveys are entirely consistent with the experiences reported by our own informants, who work in the New York–New Jersey–Philadelphia urban corridor. In many ways low-wage work in the United States has become an underground economy that is increasingly detached from federal, state, and local regulations and that operates outside the rules of occupational, safety, health, labor, and social security law. The stories offered by our immigrant respondents thus provide a clear window on "how the other half works" (Waldinger and Lichter 2003).

Notes from Underground

To characterize the world of work faced by immigrants in our sample we compiled work histories that began with the question: "When and how did you begin working in the United States?" We paid particular attention to respondents' first and last jobs in the United States and sought to clarify the conditions of employment for each, including the amount earned, the hours worked per day, the form of payment, access to benefits, deduction of taxes, the ethnicity of the employer, and other features of the work setting. We then asked about the intervening jobs and the respondent's other experiences in the labor market. The answers to our queries reveal a world of work characterized by long hours, low wages, cash payment, few benefits, little job security, double shifts, and multiple jobs worked back to back in order to raise earnings.

Like Bernhardt and her co-authors (2009), we found that a common work setting for immigrants was the restaurant industry, especially pizzerias owned by other immigrants. Such was the case of an undocumented Mexican man in New Jersey who reported that "three days after arriving I began to work with my brothers, because they worked in a very big restaurant." He quickly moved on, however, to take a job in the kitchen of a pizzeria, where he worked "cooking pizzas, making sandwiches, everything," for twelve hours a day, six days a week, earning around $11 per hour, paid in cash with no benefits or taxes deducted. He told us that these conditions were typical in the pizza business; in his experience, "most pizzerias pay in cash."

An undocumented Ecuadoran male, also from New Jersey, reported a similar trajectory: his friends and family "all worked in restaurants," and he got his first job "through a friend that has lived here for ten years who I knew" before taking a new job as a dishwasher in a pizzeria for more money, about $325 per week. He was ambitious, however, and "there I learned, and soon I knew the English names of all the products, at least all the important ones." After two months, his growing knowledge enabled him to move into the kitchen, where "in two weeks I learned the pizza business," and his salary was raised to $500 per week. The experience and skills he acquired in the pizzeria kitchen enabled him to keep moving up, this time into a job paying around $700 per week; he located it through "a cousin who worked here, you know, and he said they needed someone." The job had no benefits, however, even though he was paid by check and had taxes deducted. The owner was Ecuadoran, and his fellow workers were also Latino, including "four Ecuadorans and also some Guatemalans," suggesting that the business was an enclave enterprise.

As these vignettes suggest, a common theme throughout our interviews was the use of social ties to friends and relatives to gain access to U.S. employment—or, in theoretical terms, immigrants mobilized their interpersonal ties to extract social capital that furthered their material interests. A documented Ecuadoran male from New Jersey reported that he quickly got his first job in a restaurant "by means of a friend." Working as a busboy, he reported earning $600 per week for working a ten-hour shift from 10:00 in the morning until 8:00 at night, five to six days a week. Although he received no benefits, he was paid by check, and taxes and other charges were deducted.

Working long hours is a characteristic feature of the jobs held by the immigrants in our sample. An undocumented Mexican man in New York, who was a waiter in a Chinese restaurant, earned "something around $500 per week" working a schedule that he said was not "fixed" but generally involved long days, "sometimes twelve or fourteen hours per day," and "sometimes I work five or six days per week." He was paid in cash, and though no deductions were made for benefits or taxes, he reported that his employers did provide "a little extra money" under certain circumstances—or as he put it, "Let's say that if I need something, they give it to me."

The most extreme case of long hours was reported by an undocumented Brazilian man in Philadelphia. He quickly got a job after his arrival in May 2000, but ever since then, he reported, he had had to work "seven days a week" without a break, a fact he confirmed to the incredulous interviewer:

INTERVIEWER: When did you have a day off? Sunday?

RESPONDENT: No. I never had a day off.

INTERVIEWER: No day off?

RESPONDENT: No free day. I never had a day off. Before coming here, I had two days off. Always Saturdays.

INTERVIEWER: But now nothing?

RESPONDENT: Nothing. Not now.

Given the low hourly wage associated with most jobs, extending the number of hours worked is often the only way in which immigrants can earn sufficient money to pay their bills and save a little money to send home; long hours of work are thus actively desired and sought by many immigrants. One undocumented Mexican woman who first worked in the mushroom plants outside of Philadelphia looked for other work when she discovered that she was spending more hours commuting to the plants than working there. She went to work for a cleaning service, "but there I didn't get many hours, and so I couldn't eat. I arrived, put down my things, bathed, changed, and went out again, but it wasn't enough to get by. I couldn't eat, and my aunt and uncle told me that, for very little money, something bad was going to happen." So she went to work for her aunt and uncle, who owned a small shop and paid her $6.25 an hour for a minimum eight-hour shift with no benefits or taxes deducted.

At this job, she made up for the low pay by adding extra days to her workweek, but this schedule worried her aunt and uncle, who finally prevailed on her to take at least one day off every two weeks:

RESPONDENT: And sometimes I work the whole week. To help me they give me one day off every fifteen days. They tell me, the señora and the señor, they say, "We are going to give you a day off every week—or do you want to work the whole week?" I tell them, "No, all week." So they said, "But we don't want you to get tired, or get angry and decide to leave." And I said, "No, it's fine like this." And they said, "We are going to do something, we are going to give you a day off every week." So I said, "Oh, all right."

INTERVIEWER: So you take one day off per week or maybe one every fifteen days?

RESPONDENT: Uh huh.

INTERVIEWER: And they pay by check or cash?

RESPONDENT: Cash.

Another undocumented Mexican woman from New Jersey likewise went to work as a teenager in a local bakery for $6.00 an hour, but quickly discovered that her few hours of work yielded little money. She explained how she angled to get more hours of work:

RESPONDENT: Well, I didn't like what they were paying me there. At first it seemed like something to me, but I didn't know. I thought I earned well, but no one said, "Oh, look for something better." You know? Little by little I realized that the value, the value of money and everything. I was a cashier, selling cookies, bread, and everything. After school I went there and started around four and left at seven. The bakery closed at seven, and I went home. But sometimes I stayed a few hours extra to see how they made the bread in the back and what gets delivered to bakeries at night. But I punched my time card at seven and stayed late just to learn. Then one day the manager came and said, "What are you doing?" I said, "Nothing. I'm just looking to see how they work, nothing more." And he asked if I had punched out, and I said, "Yes, it's my free time." And he said, "Okay." The thing is, he did not want me being there because I could have an accident when I wasn't working. He told me this and then asked whether I wanted more hours, and I said, "Yes," and he said, "Okay, let's see." And next week he said that if I wanted I could help the bakers and watch the bread and their boxes. Then I left around nine.

INTERVIEWER: And did you have a job other than this?

RESPONDENT: Yes, because there I only worked nights on two days that were very busy, Friday and Saturday.

Thus, even though she was able to get more hours at the bakery, her earnings still fell short of what she wished and she felt compelled to get a second job, another common strategy for boosting total earnings among those working in the secondary labor market. For example, a documented Honduran male in Philadelphia worked as a waiter in a local restaurant but also freelanced as an electrician on the side, doing odd jobs with a partner:

RESPONDENT: I worked there [as a waiter] for two years, and unfortunately then I moved. I got another job and began to work at it.

INTERVIEWER: Okay. And what do you work at now?

RESPONDENT: I am here, working as a waiter.

INTERVIEWER: Still a waiter?

RESPONDENT: As a waiter. I also work as an electrical technician on the side, but Monday through Friday, during the week, I work here.

INTERVIEWER: Do you work independently or with a company?

RESPONDENT: It's just me and another person.

INTERVIEWER: Okay.

RESPONDENT: It's like the two of us are a company.

INTERVIEWER: Okay. So, like, you have a salary?

RESPONDENT: I pay myself.

INTERVIEWER: How's it going?

RESPONDENT: It goes well.

INTERVIEWER: Do you make enough to save and all that?

RESPONDENT: Yes.

INTERVIEWER: Okay. This, and you work five days a week in the other?

RESPONDENT: Five days a week, Monday through Friday. And sometimes Saturday.

INTERVIEWER: And in all this, as well as working for yourself, do you have to deduct taxes and all that?

RESPONDENT: Of course.

INTERVIEWER: And do you have benefits? Do you give yourself benefits?

RESPONDENT: No.

Another undocumented migrant, a Guatemalan male in New Jersey, was able to bolster his earnings by working in a sandwich shop by day and as a security guard at a discotheque at night:

RESPONDENT: Well, I work here at a fancy sandwich shop, and in the evenings I work in Trenton at a discotheque.

INTERVIEWER: Ah, so you have two jobs?

RESPONDENT: Yes.

INTERVIEWER: Are you a DJ?

RESPONDENT: No, I am an assistant in security.

INTERVIEWER: Ah, okay. And now, what is your salary, more or less? Let's say, by the week. How much do you earn per week?

RESPONDENT: Look, I don't get paid weekly, but every two weeks.

INTERVIEWER: Okay, for two weeks then.

RESPONDENT: Well, it varies a lot. Let's say something around $1,100 or $1,200.

INTERVIEWER: Okay, and about how many hours do you work per day?

RESPONDENT: Well, that varies as well. Sometimes I come in at six and stay until two in the afternoon, but sometimes until five or six, and then I work again from seven in the evening until three in the morning.

INTERVIEWER: And do they pay you in cash or by check?

RESPONDENT: At night in cash, and here during the day by check.

INTERVIEWER: With the check, do they deduct taxes?

RESPONDENT: Always.

INTERVIEWER: And do you have benefits?

RESPONDENT: No.

A Puerto Rican male in New York reported that he went to work as a hairstylist when a Uruguayan acquaintance opened a salon. There he took advantage of his access to a constant stream of clients to earn extra money by distributing fliers promoting nearby clubs and bars. In his own words, he

> met this Uruguayan guy who said . . . "I want to open my own hair salon, and if you go to school, I'll give you a job." Well, so it was. This Uruguayan started a salon, and we spent eight years working together in Elizabeth. I spent time working, and then I did promotions in the clubs and did well because, here there was more work, understand me, for a promoter here distributing fliers, handing out fliers to promote clubs in the salon while washing hair, cleaning to the end of the day.

Although the three immigrants just discussed earned more money through multiple jobs, they were still unable to gain access to benefits. Another respondent, an undocumented Guatemalan man in New Jersey, solved this problem by combining one job with few hours that offered benefits with another that offered longer hours but no benefits.

INTERVIEWER: How much are they paying you here [in this latest job]?

RESPONDENT: Here they are paying me more or less $8 per hour. But I only work three days a week.

INTERVIEWER: And where are you working now? Still with the Spanish guy?

RESPONDENT: No, now I work for another place on route 206 up north. Here I also work as a busboy, but whereas there I earn cash, here I am paid by check.

INTERVIEWER: And you have benefits here?

RESPONDENT: Yes, they have benefits, and they help you with communication, human relations, health.

INTERVIEWER: Very well. How much are you taking home, or how much do you earn when you take on additional work—this work that offers benefits, security, and everything, how much do you make a month, approximately?

RESPONDENT: Well, for the three days that I work per week, every two weeks I make around $285 or $290.

INTERVIEWER: Okay, so you earn like $600 a month, but really more than this because you get benefits.

RESPONDENT: Yes, they take money out for those, and also they deduct taxes. They call them taxes for the privilege of working in this country, right? Because for us immigrants, we'll never see the benefit from those taxes.

INTERVIEWER: No, you won't, unfortunately.

In addition to working more hours per job or stringing together multiple jobs, another strategy to increase earnings is to form a small business. A documented woman from Venezuela was able to take advantage of her experience working in first a Brazilian restaurant and then a Moroccan restaurant to partner with her husband to open their own restaurant, which earned them enough to purchase private health insurance:

INTERVIEWER: You said that where you began to work was in a Brazilian restaurant, at the bar. And after this, you did what? Do you remember?

RESPONDENT: After that, I jumped to another place as a waitress, that was a Moroccan place. I worked two years in this place, which no longer exists, for two years, and from there I went to another place, also as a waitress, and there I remained a year. From time to time I have also worked a lot as a babysitter.

INTERVIEWER: And when did you establish this business, your restaurant here?

RESPONDENT: Around four and a half years ago.

INTERVIEWER: And it goes well?

RESPONDENT: Yes, thank God, it's going really well.

INTERVIEWER: So this business is yours? Your own? Do you share it? Do you have co-owners?

RESPONDENT: Just me and my husband.

INTERVIEWER: And what about the expenses? Do you work in cash? Do you reinvest? How does it work?

RESPONDENT: Well, I have my salary and my pay by check.

INTERVIEWER: How much do you earn, more or less?

RESPONDENT: Around $400 per week.

INTERVIEWER: And you have insurance and everything?

RESPONDENT: Yes, we have medical insurance, but not from this work.

Another woman, a Honduran female living in New Jersey, after being laid off from a job in a perfume factory, set up her own small shop selling specialized ethnic products to other Latinos. Despite the long hours and modest earnings, she seemed content with the independence she enjoyed as a business owner:

INTERVIEWER: Okay. And now what do you work in?

RESPONDENT: In my own business.

INTERVIEWER: In this shop?

RESPONDENT: This shop, yes.

INTERVIEWER: And how much do you make, more or less?

RESPONDENT: At least $200, sometimes $300.

INTERVIEWER: Per day?

RESPONDENT: No, per week.

INTERVIEWER: Oh, per week. And how many hours per day do you work?

RESPONDENT: Twelve.

INTERVIEWER: And seven days a week? And you are the owner?

RESPONDENT: Yes.

INTERVIEWER: Do you pay yourself by check? How do you do it?

RESPONDENT: No, in cash, calculated.

A documented Colombian male reported a thriving business as a musician around New York: he played a regular stint three to five days a week at a restaurant on Long Island and also did his own concerts as well as weddings and parties. He made good money doing work that still left him time to pursue his studies:

RESPONDENT: I've always worked for myself, playing weddings, concerts.

INTERVIEWER: So you would [classify] yourself as an independent contractor? Is that what we should say?

RESPONDENT: Yes.

INTERVIEWER: Then that's what we'll say. Do you have a company?

RESPONDENT: No, not yet.

INTERVIEWER: You sell by word of mouth?

RESPONDENT: Yes.

INTERVIEWER: From this guy or that . . . and your price is normally . . .

RESPONDENT: Well, this time it was $70 for three hours.

INTERVIEWER: Aha, but normally how much do you charge?

RESPONDENT: Oh, it depends where and when and how.

INTERVIEWER: Okay. So let's try it a different way. Can you give me your approximate earnings these days?

RESPONDENT: It varies.

INTERVIEWER: Yes, I understand, but monthly, for example, or weekly, we need a figure. Because you are independent, it is difficult.

RESPONDENT: Well, for a week it can reach $1,000.

INTERVIEWER: One thousand, okay, so we can say that you earn between $4,000 and $6,000 per month, or is that too much?

RESPONDENT: Too much. I would say around $4,000.

INTERVIEWER: Okay, $4,000, that's good money. And do you have insurance?

RESPONDENT: No.

INTERVIEWER: How many days per week do you work?

RESPONDENT: It varies, but around five.

INTERVIEWER: Five days. How many hours per day?

RESPONDENT: Around four.

INTERVIEWER: Four hours, and also, you said you studied?

RESPONDENT: Yes.

INTERVIEWER: So you are active how many hours per day?

RESPONDENT: From around nine in the morning until eleven or twelve at night.

Another man, a Venezuelan interviewed in New Jersey, likewise reported that he increased his earnings by performing as a musician after moving between several disagreeable jobs. He began as a painter but ended up cutting his hands badly because the owner refused to let him trim back the roses around the house. He then worked at a deli, but when he discovered he was being paid less than others doing the same work, he walked away and took a job in a Korean laundry, where he became an expert at ironing shirts. Although he earned the admiration of the laundry owner and made good money, the pace was relentless, and eventually he came to see it as "typical exploitation of the Latino." He grew tired of the work and moved to Miami to stay with friends for a while. There he became involved in the local Latin community.

RESPONDENT: Then I got tired, and I went to check out Miami, where I had some musician friends who said, why don't you come down here. So I got my money together, and I rented an apartment in North Miami and went to live [there] for a year.

INTERVIEWER: And what did you do while down there?

RESPONDENT: Just music, and peaceful living, pure music. At first I didn't make much money, but I got by.

INTERVIEWER: Playing what?

RESPONDENT: Music. This was a group in those days, the best gaita band in Miami. Gaita is a kind of music in Venezuela. And with this group I began to play. Then I went off by myself and made up some cards and began to leave them around restaurants, and within a month I was playing Tuesday, Thursday, Saturday, and Sunday.

INTERVIEWER: Imagine that!

RESPONDENT: And when I began to be a musician, if I charged $300, I would give $100 to the percussionist and keep $200 for myself, because I was the one who got the contract and it was my business, understand? So I would get $200 for three hours . . .

INTERVIEWER: Imagine the difference!

RESPONDENT: Just sitting in a chair . . .

INTERVIEWER: . . . and doing what you like.

RESPONDENT: And from this came other contracts, because there were always private parties, and in these I would charge $800, at times $1,000, because these were people with a lot of money. I would bring with me to these parties a bass player and another guitarist so that we were four, and then I began to make upwards of $1,200 to $1,500 cash per week.

A woman from Ecuador with questionable documents reported that she managed to earn something approaching a middle-class income by managing a restaurant owned by her brother in Philadelphia.

RESPONDENT: I became a waitress. As soon as I began to work with my brother, because he put a little responsibility on me, right away I stayed to close the restaurant and then to open it—me, all by myself. I have always wanted to be a business person, so I began to interact with the people that he had, in terms of the business, and to take charge of the requests and these things. So it was that he gave me this confidence, and I began to work with him more directly.

INTERVIEWER: Okay. Has he made you a partner, or are you still just his sister?

RESPONDENT: He is the only owner.

INTERVIEWER: Okay. Do you have any idea, more or less, how much you earn now, how much you are earning right now, when you figure it out for the year, or if you will, for the month, or however you want to give it. Approximately.

RESPONDENT: Well, I am on salary, at $9 per hour. It's a payment that I agreed upon with my brother. But apart from that we do, um, parties. We do private events in which I get a percentage of the tip that comes to, more or less, at a minimum, around forty thousand per year. Or at least it fluctuates around forty.

INTERVIEWER: So what would be the total income per year?

RESPONDENT: Something over $40,000—$46,000, $47,000.

INTERVIEWER: That's good. And you feel comfortable with this?

RESPONDENT: Yes, yes.

A few respondents, generally those with valid documents, a command of English, and some education, reported working in the primary labor market. One Dominican female in New York first began to work at summer jobs when she was a university student, but her documented status enabled her eventually to land a job in a city agency under a special program for minority workers, which allowed her to build her résumé as she completed her studies and launch her career in accounting:

> RESPONDENT: After that, when I had, like, two years of university, I had to begin to work to gain experience that was good to get another job. Ah, I worked a month in an agency of New York City. There was a program for low-wage people to obtain work through the city, and I got a job in an office of a city agency.

> INTERVIEWER: Okay, and after you got this job?

> RESPONDENT: Summer jobs that were mainly to get work experience in my specialty—I was studying accounting—different jobs, working in different places to get experience in accounting so when I graduated I could put experience on my résumé.

> INTERVIEWER: And now do you think that you are working at your level?

> RESPONDENT: Well, really a lot of time passed before that. When I graduated, I worked for the Port Authority of New York and New Jersey in the World Trade Center, and it was there that I met my husband. This was my first job, and afterward I got my accounting license, my CPA, and I went to work for Ernst and Young, one of the largest accounting firms in the United States and even the world. I worked there nine years, and then I worked at a hospital, and then two and a half years ago I came here.

> INTERVIEWER: What is your current title here?

> RESPONDENT: Assistant accountant in the Metropolitan Museum of Art.

> INTERVIEWER: I imagine that you have benefits and all this sort of thing.

> RESPONDENT: Yes, everything. From the start I have always had benefits.

Another documented Dominican woman in New York also reported being able to take advantage of public programs directed at the disadvantaged to gain valuable work experience and move ahead in work and school:

RESPONDENT: I began to work in summer jobs when I was around fourteen years old.

INTERVIEWER: Summer Jobs for Youth?

RESPONDENT: Summer Jobs for Youth. I mean, they're government jobs that every summer give work to kids, students aged fourteen to eighteen. You have to apply every summer, and you can work up to three months, and you get the minimum wage. They are office jobs. You learn how to use computers, telephones, things like that. They're still good jobs. I don't think they have these programs now. I mean, I have not run into [anyone] who said they still have these programs. But this girl I met the other day, I told her about this program. Usually they are community service jobs?

INTERVIEWER: With nonprofits?

RESPONDENT: Ummm, yes.

INTERVIEWER: And after this work, what was your first job?

RESPONDENT: When I finished high school at age sixteen.

INTERVIEWER: Oh? In what kind of things?

RESPONDENT: It was something medical, you know, something with the health department or something like that. I began working there.

INTERVIEWER: And how much did you earn more or less? Can you tell me your salary?

RESPONDENT: I don't remember, but not very much, something like $5 per hour.

INTERVIEWER: And was it full-time or part-time?

RESPONDENT: It was part-time because I was near the university. I worked two or three days per week, less than twenty-one hours per week.

INTERVIEWER: And now what kind of work do you do?

RESPONDENT: I am a client manager. I manage, like, four people who audit medical claims from hospitals and doctors. What my department does is check that the claims that arrive are appropriately paid.

INTERVIEWER: And how much do you earn?

RESPONDENT: Around seventy (thousand per year).

INTERVIEWER: And how many hours per day?

RESPONDENT: Thousands! I mean, I like to work seven and a half hours, but sometimes I stay more, like eight or nine hours, depending on the work that I have.

INTERVIEWER: And they pay by check?

RESPONDENT: Yes, a salary—not by the hour.

INTERVIEWER: With benefits and all?

RESPONDENT: Yes, everything.

Similarly, a documented Dominican female in New York began work when she was recommended for a position by a professor at college, which was followed by other part-time positions on campus as she completed her studies, including a stint in Europe teaching English to French students and culminating with an internship that she expected to launch her formal career in the United States:

RESPONDENT: Now I have an internship with a private organization for children in Harlem. Harlem is a community . . . well, I guess you know it. Well, I work there in a program in which the children have classes in the morning and in the afternoon they play baseball.

INTERVIEWER: How much do they pay you?

RESPONDENT: They pay me $100 per week.

INTERVIEWER: Okay, and you have benefits?

RESPONDENT: I don't have benefits. What kind of benefits are you talking about?

INTERVIEWER: Like social security . . .

RESPONDENT: No, nothing like that. It is an internship for college students, and more than anything it is for the experience because I want to get a job.

INTERVIEWER: Do you work to help out your parents, or do you work to pay for school? Both things?

RESPONDENT: Mainly I work to help [with] my studies, but I would say this is also helping my parents because they are paying for my schooling. I usually like to take care of everything myself so I don't have to ask my parents for personal expenses, or even school expenses. If I need to, I ask.

For those without documents and education, mobility prospects are bleak. During the 1990s, the terms of immigrant hiring shifted in response to changes instituted by the Immigration Reform and Control Act, which for the first time criminalized undocumented hiring by sanctioning employers who "knowingly" hired unauthorized migrants. In response, immigrants began purchasing false documents, and employers shifted from direct hiring to subcontracting through middlemen. Rather than hiring an immigrant directly, employers entered into a contract with a citizen or resident alien who agreed to make workers available to the employer on terms acceptable to both. If the job site was raided and undocumented immigrants were apprehended, then the subcontractor was liable to be sanctioned, not the employer. In our interviews, we often found that the subcontractor was a middleman minority group member with legal status who served as the interface between the formal business of the employer and the underground labor market.

The net effect of these arrangements was to reduce the wages and undermine the working conditions of immigrants, who were at the mercy of subcontractors and left unprotected by the laws that governed the workplace behavior of the firm where they actually worked. Such was the situation of an undocumented Mexican woman in Philadelphia who told us:

I began to work the day after I arrived in the United States, in a greenhouse, and then later we found ourselves working for a Chinese woman in Maryland. She came and picked us up at three in the morning to take us to Maryland to work in a chicken processing plant. Yes, they picked us up at three in the morning, and we arrived at around six, and we left again at around four and came back next day again at six. And I worked there for around four months, until they began to ask for my papers.

The wages she earned were low, and the conditions of work were harsh, with the Chinese subcontractor imposing strict, uncompromising discipline:

INTERVIEWER: How much did they pay you at the chicken plant?

RESPONDENT: Around $5.50 [per hour].

INTERVIEWER: And how were the conditions of work there?

RESPONDENT: Bad, because the line came with one chicken after another, some ten chickens per minute. The line ran very rapidly, and the Chinese woman was behind you checking to make sure you had done a good job on the chicken, and if you had left a bone. She fucking cussed us out all the time, and it was very hard.

INTERVIEWER: Was it dangerous? In terms of risks, what did you do? Did you grab the chicken? How did you decide?

RESPONDENT: The chicken comes down the line cooked and really hot.

INTERVIEWER: Aha.

RESPONDENT: And we had to cut it to bits, remove the leg, the thigh, the breast. [We had] to remove both because this went into hamburgers for McDonald's.

INTERVIEWER: Really?

RESPONDENT: Yes. And to take it apart and all . . .

INTERVIEWER: . . . Hot, and your hands . . .

RESPONDENT: . . . Yes, you burned your hands there.

INTERVIEWER: They didn't give you gloves or anything?

RESPONDENT: They don't give out gloves because they gave us some liquids to sterilize our hands, to wash our hands well. They don't give out gloves because with gloves you can't feel the bone. You have to be without gloves to feel the bone, to feel where the bone goes in the meat. But, yes, there are risks, because everything is so fast and you have to use a knife, and with the knife you can cut yourself, up to the point where . . .

INTERVIEWER: Doesn't it hurt you also in this part of the hands?

RESPONDENT: Yes, that, it is really nasty, and here, like this, the chicken carries a kind of liquid, so that it isn't the chicken that hurts you, really, so much as the liquid, with which . . .

INTERVIEWER: What?

RESPONDENT: I don't know what damages your hands, if it is the liquid with which you wash your hands or the chickens, because you end up with cracks and cuts and everything with the heat.

INTERVIEWER: Maybe the chicken comes to you with some material, some liquid or something.

RESPONDENT: And this, the chicken comes hot, and you have to be doing everything rapidly, everything rapid. And after a while you just zone out without being able to be rapid, and chickens back up, and the Chinese woman really curses you for letting them back up too much. . . . That was the Chinese woman. She gave us a cap to hide our hair and earplugs because the machinery made so much noise. And when even the littlest hair fell out of the cap, or the earplugs, she would arrive and, with her hands all full of chicken . . . push and pull until she put the hair back and hid the earplugs. She was very mean, very bad. We were working there for around four months, and then we left.

INTERVIEWER: Did you have benefits or anything like that?

RESPONDENT: No.

INTERVIEWER: And how did they pay you? In cash?

RESPONDENT: Cash.

INTERVIEWER: And they didn't take out anything for taxes? Or maybe since it was in cash you don't know.

RESPONDENT: No, I don't know if they deducted anything.

INTERVIEWER: You don't know.

RESPONDENT: But she said that, yes, she took out social security.

INTERVIEWER: And did she give you a receipt that said this?

RESPONDENT: No.

A Mexican male in New York also reported working for a Chinese subcontractor, in this case someone who provided workers to restaurants on short-term contracts up and down the East Coast under a special arrangement known as "outside work"—meaning work outside of New York that paid the going wage but came with housing while the workers were temporarily dispatched out of town.

RESPONDENT: Like I will say, what we called outside work, well, outside work pays more or less the same and also offers a place to stay without paying rent. You only have to pay for personal expenses.

INTERVIEWER: What do you call it? Outside work?

RESPONDENT: Outside work. Outside New York City. It's to say that, if I want a job in New Jersey or wherever, I go to the agency and I say, "I want work in this particular place," and, well, they say, "No, I don't have anything. I have something in this other location." Or you have to wait until something comes up.

INTERVIEWER: And this job in Philadelphia was like that? You call it outside work?

RESPONDENT: Outside work, yes.

INTERVIEWER: Outside of New York, but you got it from here?

RESPONDENT: From here, yes.

INTERVIEWER: Very good.

RESPONDENT: It's that the employers are outside of New York, and they call the agency by phone asking for personnel. And from here, on a blank sheet, you put, restaurant work, two people, one for Boston, the other for Philadelphia.

INTERVIEWER: And they give you a place to stay?

RESPONDENT: Yes. And they give you allowances for this and that.

INTERVIEWER: And take you in a car and everything?

RESPONDENT: They buy you a bus ticket from here to wherever you are going.

INTERVIEWER: And then they come to get you?

RESPONDENT: Arriving at the bus station, you speak by telephone to the restaurant, and someone from there comes to find you.

INTERVIEWER: And what kind of housing did they give you? Was it good or not?

RESPONDENT: It was fine. Well, in this house [where] my cousin still lives as he continues to work there. I say "cousin" because it was him I lived with there.

Despite not having to pay for housing for this outside work, the earnings prospects were meager, with a base salary of $160 every two weeks and the rest made in tips, all without benefits or taxes and all paid in cash:

RESPONDENT: Well, how should I put it? It's that my base salary is $160 every two weeks.

INTERVIEWER: And the rest you make in . . .

RESPONDENT: In tips.

INTERVIEWER: And these are good?

RESPONDENT: Sometimes.

INTERVIEWER: Sometimes, but not always? So if you had to roughly estimate per week, would you put it at around $300?

RESPONDENT: More like $400, $450 more or less.

INTERVIEWER: Do you have benefits there? At least life insurance, health insurance, and so on?

RESPONDENT: No, nothing like that.

INTERVIEWER: Do they deduct taxes?

RESPONDENT: Yes, they take out taxes.

INTERVIEWER: And when they pay you, do they pay in cash or with a check or what?

RESPONDENT: In cash.

INTERVIEWER: And they give you a little sheet of paper that tells you the hours you worked and all that, don't they?

RESPONDENT: No.

Latino immigrants dominate the workforce of the region's lawn and garden sector. One documented Mexican male reported that his first job in the United States was working for a Chinese foreman in "la yarda"—doing yard work in the wealthy suburbs outside of Philadelphia—once again for low wages, with no benefits, no taxes deducted, and payment in cash:

RESPONDENT: A man, a Chinese guy, he came to pick us up, and we went there.

INTERVIEWER: What were you growing? What did you cultivate?

RESPONDENT: No, we were cleaning, clearing leaves that had fallen on the grass.

INTERVIEWER: Aha. And where was this? In Philadelphia?

RESPONDENT: Outside of Philadelphia. They brought me there in a car.

INTERVIEWER: How much did they pay you for this?

RESPONDENT: They paid me two hundred.

INTERVIEWER: Weekly?

RESPONDENT: A little more maybe.

INTERVIEWER: How many hours did you work per day?

RESPONDENT: Ten.

INTERVIEWER: Did you get paid in cash?

RESPONDENT: Uh huh.

INTERVIEWER: Did they take out taxes?

RESPONDENT: I have no idea.

INTERVIEWER: And you didn't have benefits?

RESPONDENT: Nope.

Although harsh working conditions are associated with labor subcontracting, a difficult work environment is not limited to this kind of indirect hiring. An undocumented Mexican woman living in New Jersey complained about the conditions she endured in a frozen cake factory where she not only worked in below-freezing temperatures but had to keep up with a rapid assembly line as she decorated cakes:

RESPONDENT: From there I entered an ice cream factory, a place for frozen desserts. The work was real hard because it is extremely cold and you have to go into the freezer to get out what you need to decorate the cakes. It's like you're stuck for eight hours, and it's always the same. You have to meet a certain production to continue in your job.

INTERVIEWER: What is this production? That they ask you to wash at least thirty baking sheets per minute?

RESPONDENT: Yes, like that. Baking sheets per hour and cakes when we made them there we froze them. The cakes were 350 per hour [had to finish 350 per hour]. Depending on the size of the cakes, sometimes for the smallest ones it was 700 per hour.

INTERVIEWER: What did you do?

RESPONDENT: You are decorating them, putting HAPPY BIRTHDAY on them, putting on the balloons and all the little figures.

INTERVIEWER: Okay, and how much did they pay you there in the dessert factory?

RESPONDENT: They paid me $7 [per hour].

INTERVIEWER: That was a little better than your first job?

RESPONDENT: A little better.

INTERVIEWER: And did they provide benefits?

RESPONDENT: Oh, no. There we had no benefits.

Not all respondents gave us unremitting tales of hardship and exploitation. One young Mexican man in Philadelphia had very nice things to say about the owner of the upscale Asian fusion restaurant where he worked:

INTERVIEWER: Do they pay you well?

RESPONDENT: I'd say so.

INTERVIEWER: How much are you earning now?

RESPONDENT: Almost $8 [per hour].

INTERVIEWER: And how many days a week do you work?

RESPONDENT: I work six days. Six days, and they treat me well. The owner, she is terrific, and the chef as well.

INTERVIEWER: The chef is Latino?

RESPONDENT: His parents are Cuban, and he speaks a little English, but the owner treats me very well. When I began working there, I washed dishes and all that.

INTERVIEWER: And you have risen?

RESPONDENT: She gave me the opportunity to work as a busboy, and she trained me in everything. I knew nothing. She trained me how to do things, and then later I went to the kitchen, doing preparations and the rest, and then she gave me another little push up the line, and now I do everything around here. I clean, I paint.

Roads to Nowhere

Despite the hope and gratitude revealed in the last interview, the prevailing picture we derive from our in-depth interviews with Latino immigrants in the northeastern United States is less than sanguine about the prospects for occupational mobility and earnings growth, consistent with the recent findings of Bernhardt and her colleagues (2009). The narratives mostly reveal that immigrants are entangled in a repetitive cycle of dead-end jobs whose demands take a physical and emotional toll while offering few chances for earning more money or moving ahead occupationally, a profile that is characteristic of the circumstances that prevail in the secondary labor market. The only immigrants who seem to be able to get better jobs in the primary labor sector are those with documents and education, a requirement that excludes the large majority of recent Latino immigrants and many in the second generation as well. In this section, we draw on a quantitative coding of our qualitative interview data to clarify and measure precisely what being mired in the secondary labor market means in terms of status and wages.

Labor Force Participation

To achieve occupational mobility and earnings growth, one must first enter the labor force. We therefore begin our analysis with a consideration of the patterns and determinants of labor force participation. The top panel of table 4.1 presents two measures of the amount of labor supplied to U.S. markets by respondents. Given the salience of the economic goals discerned in the interview narratives, it is not surprising to find a high rate of labor force participation among the immigrants in our sample, a rate that varies little by legal status. Overall, 77 percent of respondents reported that they were employed or looking for work at the time of the survey. Among documented migrants the figure was 75 percent, and among undocumented migrants it was 78 percent. The top panel of table 4.1 also shows the number of hours that respondents reported working per day. In general, immigrants put in rather long workdays: the overall average was 8.7 hours, but undocumented migrants put in significantly more time (9.1 hours) than those with documents (7.9 hours).

Labor supply, of course, is affected by a variety of individual characteristics that remain uncontrolled in the simple tabulations reported in table 4.1, so in table 4.2 we report the results of a multivariate analysis of labor force participation and hours of work. In the left-hand columns we show the results of a logistic regression equation estimated to predict a dichotomous variable that equaled one if the respondent was in the workforce and zero otherwise, using selected indicators of human capital, demographic background, immigrant's status, regional origins, racial and ethnic roots, motivations for migration, migratory intentions, and perceptions of opportunities in the United States. The fit of the model is quite good, with a pseudo-R-squared of 0.67, meaning that the predictors explain about two-thirds of the variance in labor force participation.

As can be seen, participation in the U.S. labor force is predicted by having more education, being older, being from Central America (relative to being from Mexico), perceiving the United States as a land of opportunity, and coming to the United States for family or network reasons as opposed to other reasons. Labor force participation is negatively associated with migratory motivations focused on opportunities in the

Table 4.1   Labor Market Outcomes for Latin American Migrants to the United States, by Legal Status

Labor Market Outcome	Documented	Undocumented	Total
U.S. labor force participation			
In labor force	0.754	0.775	0.767
Hours worked per day	7.857	9.149	8.705
U.S. occupational outcomes			
Parental occupational status	42.19	36.44	38.53
Status of first U.S. occupation	44.65	39.53	41.35
Status of current U.S. occupation	51.25	44.63	46.98
Occupational mobility in the United States			
Downward	0.116	0.128	0.124
Upward	0.419	0.436	0.430
Same	0.465	0.436	0.446
U.S. wage outcomes			
First hourly wage	8.92	12.50	11.22
Current hourly wage	9.32	12.98	11.66
Earns under minimum wage	0.325	0.282	0.298
U.S. wage mobility			
Downward	0.000	0.000	0.000
Upward	0.070	0.090	0.083
Same	0.930	0.910	0.917
Difference	0.39	0.48	0.45

Source: Immigrant Identity Project (Office of Population Research 2009).

United States, having intentions to return home, and having good English skills (the last probably because English ability opens up countervailing opportunities in education). Labor force participation does not vary by race, gender, documentation status, or years in the United States. Thus, entry into the labor force is most strongly a matter of age, human capital, and perceptions and motivations about the United States and is not a matter of race, gender, or documentation.

The right-hand columns of table 4.2 show the results of an ordinary least squares (OLS) regression equation estimated to predict hours of work from the same set of variables. The fit of this model is somewhat poorer, with an R-squared of 0.44, meaning that the predictors explain a little over 40 percent of the variance in the hours worked. As can be seen, hours worked per day rise with age but do not differ by gender. Unlike labor force participation, the length of the workday is generally unaffected by human capital characteristics. In general, the workday is significantly longer for those who migrated because of economic exigencies at home and for those who reported experiences of discrimination in the

Table 4.2   Regression of Selected Variables on Labor Force Participation (Logit) and Hours Worked per Week (OLS) at the Time of the Survey

Predictors	Labor Force Participation		Hours Worked per Day	
	Regression Coefficient	Standard Error	Regression Coefficient	Standard Error
Class background				
Parental occupational status	−0.023	0.038	0.004	0.017
Human capital				
Years of schooling	0.281[+]	0.161	−0.018	0.025
Good English	−2.719*	1.346	−0.765	0.572
Perceptions of United States				
More opportunity	6.055**	1.980	−1.101	0.687
More inequality	−1.033	1.001	0.551	0.491
Experienced discrimination	1.122	0.926	1.103*	0.036
Motivation for migration				
Origin conditions	−1.879	1.638	1.731*	0.865
U.S. conditions	−2.552[+]	1.540	0.158	0.882
Family or network	2.858*	1.279	0.724	0.789
Other	—	—	—	—
Intentions				
Intends to return	−2.171**	1.055	0.388	0.452
Racial-ethnic roots				
African	0.291	1.580	−0.237	0.645
Indigenous	—	—	−0.118	1.028
Dark-skinned	1.333	1.131	−1.058*	0.506
Region of origin				
Mexico	—	—	—	—
Caribbean	2.222	1.946	0.120	0.957
Central America	4.330*	1.986	−1.573[+]	0.826
South America	2.241	1.667	−0.235	0.682
Demographics				
Age	0.728***	0.188	0.162***	0.044
Male	0.593	1.057	0.741	0.465
Immigrant status				
Documented	−0.226	1.453	−0.007	0.752
Years in United States	−0.009	0.018	−0.006	0.012
Intercept	−21.850***	6.418	4.471*	1.975
Likelihood ratio X^2	97.510***		—	
R-squared	0.665***		0.443***	
Sample size (N)	137		95	

Source: Immigrant Identity Project (Office of Population Research 2009).
[+]p < .10; *p < .05; **p < .01; ***p < .001

United States. Holding actual discrimination constant, however, dark-skinned migrants and those from Central America reported shorter workdays. The positive effect of discrimination on hours of work suggests the exploitive terms of employment faced by immigrants in the secondary labor market of the United States.

Occupational Mobility

Having entered the labor market, most immigrants readily find a job and begin to move through the U.S. occupational hierarchy in pursuit of greater status and higher earnings. The second and third panels of table 4.1 summarize the occupational outcomes for the immigrants in our sample. We coded occupations into one of eleven broad categories: unpaid laborers, students, farm workers, unskilled manufacturing, skilled manufacturing, transport workers, unskilled service workers, skilled service workers, small-business owners, a combined white-collar category of professional-technical-managerial workers, and retired workers.

This classification follows that used by the Mexican Migration Project and the Latin American Migration Project and is based on the 1996 Clasificación Mexicana de Ocupaciones (Mexican Classification of Occupations) developed by the Mexican government's Instituto Nacional de Estadística y Geografía Informática (National Institute of Statistics and Geographical Information). To summarize the data, each occupational category was matched with its associated international socioeconomic status index (from Ganzeboom and Treiman 1996), yielding a scale that ranged from 16 (unpaid workers) to 70 (professional-technical-managerial workers).

To establish a baseline for the assessment of occupational mobility, we first considered parental occupational status, relying primarily on the status of the father, though if the father's occupation was missing we substituted the mother's. The parental average of 38.5 on the scale of 16 to 70 suggests that family origins were mostly in the middle of the occupational distribution, though documented migrants did display a slightly higher status at home (index value 42) compared with undocumented migrants (average value 36). In migrating to the United States for work, the average migrant does not move very far from the occupational status of his or her parents. On average, occupational status on the first U.S. job was 41, compared with 39 for parents. In terms of overall status, therefore, entry into the U.S. labor market generally seemed to involve a lateral move relative to the status of parents.

Over time, however, there is a modest amount of occupational mobility, though it does appear to be somewhat greater for documented than undocumented migrants. Overall, average occupational status shifts from 41 on the first U.S. job to 47 on the current job. Among undocumented migrants, however, the shift is only five points, from 40 to 45, whereas among documented migrants the shift is from 45 to 51 points.

The next panel in table 4.1 pairs first and current U.S. jobs and classifies the pairing by whether it involved a move upward or downward in terms of status. In general, there was little downward mobility in the United States. Only some 12 percent of respondents moved downward in status between their first U.S. job and most recent U.S. job. In contrast, 43 percent moved upward, with the rate being slightly lower for documented compared with undocumented migrants: whereas 44 percent of undocumented migrants moved upward, the figure was 42 percent for those with documents. Despite this evidence of upward mobility, the modal category was stasis. Across all columns in the table, the percentage remaining at the same status equaled or exceeded the share moving upward, with the share remaining the same ranging from 44 percent to 47 percent. If we add the percentage staying at the same status to the percentage moving downward, we can see clearly that the odds are stacked against occupational mobility. Overall, 57 percent of all respondents moved downward or stayed the same in the occupational hierarchy, with corresponding figures of 58 percent for documented migrants and 56 percent for those lacking documents.

Considering the data adduced so far, we find rather strong constraints on possibilities for occupational mobility among Latino immigrants in the urban labor markets of the northeastern United States. A majority of migrants experienced either downward mobility or no mobility at all, and the average increase was only in the range of four or five points on a 54-point scale. Table 4.3 examines patterns of occupational mobility in greater detail by displaying a mobility matrix that cross-classifies the first and latest U.S. occupations reported by our respondents. Occupational categories are arranged from top to bottom and from left to right in order of increasing status. The diagonal cells indicate status immobility and are highlighted in boldface for easy reference.

Those who did not enter the labor force when they first arrived in the United States were very likely to still be outside of it at the time of the survey, with 84 percent of these people neither working nor looking for work at both dates. For those who were employed on arrival in the United States, the matrix shows that status immobility tends to increase as they move up the occupational hierarchy. Although patterns are somewhat obscured by the small cell sizes in several categories, the overall pattern becomes evident when we consider the three largest occupations: unskilled laborers ($N = 23$, status = 31), unskilled service workers ($N = 73$, status = 40), and skilled services ($N = 15$, status = 54). Among those who entered the U.S. workforce as unskilled laborers, only 13 percent remained in the same category by the time of the survey: 13 percent moved out of the labor force, and the rest moved upward in the

Table 4.3 Comparison of Status Between Respondent's First and Current U.S. Occupation

Status of First U.S. Occupation	Status of Current U.S. Occupation										
	Not Working	16	18	31	34	36	40	51	54	70	N
Not working	**84.4**	0.0	0.0	0.0	0.0	0.0	6.4	0.0	6.4	3.1	32
Farm worker (18)	20.0	0.0	**0.0**	0.0	0.0	0.0	60.0	0.0	20.0	0.0	5
Unskilled laborer (31)	13.0	0.0	0.0	**13.0**	0.0	0.0	43.5	8.7	13.0	8.7	23
Transport worker (34)	0.0	0.0	0.0	0.0	**0.0**	0.0	100.0	0.0	0.0	0.0	1
Skilled laborer (36)	0.0	0.0	0.0	0.0	0.0	**0.0**	0.0	0.0	100.0	0.0	1
Unskilled services (40)	2.7	4.1	0.0	5.5	0.0	0.0	**49.3**	6.9	20.6	11.0	73
Small-business owner (51)	0.0	0.0	0.0	0.0	0.0	0.0	50.0	**50.0**	0.0	0.0	3
Skilled services (54)	0.0	0.0	0.0	0.0	0.0	0.0	6.7	13.3	**73.3**	6.7	15
Professional (70)	0.0	14.3	0.0	0.0	0.0	0.0	0.0	14.3	28.6	**42.9**	7
Total	20.8	2.5	0.0	4.4	0.0	0.0	34.0	6.9	22.0	9.4	159

Source: Immigrant Identity Project (Office of Population Research 2009).
Note: Numbers in bold help facilitate interpretation of the discussion in the text.

occupational hierarchy, mostly into unskilled services. Among those who began in unskilled services, in contrast, 49 percent remained in the same category at the time of the survey, with just 3 percent withdrawing from the labor force and 10 percent moving downward, but 39 percent moving upward, most commonly into skilled services. Among those who began in skilled services, 73 percent remained in the same category at the time of the survey, with 20 percent moving downward, most commonly into the category of small-business owner, and only 7 percent moving up into the professional category.

This pattern of rising immobility with increasing occupational status is structural, in the sense that at the low end of the occupational hierarchy there are many positions to occupy above but few below, whereas at the high end there are few above and many below. The patterns revealed in tables 4.1 and 4.3, however, are unconditioned by a variety of other factors likely to be relevant in determining mobility patterns, such as age, education, gender, experience, and documentation. Table 4.4 therefore shows the results of a multinomial logistic regression model estimated to predict the likelihood of upward and downward occupational mobility between the first and last U.S. jobs (with the reference category being "no change"), using the same set of predictor variables employed in earlier tables.

The model has a moderately good fit to the data, with a pseudo-R-squared of around 0.42, meaning that the variables account for around 42 percent of the observed variance in occupational mobility. Despite the significant variance explained, relatively few variables are actually important in determining occupational mobility among Latino immigrants. In this model, seemingly obvious factors that one would expect to influence occupational mobility—such as age, gender, documentation, and English-language ability—have no significant effect on the odds of either upward or downward mobility in the United States, nor do more subjective variables such as perceptions, motivations, or intentions. What appears to matter most is parental status, race, years in the United States, and, to a lesser extent, education and regional origins.

As one would expect given the structural constraints of hierarchy, downward mobility over time is significantly more likely among people who come from a higher class background. The higher the occupational status of immigrants' parents, the more likely it is that they will experience downward mobility, and the lesser the probability of their upward mobility. The odds of downward mobility decrease with time spent in the United States, however, although U.S. experience has no effect on the odds of upward mobility. In terms of race, indigenous origins strongly predict downward mobility over time. Being dark-skinned, however, is associated with a somewhat greater likelihood of moving upward. Mobility upward is also positively predicted by education, but negatively

Table 4.4   Multinomial Logistic Regression Predicting Change in Status Between First and Current U.S. Occupation

Predictors	Downward Mobility		Upward Mobility	
	Regression Coefficient	Standard Error	Regression Coefficient	Standard Error
Class background				
Parental occupational status	0.135*	0.058	−0.340***	0.089
Human capital				
Years of schooling	−0.080	0.079	0.065+	0.039
Good English	1.185	1.052	1.272	0.851
Perceptions of United States				
More opportunity	2.289	1.472	1.434	0.942
More inequality	0.844	0.982	−0.683	0.693
Experienced discrimination	0.642	0.981	0.447	0.631
Motivation for migration				
Origin conditions	−1.743	1.734	−0.673	1.182
U.S. conditions	−2.347	1.743	−1.487	1.271
Family or network	−2.251	1.554	−1.144	1.126
Other	—	—	—	—
Intentions				
Intends to return	0.642	0.897	0.675	0.609
Racial-ethnic roots				
African	1.396	1.098	−0.907	0.847
Indigenous	20.119***	4.020	0.472	1.278
Dark-skinned	1.376	0.966	1.398*	0.695
Region of origin				
Mexico	—	—	—	—
Caribbean	−2.335	1.753	−2.985+	1.703
Central America	−0.438	1.389	0.934	1.041
South America	−1.207	1.379	1.327	0.908
Demographics				
Age	0.011	0.084	−0.001	0.059
Male	−0.408	0.877	−1.100	0.702
Immigrant status				
Documented	0.160	1.379	1.331	1.059
Years in United States	−0.055*	0.028	−0.002	0.019
Intercept	−28.270***	9.212	10.934***	4.562
Likelihood ratio X^2	95.880***			
Pseudo-R-squared	0.415			
Sample size (N)	117			

Source: Immigrant Identity Project (Office of Population Research 2009).
+p < .10; *p < .05; **p < .01; ***p < .001

predicted by Caribbean origins, although both effects are only marginally significant.

In sum, patterns of upward and downward occupational mobility in the U.S. labor market are structured primarily by class origins, racial-ethnic roots, and time spent in the United States. The equations in table 4.4 predict the *direction* of change, however, not the *amount* of change in occupational status. Table 4.5 completes our analysis of occupational mobility by showing the results of an OLS regression estimated to predict absolute change in occupational status between first and last jobs in the United States. When occupational trajectories are specified in this way, the importance of documentation and education emerges more clearly, as does the importance of the ceiling and floor effects noted earlier. Once again, the higher the status of the immigrant's initial U.S. occupation, the less additional status he or she had achieved by the time of the survey. Holding constant the effect of initial status, however, education and documentation both strongly and significantly predict a positive change in occupational status, as does origin in South America compared with other regions. In contrast, African roots and the perception of the United States as a place of inequality are negatively associated with change in occupational status. The former effect, however, lies at the margins of statistical significance; with respect to the latter effect, it is not clear whether perceptions of inequality follow or predict a lack of occupational mobility, but they are clearly associated with it.

Wages and Earnings Growth

To this point, our statistical analyses reveal that stability is relatively high when comparing first and current U.S. occupations and that the prospects of mobility revolve around documentation, education, U.S. experience, regional origin, and racial-ethnic roots. Except for perceptions about U.S. inequality, where the direction of causality is ambiguous, it seems that individual motivations, perceptions, and intentions do not play a significant role in determining occupational mobility in the United States. In terms of labor market outcomes, however, the other dimension of interest is earnings. Rising occupational status is all well and good, but at the end of the day wages are more central to immigrants' economic projects, whether those projects are centered at home or in the United States. The bottom panels of table 4.1 therefore focus on wages earned in the United States.

On average, immigrants reported hourly earnings well above the legal minimum wage that prevailed at the time of data collection, which was $5.15 per hour. The average wage reported on the first U.S. job was $11.22 per hour, with a figure of $12.50 for undocumented mi-

Table 4.5   **OLS Regression Predicting Change in Occupational Status and Change in Wage Earned Between First and Current U.S. Occupation**

Predictors	Change in Occupational Status		Change in U.S. Wage	
	Regression Coefficient	Standard Error	Regression Coefficient	Standard Error
Initial U.S. job				
First U.S. occupation status	−0.843***	0.109	−0.005	0.019
First U.S. wage	—	—	−0.008	0.009
Human capital				
Years of schooling	0.187*	0.097	−0.010	0.017
Good English	3.932	2.648	−0.286	0.472
Perceptions of United States				
More opportunity	1.746	3.331	0.104	0.598
More inequality	−4.484*	2.344	0.102	0.413
Experienced discrimination	1.576	2.420	−0.423	0.424
Motivation for migration				
Origin conditions	−4.550	4.107	0.562	0.717
U.S. conditions	−2.503	4.115	−0.321	0.720
Family or network	−2.909	3.663	0.108	0.643
Other	—	—	—	—
Intentions				
Intends to return	0.703	2.211	−0.019	0.388
Racial-ethnic roots				
African	−5.359+	2.997	−0.171	0.547
Indigenous	3.915	5.271	0.872	0.921
Dark-skinned	2.828	2.372	−0.534	0.415
Region of origin				
Mexico	—	—	—	—
Caribbean	0.395	4.426	0.187	0.793
Central America	3.759	3.724	−0.494	0.661
South America	5.941+	3.156	0.906	0.564
Demographics				
Age	0.351+	0.201	−0.015	0.036
Male	−0.024	2.259	−0.085	0.395
Immigrant status				
Documented	6.531*	3.436	0.280	0.606
Years in United States	−0.013	0.057	0.004	0.010
Intercept	20.550*	9.328	0.670	1.642
Adjusted R-squared	0.367***		0.001	
Sample size (N)	117		116	

Source: Immigrant Identity Project (Office of Population Research 2009).
+p < .10; *p < .05; **p < .01; ***p < .001

grants and $8.92 for those possessing documents. By the time of the survey, wages had risen for both groups of migrants, but very modestly. Among legal immigrants the average hourly wage had risen by 40 cents to $9.32, whereas among undocumented migrants the average had risen by 48 cents to reach $12.98. Although average wages may have exceeded the minimum at both points in time, this does not mean that no one earned less than the legal minimum. Indeed, there was great dispersion in the distribution of wages, and quite a few respondents reported earning subminimum wages on their current job. Among the documented, the figure was 33 percent, and among the undocumented it was 28 percent; these figures correspond closely to the respective values of 26 percent and 38 percent obtained by Bernhardt and her colleagues (2009).

We thus see considerable evidence of wage exploitation among the immigrants in our sample and little evidence of earnings mobility over time. Across all immigrants the shift in wages from first to current job was $11.22 to $11.66—just 44 cents, or 4 percent. Given that the average respondent had spent seven years in the United States, this implies a wage gain of only 0.6 percent per year—not enough to keep up with inflation. More troubling is the fact that the wage gains we do observe seem to be utterly random and unrelated to any of the variables one would normally expect to predict earnings. The right-hand columns of table 4.5 regress the change in wages earned between the first and current U.S. occupations on the same set of variables used to predict change in occupational status. Unlike the status equation, we find that *no variables* in the wage equation significantly predict earnings mobility. With an adjusted R-squared of 0.001, the increase in wages appears to be totally random.

We obtained the same null result when we estimated the probability of earning subminimum wages and regressed the natural log of wages on the same set of variables, shown in table 4.6. Both equations fit the data poorly, and the variables taken as a whole do not significantly predict either outcome. The only individual variables to attain even marginal significance are age and indigenous origins. Older workers earned lower wages and were more likely to be paid below the legal minimum, whereas those with indigenous roots earned higher wages and were less likely to earn below the minimum.

In the secondary labor market, therefore, wage mobility has little to do with concrete factors such as education, English-language ability, U.S. experience, or documentation, or even with subjective factors such as perceptions, motivations, or intentions. Being able to raise one's hourly wage, even by the modest average of 44 cents over seven years, appears to be mostly a matter of luck rather than of skill, ability, or motivation, even for legal immigrants.

Table 4.6   Regressions Predicting the Likelihood of Earning Below the Minimum Wage and the Natural Log of Wages on Current U.S. Job

Predictors	Earned Below Minimum Wage		Log of Hourly Wage	
	Regression Coefficient	Standard Error	Regression Coefficient	Standard Error
Labor supply				
Hours worked per day	−0.176	0.138	0.031	0.027
Human capital				
Years of schooling	−0.044	0.092	−0.006	0.006
Good English	0.532	0.694	−0.122	0.134
Perceptions of United States				
More opportunity	−0.529	0.823	0.157	0.163
More inequality	−0.034	0.577	0.141	0.114
Experienced discrimination	−0.408	0.594	−0.012	0.118
Motivation for migration				
Origin conditions	0.871	0.953	−0.072	0.204
U.S. conditions	0.200	0.974	0.032	0.206
Family or network	0.601	0.878	−0.038	0.190
Other	—	—	—	—
Intentions				
Intends to return	1.017[+]	0.547	−0.084	0.104
Racial-ethnic roots				
African	0.026	0.754	−0.051	0.157
Indigenous	−2.302*	1.172	0.583*	0.237
Dark-skinned	−0.006	0.567	−0.017	0.118
Region of origin				
Mexico	—	—	—	—
Caribbean	−1.746	1.129	0.291	0.215
Central America	−1.374	0.968	0.098	0.189
South America	−1.278	0.801	0.155	0.147
Demographics				
Age	0.140**	0.054	−0.018[+]	0.010
Male	−0.561	0.527	0.067	0.108
Immigrant status				
Documented	0.289	0.861	−0.078	0.167
Years in United States	0.004	0.015	0.004	0.003
Intercept	0.148	2.441	1.353**	0.439
Likelihood ratio X^2	52.890		—	
Pseudo-or adjusted R-squared	0.390		0.044	
Sample size (N)	102		97	

Source: Immigrant Identity Project (Office of Population Research 2009).
[+]p < .10; *p < .05; **p < .01; ***p < .001

Entrepreneurial Exits

For the majority of the immigrants in our sample, a job in the primary labor market is out of reach owing to a lack of education, documents, or both; most of them find themselves working at a succession of dead-end jobs that pay low wages for long hours, offer little security, and hold few prospects for advancement. Under these circumstances, participation in the secondary labor market becomes a repetitive cycle of jobs leading nowhere, and many people we spoke to were simply resigned to this fate, though not without bitterness, as we shall see in the next chapter. A few respondents sought a way out of the secondary labor market trap, not by breaking into the primary sector but through entrepreneurship, often within the ethnic enclave. Indeed, eleven respondents had established a small business catering to their fellow immigrants by the time of the survey. To examine which factors facilitate this pathway to mobility, table 4.7 shows the results of a logistic regression model estimated to predict business ownership.

Although the overall fit of the model is at the margins of statistical significance, the pseudo-R-squared indicates that the independent variables account for about 40 percent of the variation in business ownership. Moreover, one variable—indigenous roots—predicted the outcome perfectly and therefore could not be included in the equation. Not one person with indigenous origins was a business owner, meaning that, for whatever reason, mestizos are very unlikely to become entrepreneurs. (There were no pure-blooded Amerindians in the sample.) Aside from indigenous origins, other factors lowering the likelihood of business ownership were youth, low status on the initial U.S. occupation, education, and being male.

In general, the odds of business ownership rose with occupational status and age and fell with rising education, probably because education opens up opportunities in the primary sector, thereby obviating the need for an alternative mobility path through entrepreneurship. In addition, women are more likely to own a business than men, who appear to remain stuck in the low-level equilibrium trap of dead-end jobs in the secondary sector. According to our data, in other words, the person most likely to set up a business is an older, poorly educated woman who somehow managed to land a relatively high-status first job in the United States.

Structures of Inequality

This chapter has painted a clear if rather depressing picture of the working lives of Latin American immigrants in the secondary labor markets of the urban Northeast. The narratives transcribed from detailed inter-

Table 4.7   Logistic Regressions Predicting Business Ownership in the United States

Predictors	Regression Coefficient	Standard Error
Initial U.S. job		
First U.S. wage	−0.207	0.153
First occupational status	0.123*	0.061
Human capital		
Years of schooling	−0.364[+]	0.215
Good English	−3.504	2.440
Perceptions of United States		
More opportunity	−0.203	1.939
More inequality	0.889	1.047
Experienced discrimination	−1.263	1.201
Motivation for migration		
Origin conditions	2.887	2.469
U.S. conditions	3.793	2.707
Family or network	2.485	2.478
Other	—	—
Intentions		
Intends to return	−1.952	1.369
Racial-ethnic roots		
African	−0.567	1.747
Dark-skinned	0.311	0.973
Region of origin		
Mexico	—	—
Caribbean	−0.234	2.167
Central America	−0.579	1.958
South America	1.071	1.798
Demographics		
Age	0.198[+]	0.109
Male	−2.889[+]	1.151
Immigrant status		
Documented	1.031	1.438
Years in United States	0.067	0.051
Intercept	−8.497[+]	0.215
Likelihood ratio X^2	26.57[+]	
Pseudo-R-squared	0.396	
Sample size (N)	110	

Source: Immigrant Identity Project (Office of Population Research 2009).
[+]p < .10; *p < .05; **p < .01; ***p < .001

views with 159 Latino respondents reveal a world of unstable jobs that pay low wages for work under stressful and often unpleasant conditions, with terms of employment that take advantage of workers' vulnerability as undocumented minority group members. Most work through labor subcontractors and are paid in cash, with no benefits or taxes taken out. In those instances where taxes are deducted by employers or subcontractors, migrant workers generally receive no formal accounting in terms of a written receipt or pay stub, and most have no idea whether or how much money was deducted and for what purposes. Not surprisingly, they do not expect to see the money again or to receive anything in return.

A few respondents with education, English-language ability, and documentation reported employment in the primary labor market, a few reported good treatment and mobility in the secondary sector, and some were able to advance through entrepreneurship; the vast majority of our sample, however, told stores of circulating through a seemingly endless series of dead-end jobs without being able to gain much in the way of greater status or income. The only practical way to raise aggregate earnings was to increase hours of work, but in most cases the hours grew so long that workers simply wore out, despite earning the greater income. Although most respondents were proud of being good workers, were dedicated employees, and rarely volunteered complaints about their situation, they did perceive rampant inequalities in the worlds of work they witnessed around them and had few illusions about getting very far ahead in American society.

The narrative reports of our respondents were generally confirmed by our quantitative analyses of occupations and wages. Consistent with the economic motives discerned in earlier chapters, the vast majority of immigrants—more than three-quarters—were working at the time of the survey, mostly in jobs that required long hours. The large majority worked as unskilled manual laborers or service workers, and only a minority were able to improve their occupational status between their first and current U.S. jobs. Close to 60 percent either had moved downward or remained at the same occupational status on their first U.S. job and their latest U.S. job. Status immobility was greater the higher the status of their initial position in the United States.

Downward occupational mobility was most common for immigrants with indigenous roots and limited U.S. experience, whereas upward mobility was predicted by education, skin color, and Caribbean origins. Absolute gains in occupational status were positively predicted by education, the possession of legal documents, and South American origins, but negatively predicted by African origins and perceptions of inequality in the United States. Patterns of occupational mobility thus appear to be structured around the factors of education, documentation, regional origins, and race.

Although upward occupational mobility was possible for certain kinds of immigrants, the gains in occupational status were generally small and did not translate into higher earnings. Average earnings were above the legal minimum, but there was great variability in wages, and around 30 percent of respondents earned below the legal minimum on their current U.S. job. Moreover, the average increase was only 0.6 percent per year, and this tiny increase was unrelated to any of the variables we considered, including standard human capital variables such as education, experience, English-language ability, and occupational skill, as well as subjective factors such as perceptions, motivations, and intentions. Wage gains were also unrelated to legal status, racial-ethnic roots, or regional origins. Indeed, experiencing a wage gain in the course of a migratory career seemed to be almost entirely a matter of chance. Enclave entrepreneurship constituted an alternative mobility path for a small number of people, but most respondents seemed to be relegated to life in the secondary labor market with no apparent exit.

═Chapter 5═

Dreams and Disappointments

Although the specific motivations for migration may vary from
person to person, most Latin American immigrants have one
broad goal in common in coming to the United States: one way
or another, they are seeking to improve their lives. It is the details that
differ. Whether they are pushed out by poverty and violence or pulled
in by economic opportunity and family ties north of the border, migrating to the United States usually involves some dream of self or family
improvement. Indeed, our respondents often referred to their "dreams"
in talking about their decision to migrate to the United States, and one
person explicitly referred to the "American Dream." The dream meta-
phor implies some kind of cognitive comparison of conditions at home
and abroad. In the interviews we therefore directly asked respondents
to describe their perception of opportunities in the United States versus their country of origin; this question yielded a rich body of qualitative data on what immigrants expected to achieve by migrating to the
United States.

Dreams are always tempered by reality, however, and in chapter 4 we
found that most immigrants reported being mired in a succession of
low-wage jobs that offered little stability, few benefits, and limited prospects for advancement. Thus, after discussing opportunities in the
United States, we also asked respondents to reflect on the inequalities
they perceived in the United States versus their origin country. By asking this question, we sought to learn about the constraints on social mobility they perceived before and after migration; delving further into
possible gaps between their dreams and realities, we also asked respondents whether they had experienced discrimination in the United States.
Answers to these three questions enable us to assess both the dreams
and disappointments faced by immigrants in the United States.

Dreams of Opportunity

One section of the interview guide leads off with the question: "In terms of opportunities, do you see more here or there?" In the context of the interview, "here" clearly referred to the United States and "there" to the country of origin. We deliberately left the term "opportunities" undefined in order to let respondents tell us which opportunities were most salient to them. Given the salience of economic motivations, as noted in the last chapter, it is not surprising that the vast majority of respondents defined opportunities in economic terms: 85 percent cited earnings opportunities, and 2 percent mentioned work or career opportunities, in comparison with 6 percent who mentioned personal growth or fulfillment and 1 percent each who referred to educational opportunities and political issues. Roughly 6 percent did not offer a usable answer to the question.

Whatever the specific definition of opportunities, respondents generally saw more of them in the United States than at home. Table 5.1 shows the distribution of answers to our query about where opportunities were seen to be greatest. Overall, 81 percent said that opportunities were greater in the United States, compared with just 4 percent who judged them to be more abundant at home and 9 percent who indicated that they were the same in both places. A key component of the immigrant dream, therefore, is the conceptual framing of the United States as a land of opportunity. Although the perception of greater opportunity in the United States was slightly more common among documented migrants (88 percent) than among undocumented migrants (80 percent), it was nonetheless very high in both cases.

In describing the greater economic opportunities here, one prominent theme was the drawing power of the dollar, which we take to refer to the comparative value of dollar-denominated earnings. A Brazilian man, for example, was adamant in his perception that there is more opportunity "here ... because here the dollar, the dollar commands capitalism throughout the world. Only for this reason." A young Brazilian woman was more ambivalent; she noted that in the United States there are only "a few more opportunities" for work, and that although economic conditions in Latin America are "very difficult and things are very bad ... it's not always so great here either." She concluded, however, that "always there are the dollars."

Although a male respondent from Argentina did not mention dollars explicitly, he nonetheless concluded that "there are many, many, many more possibilities to earn more money here." A Venezuelan man similarly noted that "here at least, even if you work in a small shop, you earn something," though he also underscored the key importance of legal documents in getting ahead, stating that "the important factor is having

Table 5.1   Perceptions of Relative Economic Opportunities in the United States and in the Country of Origin

Opportunity	Documented	Undocumented	Total
Greater in United States	87.7%	79.6%	80.5%
Greater at origin	1.8	5.1	4.4
Same in both	3.5	12.2	8.8
No answer	7.0	3.1	6.3
Sample size (N)	57	98	159

Source: Immigrant Identity Project (Office of Population Research 2009).

papers, because if you have a good document, then you will not have [the problem] of lacking work. They give it to you."

Other respondents focused not on the money they could earn in the United States but on low wages at home as the key factor accounting for the differential in opportunities. When asked about the relative opportunities "here" or "there," an Ecuadoran female was quick to answer: "Here . . . because Ecuador, you know, is a country with low pay. There is much poverty in my country." A woman from Mexico framed the issue similarly, seeing more opportunity "here, especially because in Mexico the wages you get are really low; because here you earn in one day what it would take you a week to earn in Mexico." A male compatriot's view of wages at home was even more contemptuous; he noted that his nephew had just finished training as an auto mechanic, and although he quickly found a job, "the salary he earns is a humiliation." He went on to express some anger at Mexican politicians who in their campaigns emphasize the nation's economic progress, arguing that "it is a stupidity of the Mexican president or whoever . . . it is a humiliation to have one's studies cost more than what one earns afterward."

Many respondents viewed American opportunity in terms of a strong demand for labor and the wider possibilities for occupational mobility. According to an Ecuadoran woman, "Well, if we are realistic, we know that the opportunities are here. At present, no matter what kind of work you consider, there is employment." Indeed, although she noted that the United States was experiencing an economic downturn, she insisted that, "even so, there are more opportunities than in our own countries." This sentiment was echoed by a young Mexican male who said unequivocally that, despite his lack of documents, "I perceive more opportunities here." When pushed to elaborate, he said, "I'll tell you this, that whatever one wishes to do here, one can achieve it." This positive attitude was shared by another undocumented Mexican who underscored her belief in greater opportunities "here, because here, for example, you can do what you want to get ahead."

One young male respondent described in some detail the contrasting opportunity structures he perceived in the United States and his native Brazil, noting that

> the social pyramid of the United States is generally very different from the social pyramid in a Third World country. If you look, for example, at the pyramid in Brazil, it is almost the same as the pyramid in Egypt, with a few rich at the top and wider at the bottom because the middle class is restricted and the poor classes [are] large. Here it is the opposite. Here the middle is the biggest, the rich class is a little smaller, and the poor class is the smaller, such that the base of the pyramid is smaller. Well, it is a healthier economy when you have a larger middle class, because money moves from hand to hand. Capital, it moves and generates wealth and creates work and the economy grows and yields better conditions of opportunity.

Even when they perceived greater opportunities in the United States, some respondents pointedly noted that earning higher wages and moving ahead is not always easy and often requires hardship and sacrifice. According to one Honduran woman, taking advantage of U.S. opportunities "can cost you a lot. . . . Here you, if sometimes you don't know much English, they take you for a fool, for a delinquent. For better or worse, sometimes they take offense. And sometimes when you want to do good, you end up doing bad, and even on a good day they take a smile the wrong way. So here, even though you have good intentions, it can turn out badly, so for this reason one has to be careful."

An Ecuadoran woman likewise emphasized that success in the United States requires struggle, especially for those who lack documents. Although conceding that she lacked employment at home and that "opportunities are definitely better here," she pointed out that here "you have to struggle, especially if you lack papers and friends, because in your own country they help you because you are a friend and you move on to a better position or something. Here you begin from zero. It doesn't matter if your friend is above. You begin from zero, and you have to go climbing upward."

Although the most common perception was of greater opportunities in the United States, a few respondents nonetheless saw more possibilities for advancement in their home country. Particularly for those with education, upward mobility in the United States was often blocked by a lack of documents. It is very difficult for those in an irregular status to achieve a full return on their investment in years of schooling. As one Dominican male put it, "Well, no, to be perfectly honest, I think that there are more opportunities for me, with the education I have, in the Dominican Republic than in the United States. Here many people are well prepared, and nearly always if you don't have . . . a green card, it is very difficult to find work. For me it is double the work compared with a person who has a green card because, first, not only do I have to find a company that will hire me, but also one that is willing to sponsor me."

The lack of documents also loomed large in the perceptions of another immigrant, an Ecuadoran male who explicitly commented on the many barriers to mobility faced by people in illegal status. As he put it, "Here you have certain restrictions if you are undocumented, and this is what puts you most [at risk]. . . . If you wish to continue your studies, if you wish to create a business, you can't do anything if you are undocumented." A Mexican man focused not on the issue of documentation but on the difficulty of getting a good education north of the border, owing to its cost; in Mexico "schooling wasn't so expensive, and with a job one could afford it—but here no."

Finally, others were ambivalent: they perceived opportunities both at home and abroad and were generally unable to make a clear evaluation as to where opportunities were greatest. One man from Honduras pointed out that, on the one hand, "I think there is more opportunity in one's country, in terms of work or things like that . . . yes, in terms of work . . . you look for work, and quickly you get work," but on the other hand, he admitted, "in terms of earnings opportunities, it's better here." In the end he was left in a quandary about relative opportunities here and there and simply concluded, "Well, I don't know."

Another respondent, a woman from Ecuador, saw the trade-off as not between work and wages but between earnings growth and personal growth. Although she quickly admitted that she had come to the United States "to make money"—"I think that here there's nothing else"—she believed that "for spiritual growth and everything, I think that in, in my country, in my hometown, there are more opportunities." A Nicaraguan woman who had well-placed family members able to boost her career in both countries seemed to have the best of both worlds. Asked about relative opportunities here and there, she answered, without hesitation, "On both sides." When pressed to elaborate, she described her unusual access to hospital work in both Nicaragua and the United States because of family connections in both places: "There I have more opportunity because my uncles are doctors and all that and I can work in the hospital where they work, and here in the same school where my sister is studying medicine I can also work there."

Perceptions of Inequality

The foregoing analysis suggests that the vast majority of immigrants come to the United States believing it to be a land of economic opportunity, with plentiful work at wages that are high by comparison to what could be earned at home. Hence, the prevailing dream among immigrants is to capitalize on higher American wages to advance their material interests, either to improve their economic circumstances at home (for example, financing a home, starting a business, investing in education, improving the health of family members or their own, acquiring land, or elevating household consumption) or to pursue mobility in the United States itself (for example, moving up the income and occupational scales to raise their living standards, accumulating assets, or making investments in family members living north of the border).

Despite the perception of widespread American opportunity among Latin American immigrants, economic success in the United States is hardly a given, especially for those who lack education and documentation. We therefore followed up by asking respondents whether they saw more inequalities at home or in the United States. Empirically, of course, inequalities of wealth and income are much greater in Mexico, Brazil, and other Latin American countries than in the United States (Smeeding 2005), but we are not interested in facts so much as perceptions. If inequalities are *perceived* to be sharper in the United States, this perception could very well cast a shadow on the brightness of the American Dream.

The very real potential for such a shadow is suggested by the data in table 5.2, which summarizes responses to our question on comparative inequality. Even though the vast majority of respondents perceived more opportunity in the United States than at home, the figures here suggest that most of them did not see it as a place of lower inequality. On the contrary, a majority of respondents (58 percent) did not perceive the United States to be any more egalitarian than their own country, with 23 percent seeing U.S. inequality as the same and 35 percent viewing it as more unequal. Thus, a little more than one-third of all respondents saw inequality as greater in the United States, and surprisingly, this perception did not vary markedly by legal status. Whereas 33 percent of documented migrants saw the United States as more unequal, the figure was only slightly higher, at 37 percent, among those without documents.

Although Latin American immigrants overwhelmingly perceive the United States as a land of opportunity, a large share of them also see it as a place of greater inequality. A salient theme in the comments about inequality was the high degree of prejudice in the United States against minorities, the poor, and those who do not speak English. Indeed, perceptions of inequality in the United States appear to be connected quite closely to a perception of greater American racism, which in the minds of immigrants makes the inequalities here seem worse than those at home. One woman from Colombia was positively shocked by what she perceived as the routine mistreatment of poor minorities in the United

Table 5.2   Perceptions of Relative Inequality in the United States and the Country of Origin

Opportunity	Documented	Undocumented	Total
Greater in United States	33.3%	36.8%	34.6%
Greater in country of origin	29.8	38.8	35.2
Same in both	26.3	21.4	22.6
No answer	10.5	3.1	7.5
Sample size (N)	57	98	159

Source: Immigrant Identity Project (Office of Population Research 2009).

States: "Here . . . the very, very poor here, they treat them very badly. In my neighborhood they are all black, and it's terrible how they treat them. From the time you get on the bus, the blacks are apart, and as they are so very poor, they cannot get ahead. The idea of poverty for them is very deep-rooted, and they do not rise." She saw this poor treatment in stark contrast to what she knew from her home country: "You see a poor person in Colombia, and he is a happy poor person. . . . A poor person in Colombia is someone you like, who knows how to take advantage of what he's got, appreciate what he's got, values what he has, and helps other people. . . . The poor person here is cold and bitter."

Like the United States, Brazil is a former slave society with a large African-origin population. Although dark-skinned Brazilians do suffer exclusion from jobs and education, in social terms skin tone is not as sharp a marker of social status in Brazil, and interpersonal relations are more fluid between blacks, browns, and whites, with substantially lower levels of segregation compared with the United States (Telles 2004). The difference between a color line and a color continuum probably accounts for the shock of the Brazilian man who very emphatically told us that "inequality here exists. It exists because American society is very segmented." He went on to discuss what he saw as the American "philosophy" of race and how it made him feel as a Brazilian:

Here people have the philosophy of putting themselves into a group—for example, Latinos with Latinos, blacks with blacks, whites with whites, Indians with Indians, and so on—because they feel good together. Maybe they think, "I am in the middle of people like me, of my Latin friends and everything." And at times you feel a little bit low because culturally it generates prejudice and preconceptions, like when people don't know how to get on with another group.

The Dominican Republic is another former slave society with a strong African presence, first from the importation of Africans under colonial

rule and later from the immigration of people from Haiti. Like the Brazilian man just quoted, a young Dominican man was clearly struck by
the starkness of the color line in the United States and the high degree of
segregation that prevails in American cities:

> Here there is more inequality. . . . Although down there it is a common oc-
> currence to see people begging, here there is racism, more racism than
> down there. In Santo Domingo there are blacks and whites everywhere.
> Here, no. Here you have your black area, your Hispanic area, your white
> area, you know, everyone segregated. Here everyone is separated. In
> Santo Domingo [the] poor and [the] rich people cannot live in the same
> neighborhood, but at least they will see each other daily.

A Venezuelan woman was similarly taken aback by the ubiquity of
racial judgments and evaluations in American social life:

> Look, in this I have to be clear. The first time that I came to the United
> States, I came with the understanding that I had friends of both colors, of
> all colors and all types, but then a native of this country took note and
> said, ah, but this person is black, this person is mestizo, this person is fat,
> this person is skinny. Because we, in truth, at home we don't speak of rac-
> ism and are not so dependent on the external conditions of a person.

Although a young Peruvian male framed American inequality primarily in class terms, noting that "here there is a lot of poverty, and the
different economic levels are very sharp . . . the poor, middle, and upper
classes, the divisions are pronounced," he was also struck by how, with
"the dark ones, people discriminate a lot against them."

For some respondents, the perception of prejudice was not abstract
but personal—it was something they saw as not directed solely at others
but as also affecting them. Thus, a Mexican man was referring not to
African Americans but to minorities in general, a class in which he
clearly placed himself, when he stated flatly: "Here we are minorities,
and we don't have many opportunities. We have doors shut because we
are minorities, and we have to work hard to open the doors, whereas if
we go to Mexico, there we are all equal, you know?"

A Dominican woman also experienced American prejudice as something personal; she related her feeling that "here the people, they look at
you differently. If you arrive at a job, the first thing they ask, instead of
asking your name, they say, 'Where are you from? What language do
you speak?' and when I say, 'I am Hispanic,' okay, a moment passes, and
then they say, 'There is no work.'" This woman was one of many people
who perceived prejudice against Spanish speakers; indeed, exclusion on
the basis of language was a common theme among respondents. One

Ecuadoran male went so far as to assert that, "in practical terms, I see some inequality here on the basis of language. Because of language, one cannot be equal, because of differences of language, and one has to maintain some distance because of it."

Others perceived inequality in the United States in terms of values. According to one Dominican man, in the United States "there is more inequality because here people have lost their values. You go out on the street, and no one says hello. No, nothing. They don't have this tradition, and the more you try here the more they just look at you strangely. So one feels foreign and often, lamentably, just part of the system. Even if you get used to it here, it's not much fun, and I feel estranged from it." In other words, racial, ethnic, linguistic, and cultural differences sharpen economic divisions in the United States in the view of many Latin American immigrants. As a Mexican man put it, "In terms of inequality, well, here there is a lot. Everything is less equal, everything more sharply divided, as much politically as legally."

The relative number of people who saw more inequality at home was about the same as the relative number who saw more in the United States. Among the former, respondents seemed to focus more on poverty in their country of origin than on affluence in the United States. One Ecuadoran man averred that "in my country, you know, poor is poor and rich is rich. I don't know about your country, but in mine the poor continue getting poorer and the rich richer." Whereas he saw Ecuador as starkly divided between rich and poor, he perceived more of a gradation of classes in the United States, where "there are the poor, the middle class, the rich, and the millionaires." A Mexican male attributed inequality at home to a surfeit of invidious comparison, noting that "people, I would say, have a lot of envy where I am from." Likewise, a Dominican woman who grew up in New York told us of the shock she experienced when visiting relatives back on the island:

> In Santo Domingo the social inequality is incredible. It is such that those who are dark are most poor and those who are most white have more money. And you can see, like, in the neighborhood people who are darker are really, really poor, and you can see, like, among standard people very few that have money, that live in, like, in good places and, like, there are good neighborhoods, but the rest of them are, like, well, the lightest-skinned . . . live in this good neighborhood and, like, have mansions and BMWs.

Some respondents were more nuanced, seeing their country of origin as economically divided only in comparison with the United States. Although one Salvadoran man had no trouble seeing economic problems at home, he had more trouble envisioning poverty in the United States.

For him, "in El Salvador, this here is a lot of poverty," but "in this country, the economy looks good even when the government says it is bad." Similarly, a young Dominican female who grew up in the United States commented that "when I think of the Dominican Republic I think of . . . a lot of poverty and the problems there. And this I can't see in America. I think of rich people when I think of America." When asked where inequality was greater, a young Colombian male quickly answered, "Well, in Colombia," and then said, "I don't know people here that you could call poor. There are poor, but here more than anything there are regular people. Although some are rich and some are poor, I see them as the same."

Some respondents explicitly compared the class and status systems they perceived at home and abroad, like the Nicaraguan woman who complained that, "there, to get the same necessities, the same things, only the strongest survive. Here, no. Here we all struggle as best we can, and we are in a free, large, and extensive nation. There are always opportunities for one to grab on to one way or another." A Venezuelan man saw the critical difference in terms of the competition for status and prestige: "In Venezuela you see this kind of thing—the distinction between social classes. There is a perception that you have to stand out and achieve status X to be able to be an accepted person. Here in the United States I don't see this as a requirement. Society is not structured so that you fight and fight and fight to achieve a certain social status." One Colombian woman focused on the contrast between guerrilla violence at home and benevolent governance in the United States, emphasizing that in Colombia there are dangers "that really affect your life, the guerrillas. Here, no guerrillas. We don't see them because, thank God, the government here tries to help the city and different places in the U.S."

A smaller but still significant number of people saw inequalities as roughly the same in both countries. One particularly entrepreneurial Ecuadoran man saw opportunities as equal and insisted that he could get ahead anywhere, "even if it is the poorest country." For him, "here it's the same as there. If you work, you can make money in any part of the world. If you work hard and have a good capacity to create, then you can do many things. . . . It doesn't matter [where]."

Mexicans were particularly prone to say that inequality was pervasive on both sides of the border, like the young Mexican man who saw inequality "on both sides. In Mexico there are rich people and poor people, and here as well, though I don't know if there are Americans who are very poor." A young Mexican woman who had grown up in New York also saw inequality "in both places. In Mexico there are also rich people with capital, and there are people who have less, as well as very poor people. And here there are also poor people who live in the streets as well as rich and others that are getting by more or less." This sentiment was echoed by another second-generation Mexican from New York, a man who admitted that "here there's poor people, yeah, but there's poor people in Mexico as well. Poverty is always going to be there." Likewise, a Mexican man in Philadelphia told us that "both countries are unequal. The United States is one of the richest countries of the world, if not the richest, but a lot of poverty exists. You can see it in the streets."

Several people thought that poverty was not more pervasive at home, just more visible. In the words of one young Dominican man, "There, the inequality is more obvious. I am not going to say I have taken full account of it here, but there is economic inequality. Down there, one sees it more." Another Dominican man saw things in a similar vein, noting that "in the Dominican Republic there is a class that is high, which nearly always does not give much opportunity to the middle class," but "here in the United States you don't see it so much because the upper class is so high that you never see it." He went on to say that here "the upper class—Donald Trump and Bill Gates—you never see them, never rub elbows with them. You don't go to a bar with them."

Among those who perceived equal inequality both at home and in the United States, racism and prejudice once again seemed to play a critical role in shaping their perceptions. Several respondents felt that sharper economic inequalities at home were balanced by harsher racial and ethnic inequalities in the United States. As one Mexican woman put it, "Here there is a lot of discrimination if you don't have money." According to a Mexican male living in Philadelphia, "I think that there is more socioeconomic inequality in Mexico but more racial inequality here in the United States. They pay a lot of attention here to who is of a different race or color and who belongs to a different socioeconomic stratum, especially in the northeastern United States. But in Mexico inequality is more at an economic level."

The same trade-off was noted by a male immigrant from Guatemala in this exchange with the interviewer:

RESPONDENT: Yes, there is a lot of inequality there, I think.

INTERVIEWER: But here also?

RESPONDENT: Yes, also here.

INTERVIEWER: There in Guatemala, or maybe here? There is more inequality here than there—is this what you're trying to say?

RESPONDENT: Yes, it's the same everywhere, in both places.

INTERVIEWER: The same in both?

RESPONDENT: Yes.

INTERVIEWER: There because it would be for socioeconomic reasons?

RESPONDENT: Yes, on the economic side, yes, it would be.

INTERVIEWER: And here it would be on the racial side?

RESPONDENT: What do you mean by "racial side"?

INTERVIEWER: The fact of being Latino?

RESPONDENT: Yes.

Experiencing Discrimination

As the foregoing discussion suggests, perceptions of inequality in the United States are strongly connected to perceptions of the country as a biased and racially prejudiced society. Our final follow-up in the series on inequality was thus an explicit query about discrimination in the United States—not about general perceptions but about concrete examples. Specifically, we asked, "Have you ever experienced discrimination?" The answers to this question are summarized in table 5.3. Consistent with comments in the previous section, a substantial majority of respondents, some 59 percent, reported having experienced discrimination in the United States, a figure that did not vary much by legal status.

Of those who reported experiencing discriminatory treatment, the two most common reasons given for it were race-ethnicity (national origin, skin color, phenotype) and language (speaking English poorly, with an accent, or not at all). About one-quarter of all discriminatory incidents involved language, and around one-fifth derived from race or ethnicity. The most common contexts for encountering discrimination were school, work, the streets, and medical settings. One of the most common complaints was being ignored and left unattended because of a real or presumed lack of fluency in English, such as the Bolivian man who said that "because I didn't know English, and they didn't wait on me. And I asked myself why? I guess because that's the way people are, if they know someone is new here, in this way they can discriminate." When we asked where this treatment occurred, he answered simply, "In all the stores."

A Mexican male reported a similar experience: "Just after you arrive here, you don't speak English, and so on the job you don't understand what they are telling you to do, and you don't know how to defend yourself because you don't understand." Sometimes, however, the problem is not a lack of English fluency but having accented English, as related by a Colombian woman who noted that, when "you arrive here

Table 5.3   **Experiences of Discrimination in the United States**

Opportunity	Documented	Undocumented	Total
Discrimination	59.6%	60.2%	59.8%
No discrimination	35.1	38.8	36.5
No answer	5.2	1.0	3.7
Sample size (N)	57	98	159

Source: Immigrant Identity Project (Office of Population Research 2009).

[you] don't have a good accent, do not speak English well. So when you speak it the person on the other side of the window doesn't understand." Like many other respondents, she was particularly upset by the lack of courtesy and sympathy for someone who is trying hard and doing the best they can in a second language:

> Here the Americans talk very fast and all. You have to quickly say exactly what you need, and then someone with a thick tongue arrives, and the person on the other side of the window has no patience, and, and then they treat you like, like . . . they don't let you try to speak. They just cast you aside or something. Above all it has happened to me, like, in offices, in offices where I went, for example, to get my social security, public of-fices. They have no patience.

Respondents reported sometimes feeling shunned or stigmatized for the simple act of speaking Spanish with other Latinos in public, like the Peruvian man who related that "I was speaking Spanish, and this guy—I was with my friends—and he said something in English, and all of us, we were speaking Spanish. When we are around other people speaking English, they give us a hard look, as if they wanted to say something bad about us or something." This sort of treatment often produced hurt feel-ings and bruised egos, as with a Mexican woman who admitted that "it's not that they treat you badly, just that they don't offer you decent help, and for this reason one is made to feel bad for not speaking the language." She described a particularly humiliating incident in which she was stopped for a traffic violation and the police officer "just shouted that I had to speak English, and I just say, 'I don't speak English,' but he says, 'You have to speak English because you are living here now.'. . . But he just yelled at me, which was humiliating for me because I also would like to speak the language and to be able to take care of myself when these things happen."

A Dominican man expounded on his perception of how Americans discriminate on the basis of accent: "They believe that when you speak with an accent you are, like, retarded, stupid." This jaundiced perception, in his view, makes it difficult to get ahead in the job market and triggers employment discrimination:

> They speak differently to you when you go looking for work. If it is in an office, they give the job to someone else. If they can, they give it to an Anglo-Saxon, and if not, then to a person who does not speak with an accent. If they are going to give it to you, you have to have much more training than the white person, but when you are at the same level of education, they give it to the one without an accent or who is Anglo-Saxon.

Similar treatment was reported by a Mexican man who told us that because he did not speak English well, "they just didn't give me any work." A Dominican woman also reported being shunned for speaking with an accent, though not to the extent of being denied a job. Her problems were not at work, but "more than anything you go to some places and a person will look at you sideways, differently, you know, if they hear you speak Spanish. . . . I have noted differences in how they treat you. They say something about your accent: 'Oh, you are Spanish, oh, my God, you have an accent.'" Fortunately she was fairly indifferent to this reaction, telling us, "You know, things like that don't really bother [me]. Yes, I have an accent, so what?"

Several respondents reported discrimination on the basis of a presumed lack of English ability based solely on their appearance. According to one Ecuadoran man, "They look at you with a Latino face and think that you can't speak English, that you are not capable of speaking English. This happens to me many times in stores." It also happened to a Mexican man who visited a lawyer's office:

> I had to deal with some bureaucratic issues, and the receptionist asked, "Can I help you?" in Spanish. I said to her that I had come to see the lawyer. "Okay, then sit down," she said and went about her business. I tell you, twenty minutes pass, then thirty, and finally, after an hour, a Hispanic woman came out, and the receptionist said, "Look, he is the one who is here waiting." So this lady said that she would be interpreting in the conversation I was going to have with the lawyer. So automatically, seeing that I was Hispanic, she assumed that I needed an interpreter, and I ended up waiting nearly an hour. I thought it was the lawyer who was busy, but no, it was the interpreter.

A common venue for discrimination, both linguistic and otherwise, was a medical context, such as a clinic, hospital, or physician's office. According to one Mexican male respondent: "I have noticed that here, for myself, the fact of being Hispanic, it doesn't matter if you're Venezuelan or Mexican or whatever—they treat you worse. I have really noticed this . . . like I noticed that when I went to the hospital, they didn't pay attention to me." Often the perpetrators of discrimination are not white or black but Latino. Many medical providers and social service centers in the Northeast employ Puerto Ricans as receptionists and first-line personnel, given that they are U.S. citizens by birth and are often able to communicate in both English and Spanish. A young Mexican woman told us that she received particularly poor treatment from the intake staff at a medical center, alleging that "the women who filled out forms up front, they were the racists." When the interviewer asked whether they were black or white, she was surprised by the response:

INTERVIEWER: Ah, did they not speak Spanish? Were they black or white?

RESPONDENT: Puerto Rican.

INTERVIEWER: Puerto Rican!

RESPONDENT: Uh huh.

INTERVIEWER: And being Puerto Ricans, didn't they take good care of you, being Latinos?

RESPONDENT: No. They spoke to me in English. And I said to them, "Look, I don't understand," and then she turned away from me and said, "All right, sign here, and I want your social security number." When I said I didn't have one . . . she said, "Sit down and wait to be called until we finish everyone who does have social security." Then they called me.

INTERVIEWER: Did you feel you could protest?

RESPONDENT: No.

The same story was told by an Ecuadoran woman who experienced discrimination "in a public hospital, when I was pregnant. I was pregnant, and I agree that my English didn't make much sense at that time. But this person, she was Latino, a Puerto Rican, who made me feel discriminated because of my race." According to her, "I wasn't understood when I spoke, and they made me repeat myself several times, and after I repeated myself several times, they said they could not take care of me because they didn't understand what I was saying. But I knew they did understand me."

A Mexican man reported similar treatment at the hands of Puerto Ricans, though not on the basis of language:

RESPONDENT: I've known white people as well as Hispanic people that discriminate.

INTERVIEWER: Yeah? Hispanic people too?

RESPONDENT: Yes. I have encountered people, like Puerto Ricans, that discriminate, even though they are Hispanic just like me, but they think they are better than others.

INTERVIEWER: And how does it feel when they discriminate?

RESPONDENT: Sometimes at first I felt, I felt bad.

In fact, intergroup conflict among Hispanics was a fairly common theme among respondents, up to and including instances of violence. A young Mexican man reported that "two Puerto Ricans came by and started to swear at one of my friends, and my friend is one to stand up and fight back." When the interviewer sought to confirm the breakout of a fight, the respondent answered, "Yes, they were saying, 'You Mexicans.'. . . I don't know what." Fortunately a police patrol was nearby and intervened to break up the fight, but the experience nonetheless left the respondent baffled. When asked why Puerto Ricans seem to have such anger against Mexicans, his response was simply: "The truth is, I don't know."

A Nicaraguan woman told us that her boss, a more affluent Dominican woman, confiscated some ladies' underwear that her husband had given her to sell for extra money at work:

But this Dominican woman took them from me and sold them for $20 when each one was worth, like, $10. She got $20 for the entire dozen, and she didn't pay me a cent. I was looking at her and talking to her, and everyone had brought their lunches to eat, and me, pregnant and hungry, and she didn't pay me my money. She discriminated against me and saw me as if I were a dog. And so I left work, and that day I had my son, and I collapsed from the hunger that I suffered. So I have this bad experience.

Numerous respondents reported racial and ethnic intimidation in the form of curses and epithets directed at them in both public and private venues. One Mexican man was walking on the street with his friends when they were verbally attacked with "swear words in English." Likewise, another Mexican man told us that, "in the street, when one walks along the street, they shout, 'Hey, you!' because you are here in this country and you aren't from here." An Ecuadoran man reported that when he went to look for work, employers often said, "'No, he's Hispanic,' something like that, maybe foul-smelling, sometimes they say that." An Ecuadoran woman reported that "they insulted me . . . they tell lies—intrusive, in your face. 'You Indians come here to my country to make money. Just get out!'" A Mexican man experienced a kind of drive-by harassment when a car full of young Americans passed and someone shouted out the window, "Fucking Mexican!"

Another man, a dark-skinned Venezuelan man, told us that when he went to a working-class bar with two friends, they were met with shouts from a white patron, who yelled, "Get out, you disgusting Latinos," and excoriated them by saying, "It's enough that I have to see you at work all day, and now I just want to come to my bar and relax and not see more people like you, and nevertheless I have to see you in the bar as well. Get out. Leave." A Nicaraguan woman told us that she felt looked down upon in public and could sense "the gaze of white people on me. I have seen their looks and have felt them, as if they burned from their superiority. They see you according to the color of the skin, by the shape of your face. I have felt this, and it has hurt me a lot." A young Mexican woman similarly sensed feelings of disgust from other riders on the New York subway:

RESPONDENT: They keep on seeing you as something strange.

INTERVIEWER: How do they look at you? With disgust?

RESPONDENT: Yeah, like I was a strange bug.

INTERVIEWER: Like a bug. Where do you notice this most?

RESPONDENT: Mostly on the train.

Some respondents believed that people actually recoiled from them in public places. According to one Brazilian man, "I perceived it from the way of looking at people like me, of stepping aside when we passed. In this way I felt it. They see us in a different way because the color of the skin and eyes are different. Then they discriminate." For others, the sense of discrimination was more a vague feeling that they didn't belong, as with the Mexican man who reported that "I don't feel where I live is my neighborhood. I don't know my neighbors. I don't know anyone between home and work. . . . One does not feel at home in this country, right? You feel strange, they make you feel foreign—not all persons, right? But some people make you feel this way." Similarly, a Puerto Rican man told us that "you could sometimes go to a particular white area in the city where they look at you like, you know, more in a negative way, or you can feel tension in the area, you know, like sometimes you don't belong there."

The ongoing and very prominent airing of illegal migration as a threat to America in the national media offers new opportunities for Americans to demonize immigrants as criminals. According to one Mexican man, "They want to humiliate you. They say that you're illegal. They offend you, and so on." Another Mexican male told us that "there are times when they have said this to me directly. That one is here for evil purposes, is illegal." A Honduran man told us about being approached by a white customer in the store where he worked: "I was stopped outside and wasn't blocking his way or anything, and he began to insult me, calling me a stupid wetback."

Making invidious distinctions on the basis of legal status is not confined to white Americans, however, as one Mexican man pointed out:

RESPONDENT: I wanted to say something else about discrimination, like, for example, when a person is already a legal resident—and I am speaking of people of the same origins who already have their papers—they think that, that they can do everything or that there is a big difference between being legal and illegal. This is what strikes me as terrible, and I tell you this from experience, because it just happened not long ago.

INTERVIEWER: From other Mexicans?

RESPONDENT: Yes, from other Mexicans.

INTERVIEWER: Do you think that this happens among other Latinos?

RESPONDENT: Yes.

INTERVIEWER: Really, you think among all?

RESPONDENT: Yes, among all.

One of our respondents, a particularly thoughtful Dominican male, explained why prejudice cuts across group boundaries; he saw it as stemming from a lack of education as well as from cultural insularity:

I think that the majority of people who discriminate do not have education. In general, these people don't have an education or any kind of international exposure. Everyone who travels and sees other cultures does not discriminate. Regardless of how white or black you are, you don't discriminate. But the people who don't like me are those without education, be they white, black, Latino, or even a person who walks down the street littering.

Many respondents told us about their experience of discrimination while on the job or looking for work. One young Mexican man complained that "they give you a job where you have extra work, and if you can't do it, they yell at you, tell you that you should hurry up. It is for this reason that you often quit." A Salvadoran man opined that in the United States "we are in a country where you don't get what you're owed." A Venezuelan dancing instructor explained why he could not get a job in more upscale studios: "They didn't give me certain jobs because I was Hispanic—jobs that I wanted to take. . . . Like, I want to teach dance at certain locations, and I have done so in others, but not in the schools that I want because I am Hispanic." Similarly, an Ecuadoran man did not receive a vacation or a raise, despite the fact that these benefits were routinely given to his white coworkers. In his words, "I have asked many times. . . . I have asked for vacations at work, and they tell me, 'Wait a while—I can't give it to you now,' or later on, when I ask for a raise, it's not there. They say, 'Business is not good,' but when an American asks, it's another thing." One Mexican male reported that his white boss went so far as to snatch "the bread out of the mouth of a friend of mine. Can you believe it? In a restaurant, saying that the bread was too expensive for him to eat, understand?"

Another Mexican man reported being made fun of by his employer for doing work that Americans would not do. As he put it, "I worked in the kitchen, and I was washing cooking utensils, and there were these African Americans working there, but they were a little slow at getting things done and lazy when it came to work, so the manager, who was this white guy, said, 'Come here and lend a hand.' And so I got down to work, and I noticed that the manager was making fun of me, understand?. . . Yes, mocking me."

Sometimes the harassment comes from the customers, not the employers, as happened to a young Ecuadoran woman who was working in a fast-food restaurant when a customer "grabbed me. Some dumb, drunk American tried to pick me up by the neck. And once I was pregnant, with my big belly and all, and I had to do something urgent in the food line, and they ordered me around with insults and didn't even respect that I was pregnant. Yes, and no one said anything. No one intervened, and, well, the only thing I could do was to start crying." On another occasion, the same woman reported being verbally abused by a customer for charging sales tax on his purchase. Upon receiving the bill, he suddenly began shouting, "I'm going to call the IRS. You don't know who you're dealing with! You come here to get rich! Thief! I'm going to call the IRS! I work for the IRS!" She recalled this incident as a particularly "nasty experience."

Another common discriminatory experience was being subjected to stereotyping or profiling. As already noted, Americans often assume that Latinos cannot speak English and treat them with condescension.

Such was the experience of one Argentine male when he complained about harassment from a white police officer who mistreated him "for being Latino. Yes, for being Latino. Because if they thought that I spoke English perfectly well, they would speak to me in English and I would get a different kind of treatment, but they, like, speak to me in Spanish and all." Rather than speaking Spanish as a courtesy, in this case the officer spoke the language "cynically" and in a mocking fashion.

In addition to not knowing English, another common stereotype is that Latinos are exploitable because they do not know their rights. Even though she was a native-born U.S. citizen, one Puerto Rican woman nonetheless felt stigmatized by Americans who assumed that, "if you are Latino, you can't communicate, or you don't know your rights because they say, 'Hispanics don't know their rights, they don't know the system,' and I think that they are going to treat an American or African American a little more carefully." Another Puerto Rican agreed, noting that "we still get talked down to because they think that we're not educated. I mean, that's the only major problem. But I think there is still prejudice; you can feel it anywhere you go. When, you know, you're the only person of color there, or the only Puerto Rican there, you can hear people talking about it, giving you looks, so you still feel it. Definitely."

A Mexican woman felt that she was being stereotyped, "like we are very ignorant. For example, the other day this man came and said that he wanted Mexican workers because Mexicans do good work and he pays them very little. . . . So people classify us according to a stereotype." To the extent that Mexican immigrants are exploitable, however, it is not because they are docile and ignorant, but because of their need and legal vulnerability. One Mexican man argued that it was not that he and his companion were naturally such good workers, but that they

> really need a wage, even though it is low. And if you need the job, you take it, and if they tell you to work twenty hours without stopping, you do it, understand? From necessity, you do it. But if an American or other kind of person does the same thing, understand, they respect their rights. They have the advantage of being from here, so they are not going to earn whatever they offer. If you work an extra hour, they pay you for it. For us, even though we work one or two extra hours, we don't have these benefits. No.

A number of respondents, typically males, reported being profiled and followed whenever they entered a retail store, such as the young Puerto Rican who said that, "when I use the term 'colored person,' I mean myself, people of color, that's us. You get followed in stores, still, today." A young Mexican male similarly complained that, "when one goes to a store and they think that because you are Mexican you can't pay, you can't buy, and then they treat you as if . . . I like expensive things, and so I go to a store and I want to look, but they hardly even want to show anything to me because they think that I don't have any money." A Dominican male also found that, "when you go to buy some things, they pay less attention to you because you're Hispanic," and a Mexican male saw store settings as particularly prone to stereotyping because "they see you differently, as differently dressed, because they see your dark complexion, and quickly they say that this is a person of the Hispanic minority."

One Peruvian male reported an incident that occurred in his early teens in a Sam Goody store that he and his cousin had entered to shop for records:

RESPONDENT: I grabbed a record, and then this guy started following me all over the store. All over! And I looked at him and said, "What gives?" And he said, "Can I help you?" And I said, "No thanks, I know what I want." That's what I said, right? "Well, I am looking." I was with my cousin, and my cousin dresses like he's black.

INTERVIEWER: Like in hip-hop style?

RESPONDENT: Yeah, with a hood. He walked around, picked up a record, and then put it down. And, I don't know, like, he looked at it and didn't want it, right? That's it. Sure. And he was thirteen or fourteen. And I looked at a record and didn't like it. And then I went and got another one. The guy followed me all over. Okay. I go to pay. I pay, and he looks at me with a face like this, and when I left the store, a horn went off, an alarm. Then he says, "Go again."

INTERVIEWER: And then what happened?

RESPONDENT: I return, and this guy says, "The alarm. It went off." We went through, and it sounded again.

INTERVIEWER: And you had paid for the record?

RESPONDENT: I had paid. But like I'm telling you, he was following us for quite a while. And I said to him, "Are you guys making a joke of me?" "No." We tried again to pass, and once again the alarm sounded. And so I went through with my cousin, and then you know what this guy did?

INTERVIEWER: What?

RESPONDENT: He grabs me and takes off my jacket, he takes everything from me and says, "Pass through." He grabbed the jacket and said . . .

INTERVIEWER: What?

RESPONDENT: I returned with the jacket and acted all innocent and looked at him as if to say, "What's the problem?"

INTERVIEWER: He took your jacket!

Of course, not everyone reported personal experience with discrimination. Indeed, around 37 percent could not recall a personal incidence of discrimination. Even so, however, many of our respondents felt that discrimination was still very much a reality in the United States. Some respondents experienced the same treatment as those who reported discrimination but did not define it as such. For example, although a Dominican woman flatly stated that "up to now I have never felt discrimination," she nonetheless perceived that "sometimes there are people who look at me strangely. . . . At times on the street, or in stores at times when one comes on like one knows English, they look at you strangely, no doubt because they don't understand it or reject it."

Likewise, a Mexican woman was "almost positive, when they heard my accent, they noted that I was Hispanic. Also this—when I am speaking with people, they assume that if you are Hispanic and white, that you have money or connections, or that you have this or are that. So it is a stereotype up to a certain point—but discriminated against openly, I don't think so." Although one Dominican woman could not recall any explicit discrimination, she nonetheless felt that she and other Latinos lived in a world completely different from that of most Americans, telling us that "my life is different from many people here, principally the Americans. We don't live in the same places, don't have the same jobs, and don't have the possibility of doing the same things. But, no, it's not that I have felt discrimination myself, other than realizing that we don't have the same life. . . . Different worlds, totally different."

One Mexican man refused to acknowledge differential treatment as discrimination because he felt that it was perfectly natural; he posed a hypothetical situation:

Let's suppose there is a fight, and you have a Mexican and an American, and you can only save one of them—who would you save? Well, if you say, the Mexican, then you are discriminating, yes, because I could save either one. . . . So we are all racist inside. In spite of the ideals that they teach us as children, you protect your own way of life. It's like my family. I worry about my family and leave worrying about my neighbor's family to my neighbor.

Finally, a young second-generation Honduran woman did not consider herself to have been discriminated against, even though she described what was quite clearly a systematic pattern of discrimination against other Latinos in her high school. According to her, one of the teachers was an

> American, maybe fifty or sixty years old, and one could see she had a preference for other Americans. In fact, the majority of those who wanted to go out for the team were black, Asian, and Latino, so there were, like, four Americans out of a total of twenty. And the Americans were not assigned to swimming, just us. One could see that the non-Americans had more talent for the team, but they weren't asked whether they were going out for it because three of the four were just assigned to it, while others who really deserved it, no, they didn't make it onto the team. And I saw it—maybe not happening directly to me—but I saw discrimination against Latinos.

Diminished Dreams

In coming to the United States, most immigrants seek to advance their material interests, and they dream of America as a land of opportunity. This perception of opportunity rests on the impression of abundant work at wages that are high by Latin American standards and the power that the U.S. dollar still has in their home country. Immigrants arrive with the intention of working hard to take advantage of these opportunities, which they see, initially at least, as open and accessible to all. Over time, however, they come to perceive numerous barriers to opportunity on the basis of legal status, which most expected, and especially barriers on the basis of race, which most did not expect. Despite the superior earnings opportunities and objectively lower levels of income inequality here, a majority of respondents saw the United States as unequal or worse than their home country, and most could report personal experiences of discrimination in the United States.

On the upside, the prospects for positive identity formation, integration, and boundary-blurring would seem to be good to the extent that the American Dream seems to be alive and well and bringing highly motivated and hardworking immigrants into the country. On the downside, there is a significant risk of oppositional identity formation, social separation, and boundary-brightening to the extent that immigrants come to see the United States as permeated by categorical inequalities on the basis of class, gender, legal status, and race. The difficulty that most immigrants reported in their daily brokering of boundaries with Americans suggests a problematic trajectory of integration and more durable inequalities.

Respondent narratives suggest a variety of possible influences on these ambivalent perceptions. Some influences, such as race, language ability, and legal status, came out clearly in the words of the respondents, whereas others, such as age, class origins, and education, are less readily apparent. In any given narrative, these factors commingle, and it is difficult to know which one is key in determining perceptions of opportunity, inequality, and discrimination. For this reason, we conclude this chapter with a simple logistic regression analysis that predicts three dichotomous outcomes—whether a respondent saw more opportunity in the United States, whether he or she perceived more inequality in the United States, and whether he or she experienced discrimination—as a function of racial-ethnic roots, regional origins, demographic characteristics, immigrant status, and class origins, while controlling for motivations to migrate and return intentions.

The results of this exercise are summarized in table 5.4. The left-most columns show coefficients and standard errors for the model predicting the perception of greater opportunity in the United States. This model has a very good fit and shows that perceived opportunity is predicted by five basic factors. The two strongest and most significant are age and being motivated to migrate by economic conditions at home. Those who are young and those whose move was motivated by blocked opportunities at home were much more likely to see the United States as a place of economic opportunity. Also important are legal status and Central American origins. As one might expect, undocumented migrants are significantly less likely than those with documents to see the United States as offering opportunity, and immigrants from Central America share this view. One final variable on the margins of significance is gender, with men generally perceiving less opportunity in the United States than women.

In sum, the profile of the immigrant most likely to view the United States optimistically as a place of opportunity is a young, non–Central American woman who came to the United States with documents to escape limitations at home. In contrast, the profile of a pessimistic immigrant who would not tend to see the United States as a place of opportunity is an older, undocumented Central American male who came to the United States for reasons other than economic limitations at home. Not involved in determining perceived opportunities in the United States are variables such as return intentions, racial-ethnic roots, years in the United States, English-language ability, education, and class origins.

Although race may not be relevant in determining how immigrants perceive opportunities in the United States, it is about the *only* thing that matters in determining the perception of U.S. inequality. Coefficients

Table 5.4 Logistic Regression Equations Predicting Perceptions of Opportunity, Inequality, and Discrimination

Predictors	More Opportunity in United States		More Inequality in United States		Discrimination in United States	
	Regression Coefficient	Standard Error	Regression Coefficient	Standard Error	Regression Coefficient	Standard Error
Motivation for migration						
Origin conditions	3.679**	1.409	0.850	0.656	1.583*	0.772
U.S. conditions	0.010	0.802	0.178	0.682	0.974	0.816
Family or network	-0.096	0.775	-0.134	0.586	2.160**	0.704
Other	—	—	—	—	—	—
Intentions						
Intends to return	-0.186	0.545	0.460	0.392	-0.804+	0.425
Racial-ethnic roots						
African	-0.041	0.707	0.187	0.505	0.394	0.589
Indigenous	1.154	1.437	-0.927	0.991	-1.497	1.306
Dark-skinned	0.465	1.039	1.500*	0.756	0.215	0.900
Region of origin						
Mexico	—	—	—	—	—	—
Caribbean	-0.515	1.137	0.806	0.741	-1.095	0.831
Central America	-2.421*	1.043	0.740	0.637	0.298	0.717
South America	-0.024	0.696	0.938+	0.547	-1.477*	0.634

(Table continues on p. 144.)

Table 5.4   (Continued)

Predictors	More Opportunity in United States		More Inequality in United States		Discrimination in United States	
	Regression Coefficient	Standard Error	Regression Coefficient	Standard Error	Regression Coefficient	Standard Error
Demographics						
Age	-0.152**	0.052	-0.035	0.032	0.134**	0.043
Male	-1.033+	0.629	-0.181	0.394	0.369	0.452
Immigrant status						
Documented	1.093*	0.899	-0.848	0.607	0.631	0.705
Years in United States	-0.013	0.012	0.012	0.008	0.007	0.010
Good English	0.301	0.635	-0.028	0.476	0.730	0.558
Class origins						
Years of schooling	-0.012	0.019	0.000	0.017	0.000	0.018
Parental International Socioeconomic Index	-0.004	0.017	0.003	0.013	-0.018	0.015
Intercept	5.270	2.412	0.102	1.484	-1.838	1.823
Log-likelihood	-55.511**		-87.141*		-77.051***	
Pseudo-R-squared	0.248**		0.087*		0.225***	
Sample size (N)	147		147		147	

Source: Immigrant Identity Project (Office of Population Research 2009).
+p < .10; *p < .05; **p < .01; ***p < .001

and standard errors for the model predicting perceived inequality in the United States are shown in the middle columns of table 5.4. Overall, this equation fits the data much less well than the equation predicting the perception of American opportunity. Only one variable is statistically significant at conventional levels, and that is skin color. All else being equal, darker-skinned people perceive the United States to be much more unequal than those with lighter skins. There also is a weak tendency for immigrants from South America to perceive the United States as more unequal, but this effect is on the margins of statistical significance.

Finally, the right-hand columns show coefficients and standard errors for the model predicting the experience of discrimination in the United States. Once again, the fit for this model is very good, and five variables account for its explanatory power. The strongest effects are age and being motivated to migrate because of family connections or network ties. In general, older migrants and those who come for family or network reasons are more likely to report an experience of discrimination. Less strong but still significant effects accrue to regional origins and motivation that stems from origin circumstances. South American migrants are less likely to have felt discrimination in the United States, whereas those who left to escape economic limitations at home are more likely to report it. Close to the 5 percent level of statistical significance are return intentions—those who want to return home are less likely to perceive discrimination in the United States. Perhaps surprisingly, given the narratives reviewed in this chapter, neither racial-ethnic roots, skin tone, nor legal status had any effect on perceived discrimination.

Taken together, the results of these three equation estimates suggest that perceptions of opportunity, inequality, and discrimination are conditioned as much by intangible factors such as the motivation for migration and return intentions as by tangible factors such as English-language ability, education, and occupational background. Among objective traits, three factors stand out: age, legal status, and skin color. Older migrants are much less likely to see opportunity in the United States and much more likely to perceive American discrimination; documented people tend to see greater opportunity in the United States than the undocumented; and dark-skinned people are more likely to see the United States as a place of inequality.

Equally important, however, are the original motivations for migration. Those who said that they moved to overcome economic limitations at home were simultaneously more likely to perceive opportunity in the United States and more likely to report discrimination, suggesting a scenario of optimistic dreams diminished by the realities of experience. The experience of discrimination was also more common among "tied" movers—those migrants whose reason for coming to the United States was family reunification or network ties; many of these respondents offered narratives of unwillingness or reluctance, suggesting a phenomenon of self-fulfilling negative expectations. Finally, as one might expect, those migrants who expect to return are significantly less likely to report discrimination. It is much easier to put up with discrimination when it is seen as a short-term trade-off for financial advantage rather than as a permanent feature of one's existence.

=Chapter 6=

Transnational Options

The last two chapters painted a rather stark picture of how America's society and its economy are experienced by Latino immigrants in urban areas of the Northeast. Although a few were able to land positions in the primary labor market and enjoy stable jobs with good pay, benefits, and real prospects for advancement, most were consigned to a string of poorly paid jobs in the secondary labor market that offered little hope of increased earnings or occupational advancement. We found that among those migrants who lacked education, one avenue of escape from a seemingly endless cycle of dead-end jobs and low pay was entrepreneurship. Creating a profitable enterprise, however, requires business acumen and occupational experience, not to mention legal documents, which few people possess; only 7 percent of respondents in our sample engaged in any kind of income-generating enterprise.

Another potential escape from the poverty trap of the secondary labor market is through transnationalism—channeling one's hopes, dreams, efforts, and earnings into projects in the sending country. Whereas upward mobility may be blocked in the United States, the dollars earned there, although meager by American standards, still count for something at home and can be invested and spent in ways that bring real improvements in status and material well-being to migrants and their families. By financing mobility at home, immigration offers the possibility of maintaining positive identity and self-respect in the face of a U.S. experience characterized by grueling conditions, low status, and a constant threat of arrest and deportation. In this chapter, we consider the transnational dimension of immigrants' lives, analyzing the links and behaviors that connect immigrants to homes, families, communities, and countries abroad. We begin by considering what Peggy Levitt (1998) calls "social remittances"—the ideas, concepts, and information that move between immigrants and their social contacts at home.

Social Remittances

Specifically, we asked respondents a series of questions about the nature and degree of contact that they maintained with friends and relatives at home. Answers to these questions were tabulated and coded to produce the information summarized in table 6.1. We consider first whether any contact was maintained with friends and relatives at home, and second, what form that contact took. As can be seen, the vast majority of respondents said that they were in contact with someone in their country of origin. Overall, 92 percent said that they remained in contact with family or friends at home. This very high level of transnational contact varied only slightly by documentation. For example, whereas 95 percent of the undocumented reported contact with friends or relatives at home, 86 percent of those with legal documents did so as well. The degree of contact was also similar across generation: 94 percent in the first generation reported contact, and 88 percent in the second (not shown). Although transnational contact varies somewhat by social category, the differences are generally quite small, and rates of transnational contact are universally high.

The most common form of contact reported by respondents was the standard telephone: 84 percent of respondents said that they stayed in touch with friends and relatives at home via a land line phone. Although the share using a land line was the same among both first- and second-generation migrants, wider differences appeared between documented and undocumented migrants: 87 percent of undocumented migrants said that they stayed in contact via telephone, but only 77 percent of documented migrants did so. The use of new phone technologies to stay in touch was much less frequent. Across all respondents, only 5 percent reported using a cell phone to stay in touch with friends and family abroad, and just 3 percent used a calling card. Some 4 percent of respondents said that they communicated with people in the origin country using email, with a surprisingly high level of use by undocumented migrants, whose 21 percent rate was more than double the 10 percent rate observed among legal immigrants. In great contrast to what William Thomas and Florian Znaniecki (1918–1919) found earlier in the twentieth century, almost no one—just 1 percent of respondents—used regular surface mail to stay in touch.

The reason most often given for shunning regular mail as a means of communication was the inconvenience and burden of letter-writing. According to one Peruvian man in Philadelphia, "The best way was by telephone, because, like I said, I don't read or write. (*Laughs.*) Yes, I do it, but I don't practice it." Another Philadelphia male from Brazil likewise emphasized the tedium of writing letters, noting that "I don't have the patience to write. I have to talk because I lack the patience to write."

Table 6.1   Contact with Family or Friends in the Country of Origin as Reported by Latino Immigrants to the United States, by Gender, Generation, and Legal Status

Behavior	Documented	Undocumented	Total
Any contact	86.0%	95.1%	91.8%
Land phone	77.2	87.3	83.6
Cell phone	8.9	2.9	5.0
Calling card	1.8	3.9	3.1
Email	9.8	21.1	3.8
Regular mail	1.8	1.0	1.3
Sample size (N)	57	102	159

Source: Immigrant Identity Project (Office of Population Research 2009).

We asked respondents about contacts with both friends and relatives in the sending country, and some respondents said that they were in regular contact with both groups of people, such as the Colombian man from New York who said that he "regularly" talked with both his friends and his relatives: "I talk to them, and when I go there I drop by to see them." When asked if this statement applied to friends as well as family, his response was, "Naturally." Likewise, when we asked a Mexican man in New York whether he was in contact with family members at home, he answered with a simple "Yes," and when we probed about contact with friends, he assured us that he stayed in touch with "them as well." Another man, a Brazilian in Philadelphia, told us that he was in regular contact "with my mom, with my siblings, with my friends, with everyone." A Peruvian man in Philadelphia underscored the importance of regular contact in maintaining his friendships:

> I was five years in one school with all of them, secondary school, and three or four of them, yes, two guys and two girls, as the closest, and one of the girls lives here, in Florida, but I haven't seen her there yet. But she calls me sometimes, and those in Peru are always calling me, and we're always on the Internet. It has been two months since I have seen my friends. If you don't speak with them, you lose touch.

A larger number of respondents, however, reported being in more frequent contact with family than friends. According to one Dominican woman we interviewed in New York, "With family, yes, but friends, no, because I came here when I was sixteen. During the first years, yes, I did have contact with friends, but it has been a long time now since I have had any contact." When asked about maintaining contact with family, a Mexican man in New Jersey said, "Of course," but when we inquired about friends, he told us, "More with family." Another respondent, an Ecuadoran male, answered our question about transnational contacts by saying, "My family above all. More than friends. I hardly have any friends down there." Likewise, a Honduran man from Philadelphia told us that his friends were "here," whereas his family was mostly "there," pointing out that "I have friends here, like, I always have maintained contact with my family down there by telephone." A Honduran woman in New Jersey stressed contact with family but not friends even more bluntly:

INTERVIEWER: Do you stay in touch with your family there?

RESPONDENT: Always.

INTERVIEWER: Always? And your friends?

RESPONDENT: No.

"Always" was a word used by several respondents when we asked about the frequency of communication with family members abroad. One Bolivian man in New York said that he was perpetually talking "with my mother, with my brothers and sisters, with, well, with all my family. We are always talking and all that." "Always" was similarly the word used by a Venezuelan man interviewed in New Jersey who, when asked if he stayed in contact with his family at home, said: "Every week I call. Always."

Often respondents referred to a specific relative or loved one in response to our general question about contact with family. One Ecuadoran female in New Jersey, after noting that "I still have brothers and sisters, various cousins, aunts and uncles, who I haven't seen in many years," went on to state that she endeavored to stay in touch only "with my siblings, yes." Another respondent, a Mexican man in New York, underscored the importance to him of regular contact with his wife: "Yes, when she hears my voice when I call from here, I know she won't be happy until I come back, and as they say there, I am never going to be happy until I have her by my side once again, by the grace of God. I say this because at least I hear her voice and because we talk often and I speak to her, if I can, three times a week or so."

His reported frequency of calling three times a week was not at all unusual. A man we interviewed in Philadelphia from the Dominican Republic said that, "with my mom, I call around every two days, or maybe even every day." Daily contact with family abroad was also reported by a Brazilian man in Philadelphia who, when asked about contact with his family, said that he talked "every day—by telephone and email," an answer quite similar to that offered by an Ecuadoran man in New Jersey whose response was simply, "Ah, yes. Every day." An Ecuadoran woman was quite emphatic about the importance of daily contact with her family at home:

INTERVIEWER: So you keep in contact with your family and friends in Ecuador?

RESPONDENT: I call every day.

INTERVIEWER: Yes?

RESPONDENT: Or even more often, because I really miss my daughter and husband.

INTERVIEWER: Of course.

RESPONDENT: I call my daughter nearly daily, daily, daily.

Not everyone, however, is in such frequent contact with family abroad. A Mexican woman from New Jersey reported that "normally about every fifteen days I talk to my son and to my mom. They are the ones I speak to most often. My siblings, once in a while. But with my mom and son, more often." A Mexican man from Philadelphia likewise stated that "I speak with my mom once a week, or once every two weeks, more or less," and a Dominican man surveyed in Philadelphia reported that he spoke "with my family, weekly. Like three times a week."

Although technological advances and deregulation have made international calling cheaper and more accessible in recent years, it is not costless, and the expense of telephone communication was often cited as a reason for not staying in more frequent touch with friends and family at home. A Peruvian man in Philadelphia told us that "the economic situation" in Peru had separated him from his family and friends by making telephone calls too expensive, or as he put it: "It has cut us off." As a result, they were calling him "very little now," and his friends at least had shifted to email as a cheaper alternative. With friends, he communicated "by Internet more than anything. With one, two, or three with whom I have become good friends."

Similarly, a Dominican man in Philadelphia reported shifting to the Internet because "telephone bills are ruining me." When asked whether he had some kind of long-distance plan, he said, "No, lately what I've been doing is buying cards." Another respondent, a Brazilian man from Philadelphia, also reported shifting from standard telephone service to prepaid phone cards because, "with a calling card, it's cheaper." When faced with ruinous costs, a Mexican man in New York did not switch to phone cards but instead shopped around to find a cheaper long-distance service; he told us that "what I am doing now is cheaper than it was before, which was very expensive, so that I was paying $350 to $400 per month to the phone company when I had to call my family often, two or three times a week."

Only a few people said that they were no longer in contact with friends or family in the sending country. The reason most frequently cited for this lack of contact, however, was quite logical and had nothing to do with the withering of ties to friends or relatives: everyone of importance in the person's social network had relocated to the United States. Thus, when a Dominican man in New York was asked whether he was still in contact with family members at home, he answered, "No, because nearly all of my family—85 to 90 percent—live in this country." When queried about friends, however, he admitted that "I have some friends down there from childhood, but we have lost contact." In other cases, even the friends have moved northward, as with the Ecuadoran woman from Philadelphia who reported that "all my friends from those days are now here. So I have gotten in contact with certain friends here. But in truth, the last time I returned to my country, I didn't find anyone I knew there." A Honduran man from Philadelphia told us, "It is ironic. It's been a month and a half since I went to Honduras, and I went to where I grew up and no one was there."

Although we saw earlier that contact did drop somewhat in the second generation, it nonetheless remained quite robust. Although not the 94 percent rate reported in the first generation, the contact rate was still 88 percent among those born or raised from childhood in the United States. One nineteen-year-old Dominican woman from New York said, "I call down a lot," whereas a thirteen-year-old Mexican boy in New Jersey said that he spoke to family members "by telephone. Every week." An adult Colombian woman in New York told us, "I'm in very intimate interaction. Mostly through the cousins. A lot of my family has passed away, but on birthdays and holidays we interact."

Second-generation immigrants reported being in contact with a wide variety of relatives, including "aunts and uncles and grandmothers" (a Peruvian female from Philadelphia) and "my aunt, my cousins, my grandparents" (a Colombian male from New Jersey). Sometimes, however, respondents were in regular communication only with particular relatives, such as the Puerto Rican male from New York who said that he talked "just with my parents, and I ask them about the relatives, the uncles, and cousins, and stuff like that." A Mexican male from New York said that he regularly called his grandmother, but only because of pressure from his mother. As he put it, "She gives me a hard time, you know, my mom. 'Stay here,' she says. I feel bad that she gives me a hard time. My mom is not saying it directly, but in the way that she speaks. It's like I feel the lash."

One reason second-generation immigrants are sometimes reluctant to speak to relatives in their parents' country of origin is their lack of comfort with the Spanish language, especially if they have gone to school only in the United States. Thus, when we asked one young Mexican woman in Philadelphia whether she had much contact with friends and relatives in Mexico, she confessed, "um, very little. Not much, like, I don't like talking on the phone because it is hard sometimes [to talk in Spanish,] but we are trying."

As with their parents, the children of immigrants tend to communicate more with family than with friends. When we asked a young Dominican woman who came to New York as a child about her contact with people back in the Dominican Republic, she said that she spoke

> mainly with family members. Friends before. Just after I arrived, I communicated more with them, with my friends, but later, now that I have eight years living here in the United States, well, these relations have dissolved a little with the distance, even though when I go down and visit, I still feel the same spirit that I can talk with them as if they were my daily friends, even though there are some differences.

As suggested by the foregoing remark, among second-generation immigrants, traveling back to their parents' community of origin is often key to maintaining contact with people in the sending region. As one Dominican woman from New York told us when we asked whether she had much contact with family and friends in the Dominican Republic, "Yes, especially now that I went, well, I went down in 1999 and then came back like a year later with my husband so he could know the place. I have a cousin, and we always write each other emails, you know." She went on to note that even though some of her relatives had visas entitling them to legal permanent residence in the United States, for a variety of different reasons they preferred to live in the Dominican Republic and would travel back only for a yearly visit to New York so that their visas did not expire:

> INTERVIEWER: I have cousins that come up because the majority of my family is here, though some are still there. But most of those who are down there are second-generation. The parents are up here, and the children don't want to come, or they already came for a while and things were not good for them—like a person could not get a steady job or an education here. I have many cousins that come and go—they come and go on vacation so their visa won't expire.
>
> RESPONDENT: The visa they have is through their parents?
>
> INTERVIEWER: Through the parents, but they have to use it every so

often. Some only have a multiple entry visa, and they have to use it, yeah. But there are many who don't want to come.

RESPONDENT: They are down there, and you are in contact with them?

INTERVIEWER: Yes, I'm in contact by phone and email.

Although they were clearly in the minority, some second-generation respondents insisted that they had no contact with friends or family in the origin country, such as the young Dominican woman from New York who admitted that "my family has contact, and my brother, he lives there, [but] not me." Likewise, a thirteen-year-old Mexican girl living in New Jersey, when asked about relatives in Mexico, admitted, "I have them, but we're not in contact." And despite repeated probing that revealed the presence of relatives back in Puerto Rico, a young Puerto Rican woman remained firm about her lack of contact with them:

INTERVIEWER: Are you in contact with family or friends in your parents' country?

RESPONDENT: No.

INTERVIEWER: Nothing?

RESPONDENT: No.

INTERVIEWER: Okay. So you don't send money to anyone there?

RESPONDENT: No.

INTERVIEWER: You don't have any family there besides your father?

RESPONDENT: No. Well, actually, I have aunts and uncles there, but also in New York.

INTERVIEWER: So in Puerto Rico you do have family?

RESPONDENT: Yes, on my mother's side.

INTERVIEWER: But you don't communicate with them?

RESPONDENT: No.

INTERVIEWER: Nor do your parents communicate with their families in Puerto Rico?

RESPONDENT: No.

As noted earlier, by far the most common means of staying in touch with friends and relatives in the origin country was by telephone using a land line, with email a distant second, followed by cell phones and calling cards. Phone conversations are popular, of course, because they are easy, cheap, and convenient, but also because they provide an intimacy and immediacy to transnational contacts that an email or letter simply cannot duplicate. As a second-generation Puerto Rican man from Philadelphia explained to us, "You just, you just don't get that same feeling like if you're talking to someone over the phone—sometimes the Internet, but most of the time on the phone." A Venezuelan man in New Jersey told us that regular phone calls helped him maintain an intimate bond with his mother: "The person who I call most is my mom. . . . My mom is the one I love the most. . . . I always call her. It's not that I say I have to. It's that I feel, well, I always call her on Sunday, but sometimes I get choked up and I miss her a lot and I call her. I call her to tell her I love her and that I have her picture with me and she is always in my heart."

Echoing this sentiment, a Venezuelan man in Philadelphia confessed that his need for personal contact left him little choice except to communicate directly "by telephone, always by telephone. . . . Regularly. Two or sometimes three times a week. It depends, but at least twice. Because I can't, I have no other option." An Argentine man we talked to in New Jersey explained that his choice of communication medium was contingent on his mood: "It depends on how I feel at the moment, on whether I feel a need within myself to feel them close right then." A similar view was expressed by a Dominican man we interviewed in Philadelphia who used Instant Messenger and other Internet services frequently because "most of my family down there have computers," but who nonetheless also telephoned them frequently, "sometimes weekly, sometimes more. It depends how much you miss them."

Likewise, a Dominican woman in New York told us that she used email to stay in contact with her cousins, but that she preferred to use the telephone to talk to her "aunt, who is looking after my daughters, and because of this I am always talking to her daughters as well." A Colombian man in New York similarly told us that although Internet communication was fine for friends, he preferred the intimacy of a phone call to stay in touch with his relatives, or as he succinctly put it, "Internet with my friends, family more by telephone." The same sentiment was expressed by a second-generation Dominican woman in New York who said that, "with my friends that I have there, it's through email, or like chatting with MSN online, you know, stuff like that, but with email never with my family. I always call. We always call them."

Paradoxically, one migrant, a woman from Nicaragua interviewed in New Jersey, was able to establish contact with an estranged branch of her family in her home country only after she had migrated to the United States. She explained that she did not know her father while growing up, but that "someone put me in touch from here, and I went to look for them [her paternal relatives] because I was very depressed at not knowing him." She was overjoyed at establishing contact with her father's relatives and valued the intimacy created by regular phone calls and letters:

> Yes, we talk every two weeks. I talk to them by phone, and they send me letters, and it is excellent because, I tell you, they tell me everything that happened, everything that will happen tomorrow, that which happened yesterday—if the baby quieted down, if they did that thing, ate this thing, that we agreed on this or that good thing, well, very detailed, everything, everything. It is as if I am there, and, well, what I do is grab a cassette and record a tape so they can hear me laugh and sing. I have sung them songs that the Lord gave me this, so I have to tell you something important. I send this all recorded, and they have a family reunion to listen to everything I have to say to them.

Several respondents were able to take advantage of privileged access to a dedicated long-distance phone on a work line to call home frequently at little or no cost. Thus, a Brazilian man employed in Philadelphia told us that his workplace "has access to a dedicated international line, and it doesn't matter how often you call, so I call a lot from work. I call them almost every day." An Ecuadoran man in New Jersey admitted: "Really, there are friends I talk to almost daily, but with my family there, every two days. With me, because of my business, I almost speak to Ecuador every day. . . . Most of the day I spend talking."

A woman from Venezuela who lived in New Jersey related a similar story of free-riding on someone else's communication medium, but in her case it was her boyfriend's high-speed Internet service rather than her company's long-distance phone line. She was able to use this resource "every day because I have access at the house of my boyfriend, where he pays a fixed price and you can sit there without worry and without thinking about money."

For those with the technical savvy, email offers a very convenient way not only to chat but to share photos and other memorabilia with family members at home. A Colombian woman in New York noted that in the past she had relied on the telephone, but she was looking forward to making greater use of the Internet because "I think the Internet is so much easier. Um, with photos, with emailing, so that's the way I'm going to concentrate more." Of course, not everyone has relatives with an Internet connection. Several respondents said that they would have liked to make greater use of the Internet to communicate with family at home, but that their relatives could not afford a computer, had no access to one where they lived, or were not interested in learning to use one.

When we asked an Ecuadoran man in New York about email contact with his relatives, for example, he told us, "Email, no, because they don't have a computer. I told my brother to buy one, but he says he doesn't want to." The technology gap between families at home and respondents in the United States was especially prominent for second-generation migrants. A Puerto Rican man from New Jersey informed us that "calls are usually the best thing because, you know, my parents, they don't know how to mess with the Internet. The only one who does that is my daughter." Sometimes the generation gap was expressed in terms of a difference between relatives (referring to the parental generation) and friends (the respondent's generation). When asked how he communicated with family and friends, a Colombian man from New Jersey readily told us that he talked by phone card "once a week, and at times more frequently if it is someone's birthday there," but when we probed about his use of email he said, "Umm, no, because none of my family have Internet access." Nonetheless, when we asked if he used the Internet to communicate with friends, his answer was an unequivocal "Yes." Another second-generation Puerto Rican man, also from New Jersey, told us that he spoke regularly to his grandparents and cousins by telephone rather than through the Internet because they lacked a computer:

INTERVIEWER: Okay, and when you speak, to whom do you speak?

RESPONDENT: Ah, my grandmother and grandfather.

INTERVIEWER: Okay.

RESPONDENT: And sometimes my cousins.

INTERVIEWER: In Spanish?

RESPONDENT: Yes, that's all they know. Spanish in Puerto Rico anyway.

INTERVIEWER: Oh, yeah?

RESPONDENT: Yes.

INTERVIEWER: Do you communicate with them by mail or by email or something like that or no?

RESPONDENT: No, they don't have a computer.

INTERVIEWER: They don't have a computer?

RESPONDENT: No.

A similar situation was described by a young Peruvian woman in Philadelphia who reported frequent contact by phone and regular mail, but not by email:

INTERVIEWER: How frequently do you communicate with your family in Peru, more or less?

RESPONDENT: With them by calling cards like every week.

INTERVIEWER: So it is by phone?

RESPONDENT: Yes.

INTERVIEWER: And have you used the mail?

RESPONDENT: Yes, letters.

INTERVIEWER: Letters as well. And the Internet?

RESPONDENT: Um, no. They don't have computers.

Lack of access to the Internet is a special problem for those with relatives who live in rural rather than urban areas of the origin country. A second-generation Dominican man in New York told us that he communicated by both phone and email with his siblings and cousins in the capital city of Santo Domingo, but that things were different for parents and uncles who lived in smaller cities and the countryside:

INTERVIEWER: Is most of your family in Santo Domingo or in other places?

RESPONDENT: In reality they're in different places—some in Santiago, some in Santo Domingo, and some, shall we say, in the countryside. Some of my uncles still live out there and have never left the countryside for the city. I mean, they live there.

INTERVIEWER: And with them you don't communicate via email I suppose.

RESPONDENT: No, really, I really communicate mostly with my cousins via email, but by phone when my mom calls, and I say hello to whoever is there, and I call my cousins that are there who are close to my age.

In a few cases, it was the family members who had Internet access and the immigrant who preferred to use the phone. Such was the case with an Ecuadoran woman in Philadelphia who told us that her family at home actually preferred that she use email as a medium of communication, but that she herself preferred talking "by telephone. Normally by phone. Electronic mail, well, I know that they would like it very much if I would, but I don't like it, and moreover, I don't have the time to sit at the computer, except for my work at the university."

Several other respondents mentioned time constraints as a reason to prefer the phone over the Internet. When asked why he confined himself to the phone and did not use the Internet more, an Ecuadoran male from New Jersey said simply, "I don't have the time." Another migrant, a Honduran woman from New York, admitted to using the Internet "a little" to communicate with her family, but when we asked her why it was only "a little," she said, "Really, I don't have the time." A Mexican man in Philadelphia similarly complained about the time burden of communicating with relatives, noting that "every time I spoke to them they squandered things, or rather they wasted my time, wasted it—like I was thinking a lot about Mexico but I wasn't, not in Mexico and not here." To ease the burden he simply "stopped calling, and now I focus more here than Mexico"; he communicates with his family only occasionally by "postcards and email," the latter from "an Internet café."

Financial Remittances

In addition to the exchange of ideas and information, another way to assess the practice of transnationalism is by examining material exchanges between immigrants in the United States and their friends and relatives at home. In our interviews we asked directly about the sending of financial remittances, the frequency with which they were sent, and the mode of transmission; table 6.2 presents coded responses to these queries. The top panel indicates whether the respondent sent remittances and, if the respondent was in the second generation, whether one of the respondent's parents sent remittances. As can be seen from the last column, which presents tabulation for the total sample, the large majority of those we interviewed, around 79 percent, said they currently sent home remittances—somewhat less than the 92 percent who said they exchanged information, but quite substantial nonetheless. Another 7 percent reported that while they did not send remittances, their parents did. All told, then, 86 percent of respondents were involved in sending remittances, either directly themselves or indirectly through their parents.

In other words, most of the Latin American immigrants we interviewed were materially connected to their communities of origin through the regular sending of money. Among respondents, the incidence of remitting was more common among undocumented migrants (82 percent) than among documented migrants (74 percent), but the rate was not much different in the first generation (80 percent) compared with the second (77 percent—not shown). Twenty percent of second-generation migrants said that while they did not send remittances, their parents did, meaning that 98 percent of our respondents were involved in remittance-sending at least indirectly.

As important as the incidence of remitting is, the strength of material ties is probably better measured by the frequency with which remit-

Table 6.2   Information on Material Exchanges Between Latino Immigrants
to the United States and Their Family and Friends in the
Country of Origin

Behavior	Documented	Undocumented	Total
Sends remittances			
Respondent	73.7%	82.3%	79.2%
Parent	10.5	3.9	6.9
Either	84.2	86.2	86.1
Frequency of remitting			
Up to once a month	24.6	54.9	44.0
Once a month to twice a year	8.8	6.9	7.6
Twice a year to once a year	7.0	2.9	4.4
Once in a while	33.2	13.7	20.8
Only on special occasions	0.0	3.9	2.5
Never	26.3	17.7	20.8
How money is sent			
Money order	59.7	65.7	63.5
Person	3.5	3.0	3.2
Bank	7.0	8.8	8.2
Combination	4.0	3.5	3.8
Nothing sent	26.3	17.7	20.8
Has bank account			
In the United States	64.9	38.2	47.8
In the origin country	15.8	38.2	30.2
In both countries	14.0	14.7	14.5
Sends gifts to friends or family	49.1	55.9	53.5
Sample size (N)	57	102	159

Source: Immigrant Identity Project (Office of Population Research 2009).

tances are sent, and this is the subject of the second panel of table 6.2. In general, most respondents were regular contributors to the remittance flow: 44 percent said that they sent remittances at least once a month, and another 8 percent reported sending remittances at least twice a year. Thus, a majority of all respondents (52 percent) said that they sent money at least once every six months, representing two-thirds of those who remitted. Only around 23 percent said that they confined their sending to "once in a while" or to special occasions such as holidays, birthdays, and anniversaries. Whereas 55 percent of all undocumented migrants said that they sent remittances at least once a month, the figure was just 25 percent for those with legal papers. Similarly, the share of undocumented migrants who reported remitting only once in a while (14 percent) or never (18 percent) was substantially below the corresponding figures for documented migrants (33 percent and 26 percent, respectively).

The third panel in the table reports how remittances were sent, and here the overwhelming favorite across all categories was the commercial money order. Some 64 percent of all respondents said that they sent remittances in this fashion, or 82 percent of all those who reported remitting. Only 3 percent said that they entrusted the delivery of remittances to a person, such as a friend or relative who was traveling home or a commercial courier service, and just 8 percent said that they sent the money via a bank transfer. Another 4 percent reported using a combination of methods (money order and friend or relative), so that 68 percent of all respondents reported using a money order to send remittances at one time or another, representing 86 percent of those who remitted. There were relatively few differences by legal status in the mode of remitting. No matter what a person's documentation, around two-thirds used commercial money orders to send funds home.

Whether or not one uses a bank to send money internationally depends very much on whether one has a bank account to use, of course, so we also asked respondents whether they currently had a bank account in the United States and in their origin country; answers to these questions are coded in the fourth panel of table 6.2. Obviously, the small share of respondents who reported sending money via a bank transfer (8 percent overall) is explained mainly by the small share of people having bank accounts at both origin and destination (15 percent). Among those with the technical ability to send bank transfers, a clear majority (53 percent) did so. In general, respondents were more likely to report having a U.S. bank account (48 percent) than one in their country of origin (30 percent), a pattern that was accentuated among legal immigrants (65 percent in the United States versus 16 percent at home) more than among undocumented migrants (38 percent at both locations).

Finally, to round out our assessment of material exchanges we asked whether gifts were sent to family and friends in the origin country; this information is summarized in the last line of the table. A majority of respondents (54 percent) said that they sent gifts to friends or relatives outside the United States. Gift-giving was slightly more common among undocumented migrants (56 percent versus 49 percent among the documented). These numerical tabulations were coded from narrative responses to open-ended questions, of course; a more textured and nuanced appreciation for the role of remitting in the lives of migrants comes from the narrative reports themselves.

In general, immigrants were proud of their ability to support relatives and friends at home. An Ecuadoran woman from New Jersey reported with some pride that she had been supporting her brothers and sisters "since 1998" and that since she "began to work more independently I have been able to send money for my siblings' studies." Likewise, a woman from Nicaragua we talked to in New Jersey said that she had been sending money home "since we began working here." In answering our questions about remittances, our respondents frequently used the terms "regularly," "always," "of course," and "naturally," suggesting the salience of remittance-sending as a raison d'être for their presence in the United States. An Ecuadoran man from New York replied somewhat indignantly, "Yes, of course, regularly," when we asked if he sent remittances, and a Bolivian man in New York simply responded, "Yes, I send regularly," as did a Mexican man in New Jersey who said, "Yes, I send money regularly to my family." More adamant was a Venezuelan man from New Jersey who told us, "I've always sent money," as did a Guatemalan woman from New Jersey who insisted, "Well, yes, I always send money." A Honduran man in Philadelphia also emphasized the word "always" when we asked whether he remitted: "Yes, always, always. Every month I am sending to them."

Several respondents underscored the moral obligation of remittance-sending. When asked whether he was able to send money to his family in Mexico, for example, one Mexican man in New York instantly responded, "Yes, especially because for me it is an obligation, it is mandated," and another Mexican male from New York similarly stated, "Yes, definitely, because for me it is obligatory to be sending." One Honduran woman in New York even invoked God in her response, noting that she sent money home "every month, thank God. I send to my mother." A Mexican male we interviewed in Philadelphia underscored the salience of remitting in his daily calculus by emphasizing that in the United States he consumed only what was necessary and sent everything else he earned to his family:

RESPONDENT: All the money that they pay me I send to my parents, who put it in the bank.

INTERVIEWER: So what do you live on here?

RESPONDENT: Well, what I call a personal administration. . . . I have to look at my expenses and see what I have to pay, what I have to buy to eat and all that, and the money . . .

INTERVIEWER: The rest you send down there?

RESPONDENT: All the rest I send to my country.

Not all migrants are able to be so generous in remitting, and some hinted at a certain shame or disappointment at not being able to send more. Some did this by downplaying the amount they sent when reporting a high frequency of sending, such as the Mexican man in Philadelphia who answered, "Money, yes, I send regularly—a little bit." Other respondents confessed not only to sending little but to sending less often because of financial constraints; one Dominican male from New York admitted that he was only able to remit funds "very rarely." A Venezuelan woman in New York reported that, depending on circumstances, she sent money "one month, yes, the other, no," and an Ecuadoran male from New Jersey simply noted that "it depends—sometimes every two weeks, sometimes every three weeks." A Puerto Rican man from New Jersey told us that he was able to send money to his parents only "whenever."

As noted earlier, some respondents reported that they sent money only on special occasions, such as birthdays, Christmas, national holidays, or a parent's day, such as the Mexican woman in New Jersey who said that she mainly sent money to her parents on May 10, Father's Day, or the Dominican man in New York who confessed that he did not send money in any monthly amount, but only "when it is gifts for Mother's Day or Christmas." "No, not that," he confirmed.

As already noted, a minority of respondents said that they did not send remittances at all. A Mexican woman surveyed in New Jersey, when asked whether she sent money abroad to help out, replied, "No, right now, no. Presently I don't send." Moreover, although the vast majority of respondents said that they regularly remitted, there were two cases of reverse remitting—the immigrants themselves were receiving money from relatives abroad. A Dominican man in Philadelphia responded to our query about remittance-sending by exclaiming: "No, thank God! At times they are the ones sending me the money." Similarly, when we asked a Puerto Rican man in Philadelphia whether he sent money to his family back home on the island, he laughed heartily and said, "No, just the opposite."

Respondents gave a variety of reasons for not sending remittances or for sending them infrequently, the most common of which focused on financial constraints in the United States. For example, when we asked a Dominican woman in Philadelphia whether she was able to send money home, she sheepishly responded, "Not really. I can hardly send money to my mother for her medical expenses. . . . A couple times a month, more or less, but not exactly." A male Venezuelan, also in Philadelphia, was more up front about the limitations he faced, telling us, "Not really, you know, every fifteen or twenty days because here what I earn is meager. . . . As I plan to stay here quite a while, I have to be economical." A Brazilian man we talked to in Philadelphia also admitted that, "no, I hardly send. It's difficult, right? I hardly ever send money to Brazil, just to pay off what I had borrowed from my father to come here." A woman from Guatemala we interviewed in New Jersey said that she sent back only a "minimal" portion of her salary because "I have other expenses to meet," and a Venezuelan woman in Philadelphia just laughed when we asked whether she sent home money regularly, telling us, "I don't have much to send." A Mexican woman from New Jersey told us that, "when I have it, I send it, but when I don't have it, I can't send what I don't have."

In addition to financial scarcity, two other reasons were given for not sending money to friends and relatives in the origin country. The first was that family members there simply did not need the money. As one Ecuadoran man in Philadelphia told us, "We haven't had the need to send money because everyone down there has their business. Everyone is doing all right with the good economy there." Similarly, a Dominican man from New York said that he did not send money home very often because "I really haven't had the need to do it, because, like, I have businesses there, and my mother is the one in charge of them, and my brothers, they are taken care of by what I left back there."

Several respondents said that they sent money home infrequently because they only responded on an as-needed basis; a young Dominican woman in New York told us that she sent money to her family "only when they needed it," and a Peruvian man from New York told us simply that, "when they ask, we have sent." Sometimes, however, the lack of an articulated need does not reflect an absence of poverty at home. As a Puerto Rican man from New Jersey told us, "You know, my parents are very proud for themselves, so they don't really ask. But whenever they say, 'Oh, well, you know, we're going through some tough times,' all right, I go, okay, 'I'll call you back later.' And then, you know, I go to Western Union and send. There's no excuse. I say, 'Mom, go to Western Union,' and she says, 'Oh, what did you do?' Just go pick up the money. And you know what I mean."

The lack of need for remittances among relatives back home can also stem from the absence of a cash economy. When we asked one male Ecuadoran in New Jersey whether he sent money home to his family, he responded with a noncommittal "More or less." When we probed further, he said simply, "My parents are able to sustain themselves there." On further questioning, we found out that his parents had no use for money, not because they were not poor, but because they lived in a subsistence setting:

INTERVIEWER: Oh, so it's like they don't need it?

RESPONDENT: No.

INTERVIEWER: They don't depend on you?

RESPONDENT: No, no. It is another world, or rather, that I belong to an Indian world.

INTERVIEWER: Ah, that's it.

RESPONDENT: It is very different, another way of thinking, another cosmic vision.

Another major reason for not sending money home was simply having no relatives left there to send money to. One Venezuelan man in Philadelphia told us that he had stopped sending money "because my parents are now here," and a Mexican man from New Jersey reported that he "sent more then than now" because that was "when my mother was down there, and sometimes we sent to my grandmother." A woman from the Dominican Republic who had settled in New York said that she rarely sent money home "because in reality I don't have any immediate family there. They're all here."

Sometimes, of course, no relatives are left at home, not because they have emigrated, but because they have all died, as was the case with a Mexican man in Philadelphia who told us that he had sent money in the past, when "my mother's family members were having problems, and all that," but that, "unfortunately, most of my mom's relatives who needed help have now died and, well, they no longer need help." In at least one case we detected a reluctance to remit on the basis of personal animosity. An Ecuadoran man readily admitted to sending money to his son, but when we inquired about his divorced wife, the response we got was, "For her, nothing."

As noted earlier, some respondents did not themselves remit money to relatives abroad, but their parents did; this pattern was especially common among, though not restricted to, the second generation. A Honduran woman from New York told us, "Well, it is my mother who sends the money," and a female Dominican from New York admitted that she sent money "only if my mom tells me that someone needs a little something, and then I will give money to her and she will send it to the family." A Honduran woman from Philadelphia likewise reported that, "yes, my mother sends all the time," and when we asked a young Mexican from New Jersey whether he sent remittances, he answered, "My mom, she does. My grandparents are in Mexico, and so she sends to them." We got a similar response from a young Dominican woman in New York: "Not me, but my parents do it all the time." Another female New Yorker of Dominican origin answered: "Yes, my parents do."

Of course, when reporting on remittances sent by their parents, respondents often have hazy notions about the frequency of their parents' remitting and the amounts sent; a Mexican teenager from New Jersey admitted as much when we asked whether he knew how much his parents sent and he responded with a simple "No." Rather than answering so categorically, another teenager from New Jersey, a Colombian female, was exceedingly vague, telling us that her parents would "send, well, it depends . . . they'd send weekly, or whenever it was needed, every two or three weeks, they'd send whatever they need to help. I'm not sure."

The intensity of transnational ties to the origin country is indicated not only by the frequency of remitting but also by the amount sent and

Table 6.3   Relative Amount of Money Sent by Latino Immigrants to Family or Friends in the Country of Origin and How These Remittances Were Used

Behavior	Documented	Undocumented	Total
Amount remitted			
Up to one-fifth of earnings	5.3%	26.5%	18.9%
One-fifth to one-half of earnings	25.5	12.3	20.8
Varies month to month	57.9	29.4	39.6
Nothing remitted	26.3	17.7	20.8
How remittances are used			
Housing	5.3	17.7	13.2
Family	57.9	56.9	57.2
Health	12.3	5.9	8.2
Education	1.8	9.8	6.9
Savings	1.8	11.8	8.2
Debt	1.8	1.8	1.9
No remittances	26.3	17.7	20.8
Sample size (N)	57	102	159

Source: Immigrant Identity Project (Office of Population Research 2009).

the uses to which the remittances are put. Sending a lot of money and investing it productively in the origin community are concrete indicators of strong material ties and an intention to return, whereas sending modest amounts to cover current consumption may or may not indicate strong ties and an intention to return. In our conversations with respondents, we asked about the absolute amount of remittances, of course, but we also asked them to estimate the relative amount on a 1 to 10 scale, where 10 represented sending all of one's earnings and the lower numbers indicated the fraction that was sent. This device allowed us to develop a categorization of the relative amount sent, which we break down into three broad categories in the top panel of table 6.3: up to one-fifth of earnings (categories 1 and 2), between one-fifth and one-half (categories 3, 4, and 5), and variable from month to month.

Some 19 percent of respondents reported sending home up to one-fifth of their earnings; another 21 percent said that they sent between one-fifth and one-half; and 40 percent said that the amount varied from month to month. Expressed as a percentage of those who remitted, roughly one-quarter sent at least one-fifth of their earnings, and 27 percent sent between one-fifth and one-half, so a majority of those who were actively remitting sent predictable amounts. In general, first-generation migrants were more likely to report a consistent amount (not shown): 19

percent reported sending up to one-fifth of their earnings, and another 25 percent sent up to one-half, leaving just 35 percent reporting variable amounts. In contrast, 50 percent of those reporting month-to-month variation were second-generation migrants. The differential in the amount remitted was even sharper by legal status. Whereas 39 percent of undocumented migrants reported a consistent amount and 29 percent a variable amount, the respective figures for documented migrants were 31 percent and 58 percent. Differences by gender were smaller, though males displayed a slight tendency toward greater regularity.

Because the relative amounts are well summarized in the quantitative table just presented, our qualitative analysis focuses on discussions of absolute amounts. The range of remittances mentioned by respondents went from a low of around $30 to a high of $1,000, though the periodicity of payments varied from respondent to respondent, with higher amounts generally being less frequently sent and the smaller amounts more regularly transmitted. Immigrants who had just arrived and not yet paid off their travel and adjustment costs found it hardest to remit. A Dominican man from New York complained that "I still haven't sent money yet because I am not earning very much. There is the rent and the bills and taxes here, so the money is barely enough. I am just beginning, but I have been able to put together a little bit because I want to send my mother a few gifts for Mother's Day."

Even those who have accumulated considerable experience in the United States at times find it hard to send money home owing to the ongoing financial burdens of immigrant life, especially when there is a family to support. As a documented Nicaraguan woman with eighteen years of U.S. experience told us:

> Well, look, I'm going to be frank. Like here we live so close to the edge, and we have a lot of problems, but I always managed to send $30. At first, yes, we thought we could manage to send $100, so we put in $100, but then we didn't have enough for food when we sent $100, sometimes monthly. Until we saw that other people were only sending around $20, and the truth is that, we have $20 or $30 extra, we send it.

Most of the payments were in the hundreds and were sent weekly or biweekly, as with the Mexican woman in New York who said that "every fifteen days I send $50, or sometimes $100." When we asked a Dominican male in Philadelphia how much he sent his mother, he said, "Once in a while, when she needs it, $200 to $300." More reliable was the Mexican man in New Jersey who reported sending "sometimes $100 per week. Sometimes when I can, I try to give them more because I want to help my family because it is difficult to live down there." As a Dominican woman in New York pointed out, "One hundred dollars from here is a lot down there."

Another respondent, a Mexican man in New York, responded to our question on remittances by telling us, "Let's say I send $300 monthly." Another Mexican male we spoke to in New York put his remittance even higher, noting that, "when I send once a month, $500, or twice a month, $300." A Mexican woman in Philadelphia said that she saved whatever she could and sent a payment to her family every eight days. Although in times past she was able to "earn $350 and send them $300 and leave $50 for myself," she was no longer able to do that because "right now I have to pay rent, and when it is due, for example, it's a lot with the bills and everything, so it's more like $100 that I keep here for myself, so now I'm not able to send $300 because I need to leave this amount from what I send." Doing the subtraction, however, makes it apparent that she was still sending around $250 per week.

A Peruvian man in Philadelphia told us that he was able to keep his payments in the hundreds every month by pooling resources with other relatives: "[It] might be, might be every month. Sure, we are between us nephews who are eighteen or older, and cousins and uncles, and we put in $100 per person, and sometimes I put in $200. Or maybe $50—whatever you can. You send what you can."

A collective strategy was also applied by a young, second-generation Dominican man in Philadelphia who was able to send $1,000 every two weeks by pooling his $500 with $500 from his mother, though he admitted that "once in a while I send less than $500. I send whatever I can. She always sends $500."

The bottom panel of table 6.3 summarizes information on how remittances were used by family members at home. Remitted funds may be used for more than one thing, of course, and some respondents reported two uses. The data included in the table include all reported uses and are not mutually exclusive. The most common use by a wide margin was for day-to-day support for the family—food, clothes, and other necessities. Some 57 percent of respondents reported spending on family support, a percentage that did not vary much by legal status or generation, though women did report spending on families more often than men (62 percent versus 54 percent). If we discount those respondents who sent nothing, then we find that nearly three-quarters of active remitters spent on family support.

After the family, the next most important spending category was housing, at 13 percent, and here there were rather wide differentials in terms of gender, generation, and legal status. Whereas 17 percent of men reported spending remittances on housing, the figure was just 9 percent for women, and whereas 18 percent of undocumented migrants contributed to housing, just 5 percent of legal immigrants did so. Not surprisingly, spending on housing was more common among first-generation immigrants (16 percent) than among those in the second generation (6 percent).

After housing, the next three spending categories in quick succession were health and savings at 8 percent each and education at 7 percent. In general, women, the documented, and second-generation immigrants were more likely to spend on health, whereas men, the undocumented, and first-generation immigrants were more likely to spend on savings. In terms of education, spending was more common among women, the undocumented, and the first generation. Far fewer people, just 2 percent, used remittances to pay debts. If we consider spending on family maintenance to represent current consumption, and spending on housing, health, education, and savings to be investments, then overall 57 percent reported spending on consumption and 37 percent reported at least some kind of investment. When expressed as a fraction of those who reported sending remittances, these shares become 76 percent and 46 percent; although the balance of remittances appear to be devoted to consumption, investments in human and physical capital are by no means insignificant.

Students of migration and development are fond of classifying the spending of remittances as consumption versus investment, as if there is always a clear distinction between the two. In reality, the line is often blurred. As we have already noted, remittances may be put to more than one use; indeed, half of those respondents who sent remittances reported multiple uses for the funds they sent. Moreover, the distinction between consumption and investment is often quite ambiguous. Ultimately, all spending to support children or sustain a working adult may be considered an investment in human capital to the extent that it allows for current or future participation in the labor force. In this sense, food and clothing are investments if they permit a young person to grow and mature into a productive worker or enable an adult to go to work and produce each day, though most economists would probably classify such spending as consumption rather than investment.

Spending on shelter is more ambiguous still. If such spending is in the form of rent or home maintenance, then it probably lies more on the consumption side, but money used to purchase, expand, or build a home constitutes more of an investment, since it contributes to the accumulation of wealth and may be used productively. Spending on health is often considered an investment in human capital, since unhealthy people do not make very productive workers, and spending on education is almost always considered a human capital investment. Most clearly on the investment side is the use of remittances to purchase or improve productive assets, such as farmland, equipment, rental properties, or a business enterprise, or to contribute to savings with these goals in mind.

Rather than constituting a clear distinction, therefore, the spending of remittances represents more of a continuum from obviously consumption to obviously investment with a lot of hazy territory in between.

Finally, questions about the use of remittances do not really get at the underlying issue of household liquidity (see Massey et al. 1998). The arrival of dollar remittances and their use solely for family support may ease budget constraints and increase liquidity, allowing the household to channel income from other sources (local labor, farm production, retail sales) into productive investments. In this case, the respondent would report that all remittances were spent on consumption, and we could falsely conclude that this use of them was unproductive, when in fact their arrival freed up other resources in the household that went directly to investment.

The foregoing ambiguities are reflected in the narrative answers given by respondents to our questions about the use of remittances. Some spending fairly clearly fell into the category of consumption, such as that reported by the Dominican woman from Philadelphia who said, "Well, I really send it so they can buy food for my kids, to give them what they need, and to pay the rent if my husband can't, because at times he doesn't have work and I have to help him," or the Puerto Rican woman from Philadelphia who told us, "They need it because the economy down there is bad because some of the companies have relocated to other countries, making it very difficult to get work to pay for everything—for the house, for shoes for the children, everything." A little more ambiguous was the report of the Mexican man in New York who told us that his remittances went for debts and food, but also for investments in human capital in the form of "schooling for my siblings."

Also ambiguous was the situation of the Mexican man in Philadelphia who explained that his use of remittances depended on circumstances, "which may change. There was one time that I sent money to my mom so that she could buy a car, and little by little I was sending money. Another time it was an emergency because we had to pay health insurance for a cousin who wanted to go to Europe and she needed money for insurance. Another time it was, well, she just needed money to cover her expenses." This kind of spending on "expenses" and insurance would seem to be consumption, as would spending on a car—except that in Mexico cars purchased by lower-class families often are not just used for getting to work but are put to productive uses, such as running a taxi or delivery service, though this does not seem to have been the case here.

In the foregoing example, the health spending was for insurance, but far more often health spending is targeted at an unanticipated need for treatment, as with the Dominican woman in New York who told us that her remittances went to "food and clothing for sure, and an uncle of mine had an operation, money for this." Although spending on family support and medical emergencies was common, more common still was the combination of family support and spending on the home. An Ecuadoran man in New York told us, "I give everything all together to my dad, and he is in charge of all the expenses, like the payment for my son and to see what he needs." Even this migrant, however, was contemplating investment by "building a house, but I am unsure. I've changed my mind several times. I don't want to do anything there in case I stay here. . . . I have to really think seriously to see where I am going to stay and live."

Another Ecuadoran man, from New Jersey, saw spending on home maintenance as setting the stage for possible future investment in a business:

RESPONDENT: More for food, and naturally for maintenance, to maintain the home.

INTERVIEWER: The home?

RESPONDENT: Umm, the home, yes, naturally there is an amount that one sets aside to see if there will be some day in the future when one can do something with it. Who knows if I make a preparation here how nice it would be to be able to have money to develop my own, my own business.

Yet another Ecuadoran man, also from New Jersey, reported the same combination of spending on housing and family support, noting that "for two or three months I sent money for the house, which had a few details that needed to be taken care of to finish it. But now, last week I sent a little money for my grandmother. . . . I know the money is not worth much. It's just so she can buy a few clothes she might like. . . . I believe in sending cash and letting them buy what they want." Likewise, a Guatemalan man we spoke to in New Jersey told us that his remittances went "mainly to fix up the house and everything, what I wanted it to be before coming here," but that he also devoted some of the funds "for support of my mother, for the doctor, for this or that thing, keeping up the house."

A Dominican woman in New York reported that her remittances were spent "mainly on food and on building the house because, well, this has to do with my mother, and this constructing of the house, because they are still building their house, they live in a house that is not finished, so they want to finish it, but they also have to spend on food and clothing and all that." An Argentine woman working in New Jersey told us that in addition to sending remittances "to the family for their necessities," she was also sending money to her grandmother "to keep up [her] apartment because she doesn't want to sell it," as well as to her parents "to renovate the house because we left and came here always with the idea of going back to Argentina. My parents always came to work to make money, to earn money that they could send to build a little house on the land that they've always had, to build a house on the land of their parents or to add a second floor. So they made a two-bedroom house on the land of my grandparents."

In addition to improving her home and paying for family support, a Honduran woman in New Jersey made investments in her children's education, though she was not yet up to thinking about a formal business investment:

INTERVIEWER: For what is the money you send down there?

RESPONDENT: I have three kids down there—three there and four here.

INTERVIEWER: Wow. So you send money for food and clothing?

RESPONDENT: Uh huh.

INTERVIEWER: For school?

RESPONDENT: Yes, for school.

INTERVIEWER: And for fixing up your house, could we say that as well?

RESPONDENT: Yes.

INTERVIEWER: And you have a business down there?

RESPONDENT: No.

Also combining family support with investments in housing and education was a Peruvian man in New York who, in addition to paying for a year of university education for a cousin, "sent money to my uncle to rebuild the roof on his house, which had fallen in," as well as to buy "food, clothes, school uniforms, suits for all kinds of uses."

A Mexican man in Philadelphia told us that in addition to "paying off what I owed, what I borrowed to come here," and an earlier debt he had contracted "when my father couldn't work anymore," he was sending money for family support "so that my parents could go on surviving, you know?" But in spite of these acute immediate needs, he was also spending some of the money "so that my sister could study to go to the university" and "achieve her goal," which was to become a nurse—a clear investment in human capital.

Even when they are pressed by circumstances into channeling remittances mostly into consumption, respondents were often thinking ahead and setting aside some money in savings to use productively in the future, as was the plan of the Honduran man from Philadelphia who told us that his remittances were "for everything—food, clothes, housing . . .

debts, everything," but also for "savings to work with when I return." Likewise, an Ecuadoran man in New Jersey felt compelled for the moment to send money to his mother, "for her medicines, which cost a lot," but he was also "saving to open up a little store, something like that."

For some respondents, the channeling of remittances to housing, land, and real estate was not consumption at all but part of a very deliberate and well-planned business strategy. For example, when we asked a Brazilian man in Philadelphia what he used his remittances for, his answer was simple and unambiguous: "Business." He then offered a detailed description of his business plan:

RESPONDENT: You buy an apartment, to continue to pay for the apartment you have to rent it out, for example. Like you have financing here, you have financing in Brazil. Once you have the financing, you have to keep paying.

INTERVIEWER: Right.

RESPONDENT: So a little more, because the more that you earn here, the more you can pay off your investments down in Brazil.

INTERVIEWER: Yes, okay. You have rather large interests down there, right? How much do you have down there?

RESPONDENT: How long have I been financing this investment? Quite a while, but it depends—two, three, four years. One has been for two years, and the other for a little more, around six years, when I sold it after around six years. Now I have been paying a little under two years.

INTERVIEWER: So you buy real estate, like that first apartment, to later sell [it]. And what about the future? What are you going to do with the real property you accumulated?

RESPONDENT: It gives me profits. It returns profits for you, cash for you. One can, as they say, calculate to rent in Brazil, and the rents generate returns for you. You get what you want in the way of returns.

INTERVIEWER: Are you planning to go back or to keep on doing this indefinitely?

RESPONDENT: At the moment, shall we say, the best investment is in Brazil, but this is not a certainty, my word, no, it is not a controlled certainty. It depends on how the Brazilian government is doing, boom or bust, the dollar rises and falls. Then you have to do a U-turn in your investments, because others will give you nothing.

INTERVIEWER: But right now the money is in Brazil.

RESPONDENT: Exactly. Now I have my money here, for example, but I always send something to Brazil.

Equally clear about his investment strategy was a Bolivian man in New York who was working to fund an expanding cattle business and a growing portfolio of real estate acquisitions:

RESPONDENT: Yes, right now I have a piece of property that my grandmother is selling. I've got ten head of cattle bought, and now I have a house where my mother is living.

INTERVIEWER: And you bought all that?

RESPONDENT: Yes, I'm paying for it.

INTERVIEWER: You bought it or made it?

RESPONDENT: No.

INTERVIEWER: You bought it, then.

RESPONDENT: Let's just say I got a loan.

INTERVIEWER: Okay, so then the money that you send—well, you already said, but once again I have to ask you, on what do you spend the money down there? The questions are: On food? On schooling? To build or improve a house? For a business? To pay debts?

RESPONDENT: Right now I am paying for the house.

INTERVIEWER: Which house?

RESPONDENT: The one on my property that I am buying, and I spend for expenses in the house as well, but not food.

INTERVIEWER: This is the property on which you have cattle, right?

RESPONDENT: Yes, yes, that property. A fifth of a hectare.

INTERVIEWER: Very well, and you are interested in running a business there?

RESPONDENT: Cattle-raising.

INTERVIEWER: Is that right?

RESPONDENT: Yes.

In sum, remittances are typically put to a variety of uses that are often difficult to separate cleanly into categories of consumption versus production. It seems clear that the bulk of the money remitted by migrants in the United States indeed bolsters the consumption of family members back home. From remittance use data alone, however, we are unable to observe the productive effects that this spending might have by increasing liquidity and easing budget constraints to enable the productive use of other funds at the household's disposal, and we are also unable to observe the multiplier effects of the local consumption enabled by the arrival of remittances from abroad (Durand, Massey, and Parrado 1996). Spending on consumption is often paired with productive investments of various sorts, and many things that remittances buy may be considered to be consumption or investment depending on the uses to which they are put. Whatever the intentions of those doing the remitting, it is clear that the sending of remittances is part and parcel of their transnational lives and a fundamental reason for immigration in the first place.

Transnationalism As a Way of Life

The quantitative and qualitative data marshaled to this point are consistent in confirming a vibrant transnationalism among Latino immigrants to the United States that shows little sign of dissipating over time or across the generations. Virtually all respondents (92 percent) were regularly involved in sending social remittances—communicating ideas, information, concepts, and perceptions through frequent phone calls to friends and relatives in their communities of origin. Respondents found these telephone conversations to be essential for maintaining emotional bonds to friends and relatives at home. Email played a growing role in the maintenance of social ties, but more for friends than for family members. A supplement rather than a substitute for phone conversations within kin networks, the Internet enabled the rapid transmission of photographs and other mementos of family life. Virtually no one relied on postal service as a means of communication. Although language fluency was an issue for some in the second generation, social remittances to family members generally did not cease unless close relatives had either passed away or relocated to the United States.

Although not quite as universal as social remittances, the vast majority of migrants also sent financial remittances: nearly 80 percent sent cash, and 54 percent sent gifts and presents, again with only small differences across the generations. In terms of financial remittances, legal status played a larger role: documented migrants were less connected materially to their home communities than undocumented migrants. Most respondents reported that they remitted significant funds with some regularity, though both the frequency of remitting and the quantities sent were somewhat lower in the second generation. Among those who sent remittances, a majority transmitted funds at least once a month, and a majority said that they gave a steady amount; one-quarter sent between one-fifth and one-half of their earnings. The remittances were generally sent via money order, since only a tiny minority had bank accounts in the United States or the country of origin. Though U.S. accounts outnumbered foreign accounts, neither were particularly common among immigrants.

Respondents generally viewed remittances as a moral obligation—a social requirement of their existence as transnational migrants that could be suspended only for very good reasons, such as when relatives at home no longer needed support, when they had all died, or when they had all moved to the United States. The bulk of the funds went to maintenance and support, but in most cases some share of the remittances was also dedicated to productive ends in order to advance the family's economic interests within the country of origin.

It is thus clear that transnationalism plays an integral role in the lives of contemporary immigrants from Latin America and is an inextricable component of their identities. What is not clear from simple tabulations and narratives is the degree to which transnationalism constitutes an alternative source of satisfaction and self-esteem in the face of bleak mobility prospects and discriminatory barriers in the United States, or whether it constitutes a wholly independent system of valuation apart from what happens to immigrants in American society. To answer this question we estimated a series multivariate models to predict the likelihood of various transnational behaviors given a migrant's job situation, perception of inequality, and experience of discrimination in the United States. If migrants turn to transnationalism as a result of blocked mobility north of the border, then we would expect transnational behaviors to be predicted significantly by these factors If transnationalism is sui generis, however, part and parcel of the immigrant experience itself more than a reaction to blocked opportunities, then we would expect transnational behaviors to be unrelated either to a migrant's objective economic circumstances or to his or her subjective perceptions about discrimination and inequality.

We began by attempting to estimate a model predicting whether or not respondents were in contact with friends or relatives abroad, but there were so few who were not in contact that the model was empirically inestimable; we concluded that social remittances are simply a universal feature of immigrant life that does not depend on individual circumstances or characteristics. Table 6.4 presents two logistic regression equations estimated to predict the sending of remittances and gifts by respondents. In neither case was the transnational behavior related strongly to objective or subjective circumstances in the United States. Neither the sending of remittances nor the sending of gifts was related to perceptions of opportunity, inequality, or discrimination in the United States or to current wages or present occupational status. Although the sending of remittances is negatively predicted by hours worked per week, the effect is weak and probably just reflects the crowding out of remitting by time constraints.

Table 6.4   Logistic Regressions Predicting Whether Respondent Sent Remittances and Whether Respondent Sent Presents to Friends and Relatives in the Country of Origin

Predictors	Sent Remittances		Sent Gifts	
	Regression Coefficient	Standard Error	Regression Coefficient	Standard Error
U.S. job situation				
Current wage	−0.005	0.008	−0.004	0.008
Current occupational status	−0.006	0.013	−0.009	0.012
Current hours worked per week	−0.012+	0.068	−0.005	0.006
Class background				
Parental occupational status	−0.018	0.016	0.002	0.014
Human capital				
Years of schooling	−0.040	0.038	0.775	0.538
Good English	−0.335	0.564	−0.019	0.039
Perceptions of United States				
More opportunity	0.738	0.747	−0.097	0.632
More inequality	−0.411	0.472	0.174	0.428
Experienced discrimination	−0.110	0.522	−0.015	0.467
Motivation for migration				
Origin conditions	−0.325	0.824	0.418	0.712
U.S. conditions	−0.343	0.802	0.120	0.695
Family or network	0.813	0.735	1.961**	0.682
Other	—	—	—	—
Intentions				
Intends to return	0.569	0.469	0.415	0.410
Racial-ethnic roots				
African	−0.768	0.672	−1.053+	0.604
Indigenous	1.368	1.118	−0.956	1.152
Dark-skinned	0.890+	0.517	0.535	0.470
Region of origin				
Mexico	—	—	—	—
Caribbean	1.554+	0.904	1.675*	0.810
Central America	2.640**	0.997	1.800*	0.745
South America	1.357*	0.687	1.288*	0.622
Demographics				
Age	0.904+	0.052	0.005	0.041
Male	−0.311	0.488	−0.694	0.437
Immigrant status				
Documented	−0.780	0.700	−0.615	0.618
Years in United States	0.005	0.010	−0.006	0.009
Intercept	−2.397	2.001	0.437	1.849
Likelihood ratio X^2	38.050*		32.010+	
Pseudo-R-squared	0.219		0.165	
Sample size (N)	142		142	

Source: Immigrant Identity Project (Office of Population Research 2009).
+p < .10; *p < .05; **p < .01; ***p < .001

The only strong predictor of sending either gifts or remittances is re-gion of origin. Compared with Mexican immigrants, those from other regions are more likely to send both money and presents, with Central Americans exhibiting the highest likelihood followed by Caribbeans and South Americans. This contrast probably reflects the fact that Mexicans are uniquely able to bring money and goods home in person, given their country's land border with the United States. Although darker skin tone and rising age predict the sending of remittances and African roots pre-dicts the sending of gifts, the effects are weak. The only other strong ef-fect is the connection between family or network motivations for migra-tion and the sending of gifts, which probably illustrates the importance of gift-giving in the maintenance of social networks and interpersonal relationships (Mauss 1969).

Table 6.5 presents logistic regression equations estimated for respon-dents who reported remittances to predict whether or not they sent them at least once a month and whether or not they sent them via money order. Once again, there is little to suggest that these behaviors are con-nected in any way to the context of reception in the United States. The frequency of remitting is not predicted by an immigrant's U.S. job situa-tion or perceptions of opportunity, inequality, and discrimination in the United States. The only strong predictor is age: the frequency of remit-tances declines with advancing age, though there are also weak relation-ships with parental occupational status and skin tone. The choice of a money order over other modalities is strongly linked to the motivations for migration, racial-ethnic roots, and origins in the Caribbean, but there is little to suggest that this choice of modality is dictated by a person's objective or subjective situation in the United States.

Table 6.6 shows a multinomial logistic regression model estimated to predict the amount of remittances sent. The two equations correspond to a regular amount of up to one-fifth of earnings and a regular amount from one-fifth to one-half of earnings, compared with irregular month-to-month amounts. Again we observe no apparent connection between a person's U.S. job circumstances or perceptions about the United States and the amount of money remitted—that is, there is little evidence that migrants channel money into remittances as a response to blocked op-portunities in the United States. Indigenous origins and undocumented status predict the regular sending of the lower amount of remittances, whereas the intention to return and light skin tone predict regular send-ing at the higher amount.

Finally, table 6.7 shows the results of a logistic regression estimated to predict whether remittances were invested productively in the country of origin (that is, whether they were devoted to housing, education, health, or savings as opposed to family maintenance or current con-sumption). This equation is entirely consistent with the others in show-

Table 6.5   Logistic Regressions Predicting Frequency of Remittances and How
             Remittances Were Sent to Friends and Relatives in the Country of Origin

Predictors	Sent at Least Once a Month		Sent by Money Order	
	Regression Coefficient	Standard Error	Regression Coefficient	Standard Error
U.S. job situation				
Current wage	0.017	0.016	−0.033+	0.018
Current occupational status	0.008	0.016	0.028	0.029
Current hours worked per week	0.018	0.013	−0.012	0.014
Class background				
Parental occupational status	−0.045+	0.026	−0.073*	0.038
Human capital				
Years of schooling	0.080	0.123	0.159	0.173
Good English	−0.562	0.740	−0.866	1.121
Perceptions of United States				
More opportunity	−0.139	0.952	2.023	1.414
More inequality	0.633	0.698	0.614	1.045
Experienced discrimination	−0.324	0.688	−1.150	1.005
Motivation for migration				
Origin conditions	−1.078	1.079	−3.977+	2.322
U.S. conditions	0.457	1.100	−3.968+	2.375
Family or network	−0.990	0.945	−4.767*	2.202
Other	—	—	—	—
Intentions				
Intends to return	0.840	0.632	−0.358	1.006
Racial-ethnic roots				
African	0.344	0.988	5.194**	1.844
Indigenous	−0.196	1.835	4.883*	2.518
Dark-skinned	−1.223+	0.727	−0.061	0.937
Region of origin				
Mexico	—	—	—	—
Caribbean	−0.873	1.370	−4.985*	2.322
Central America	0.554	1.171	−2.049	1.450
South America	−0.696	0.974	−1.526	1.279
Demographics				
Age	−0.142**	0.056	−0.175	0.106
Male	0.587	0.633	0.160	0.975
Immigrant status				
Documented	−0.245	0.777	0.030	1.381
Years in United States	−0.015	0.013	0.059	0.037
Intercept	6.087+	3.352	5.147	4.096
Likelihood ratio X^2	37.780*		37.92*	
Pseudo-R-squared	0.294		0.404	
Sample size (N)	99		99	

Source: Immigrant Identity Project (Office of Population Research 2009).
+p < .10; *p < .05; **p < .01; ***p < .001

Table 6.6   Multinomial Logistic Regression Predicting Amount of Remittances Sent to Friends and Relatives in the Country of Origin

Predictors	Up to One-Fifth of Earnings		Up to Half of Earnings	
	Regression Coefficient	Standard Error	Regression Coefficient	Standard Error
U.S. job situation				
Current wage	−0.007	0.013	−0.021	0.016
Current occupational status	−0.018	0.020	0.025	0.020
Current hours worked per week	0.004	0.012	0.014	0.012
Class background				
Parental occupational status	−0.015	0.029	−0.046	0.030
Human capital				
Years of schooling	−0.095	0.143	−0.204	0.142
Good English	−0.014	0.828	0.104	0.857
Perceptions of United States				
More opportunity	−0.082	0.963	−0.238	0.991
More inequality	0.388	0.714	−0.256	0.773
Experienced discrimination	−0.215	0.697	−0.056	0.743
Motivation for migration				
Origin conditions	1.100	1.182	−0.303	1.283
U.S. conditions	−0.241	1.212	−0.873	1.249
Family or network	−0.591	1.031	−1.734	1.107
Other	—	—	—	—
Intentions				
Intends to return	−0.161	0.728	1.409*	0.709
Racial-ethnic roots				
African	1.145	1.033	0.967	1.048
Indigenous	19.568***	2.738	0.995	1.899
Dark-skinned	−0.700	0.799	−1.701*	0.791
Region of origin				
Mexico	—	—	—	—
Caribbean	−0.197	1.658	−1.569	1.613
Central America	−1.891	1.266	−1.294	1.194
South America	−0.513	1.095	−0.388	1.050
Demographics				
Age	−0.046	0.065	−0.041	0.065
Male	0.248	0.750	0.466	0.711
Immigrant status				
Documented	−3.586*	1.487	−0.011	1.613
Years in United States	0.015	0.018	−0.014	0.018
Intercept	−15.078	3.211	4.452*	3.708
Likelihood ratio X^2	52.770			
Pseudo-R-squared	0.247			
Sample size (N)	99			

Source: Immigrant Identity Project (Office of Population Research 2009).
$^+$p < .10; *p < .05; **p < .01; ***p < .001

Table 6.7   Logistic Regressions Predicting Bank Productive Use of
Remittances in the Country of Origin

Predictors	Regression Coefficient	Standard Error	P-Value
U.S. job situation			
Current wage	0.015	0.011	0.179
Current occupational status	−0.009	0.015	0.553
Current hours worked per week	0.003	0.009	0.697
Class background			
Parental occupational status	−0.116	0.850	0.891
Human capital			
Years of schooling	0.182	0.115	0.114
Good English	−2.030**	0.756	0.007
Perceptions of United States			
More opportunity	−0.116	0.850	0.891
More inequality	−0.645	0.602	0.283
Experienced discrimination	0.333	0.579	0.566
Motivation for migration			
Origin conditions	0.244	0.946	0.797
U.S. conditions	−0.643	1.028	0.537
Family or network	1.004	0.808	0.214
Other	—	—	—
Intentions			
Intends to return	0.423	0.550	0.566
Racial-ethnic roots			
African	−1.147	0.814	0.159
Indigenous	−1.588	2.192	0.469
Dark-skinned	−0.397	0.602	0.510
Region of origin			
Mexico	—	—	—
Caribbean	2.272+	1.266	0.073
Central America	0.910	0.930	0.328
South America	0.393	0.868	0.651
Demographics			
Age	−0.029	0.050	0.565
Male	0.098	0.594	0.869
Immigrant status			
Documented	−2.029*	0.885	0.022
Years in United States	0.025+	0.133	0.065
Intercept	1.163	4.117	0.709
Likelihood ratio X^2	27.170		
Pseudo-R-squared	0.200		
Sample size (N)	99		

Source: Immigrant Identity Project (Office of Population Research 2009).
+p < .10; *p < .05; **p < .01; ***p < .001

ing no connection between experiences in the United States and the productive use of remittances. There is no connection between productive investment and any feature of the respondent's current U.S. employment or subjective perceptions about U.S. opportunities, inequalities, and discrimination. The channeling of remittances to human capital, physical capital, or savings is primarily determined by the degree of social and cultural integration in the United States; those with documents and those who speak English well are significantly less likely to send remittances, though when we hold these two factors constant, the propensity does rise weakly with years spent in the United States.

All evidence thus suggests that transnationalism is intrinsic to the immigrant experience itself, not a reaction to difficult circumstances in the United States. There is no evidence to indicate that migrants intensify contacts with friends and relatives abroad, increase the frequency or amount of their remittances, or channel their remittances more toward productive ends in response to negative experiences or blocked mobility in the United States. Rather, immigrants view social remittances as essential to the maintenance of emotional ties that are of inherent value to them, and financial remittances as a moral obligation of kinship or friendship. Neither form of transnational exchange appears to weaken very much with time spent in the United States or across the generations. The most we can say is that as people become more socially integrated in the United States—acquiring documents and learning English well—they shift the use of their remittances more toward consumption than investment and that if they also abandon the dream of return migration they reduce the amount and regularity of their remittances. But social and financial remittances nonetheless continue as long as there are close friends or relatives at home to receive them.

=Chapter 7=

Verbalizing Identity

The evidence we have marshaled in the foregoing chapters finally puts us in a position to consider systematically the construction of identity among Latino immigrants to the United States—how they broker the group boundaries and manage the meanings they encounter as they move through American society. The data accumulated so far paint a decidedly mixed picture of life for Latin American immigrants in the United States. Most arrive with dreams of social or material improvement and initially perceive the United States as a land of opportunity. Over time, they encounter a harsh world of work and experience the indignities of prejudice, discrimination, and blocked opportunities. Eventually many come to see the United States as a place of inequality, particularly along the lines of race.

This dual reality of ongoing engagement and growing disillusionment with the United States suggests a fundamental tension between "American" and "Latino" identities that Latin American immigrants must somehow broker in their daily lives. As discussed in the opening chapter, social scientists no longer view ethnicity as a primordial sentiment handed down from the distant past or transplanted wholesale from a culture abroad. Instead, ethnic and racial identities are actively created by immigrants as they interact with each other and with the people and institutions of the host country. Identities form as immigrants discover categorical boundaries that facilitate or constrain their interactions with others and then engage in boundary work that either brightens or blurs the divisions they encounter. In this sense, ethnic identity is something that is made in America, not a foreign import.

As noted in the introduction, sociologists theorize the construction of ethnic identity as occurring in one of two ways. *Emergent ethnicity* views ethnic identity as developing out of the "structural conditions characterizing American cities and the position of groups in American social structure" (Yancey et al. 1976, 391). In contrast, *reactive ethnicity* conceives of identity as "the product of confrontation with an adverse native main-

stream and the rise of defensive identities and solidarities to counter it";
in this conception of ethnic identity, "the discourses and self-images that
it creates develop as a situational response to present realities" (Portes
and Rumbaut 2001, 284). Our conversations with Latin American immigrants suggest that both processes are at work in adapting to life in the
United States: Latino identity expresses itself as an emergent identity
soon after arrival, and then American identity is defined reactively over
time in response to an unequal and often hostile context of reception.

Latino Identity

All immigrants arrive with a specific national identity, of course—as
Mexicans, Colombians, Dominicans, Argentines, and so on. Most also
come with aspirations to pursue the American Dream and ultimately
hope to be received as fellow "Americans." After arriving in the United
States, however, immigrants undergo two formative experiences that
tend to engender in-group solidarity and a common identity. First, they
run headlong into the realities of life in the secondary labor market and
encounter the hostility of natives; second, they have these experiences
alongside other immigrants who may have different national origins but
who nonetheless share many affinities.

The sharing of experiences with similar others offers fertile ground
for the emergence of a new "Latino" identity in the United States that
extends beyond any particular country to embrace people from throughout the continent. To explore this possibility we asked respondents
whether they indeed perceived a common identity among Latin American immigrants in the United States. The coded responses to this query,
which are summarized in the top panel of table 7.1, clearly indicate that
immigrants do perceive a common identity. Overall, 82 percent of respondents perceived the existence of a shared Latino identity in the
United States, with only 7 percent denying it and just 4 percent saying
that they were unsure or did not know. The perception of a shared identity was slightly higher among undocumented migrants (84 percent)
compared with their legal counterparts (77 percent).

To delve more deeply into the subjective roots of identity formation
we asked respondents to elaborate on what a Latino identity meant to
them. In their answers, several respondents focused on the Spanish language as an important unifying factor. One man from Venezuela told us,
"Yes, it [a common identity] exists because we speak the same language,
understand?" Likewise, a Mexican man from New Jersey emphasized
that the "one thing that identifies us, that identifies all Latinos, is our
way of speaking," and an Ecuadoran woman in New Jersey explained
that, "with Latinos one identifies, one can talk to them." Even a young
Dominican man who had grown up in the United States and spoke flu-

Table 7.1   The Perceptions of Latin American Immigrants to the United
States About Sharing a Common Identity, by Legal Status

Group Identity	Documented	Undocumented	Total
Perceives a Latino identity			
Yes	77.2%	84.3%	81.8%
No	7.0	6.9	6.9
Don't know/missing	5.3	4.0	4.4
Respondent's identification			
Latino	57.9	65.7	62.0
American	15.8	25.5	22.0
Both	26.3	5.9	13.2
Don't know/missing	0.0	2.9	1.9
Sample size (N)	57	102	159

Source: Immigrant Identity Project (Office of Population Research 2009).

ent English told us that "I can be among many different groups, but always I go to find the guy who speaks Spanish, who maybe is Puerto Rican. I heard that he said 'che' or something like that, and then I'm like, oh, boy, this person speaks Spanish, and I try to get to know him."

A Honduran woman we interviewed in New Jersey explained that being able to communicate in a common tongue was critical to her perception of a shared identity with other migrants; she pointed out that "you can be Mexican and we speak Spanish. I can be Honduran, the other Argentine, and we all speak the same Spanish. Whatever else we may be, we can dialogue with one another, and we can understand one another a little more." An Ecuadoran man from New Jersey stated that what unites Latinos is simply "their language—a language loaded with Spanish." Even though outside of Brazil everyone in Latin America speaks Spanish, there are nonetheless regional differences in vocabulary and pronunciation; despite these differences, a Dominican man in Philadelphia saw a common underlying reality when he noted that, "if you take a look at the food, what in Venezuela they call 'caraoque' the Colombians call 'habichuela,' but it's the same bean. I see no difference."

In working out linguistic differences, interacting with other Latinos is essential; this same respondent explained that, after he had been in the United States for a while, "there came a time when I spoke like a Venezuelan," because he socialized with Venezuelan friends:

> Because all the time we were speaking Venezuelan. Every once in a while a few Puerto Rican words came out, and they also used them. . . . So there arrives a moment when you say, this, this is a real Latino community, because even though it is very difficult for a Dominican in the Dominican

Republic to understand the words of a Venezuelan, here everything is colloquial and I understand it. I understand all these languages.

The pull of language is so strong that even a Brazilian man felt solidarity with other Latin Americans on the basis of Spanish. When we interviewed him in Philadelphia, he told us: "I think that here there exists some kind of [identity]. I don't know, it's that, maybe the language is something that creates an identity." When we pointed out that he spoke Portuguese, not Spanish, he responded, "Yes, but it's all the same to me, because to me Spanish seems rather natural as well, so that, well, I don't know. Maybe you have a point. But I think that up to a certain point, if it is a person that I don't know, I feel a little better with a Latino."

An Ecuadoran woman from New Jersey saw evidence of Latino identity in the proliferation of Spanish in public spaces in the United States; she told us that "it's like something that is growing and each time becomes stronger. Like, I feel that Latinos came here imposing ourselves, in the sense that you go to a public office and you find forms in both Spanish and English. Not in English and Chinese, or English and Italian. You find them in Spanish and English." She pointed out that this development is "good, because we conserve our culture, but the negative side I see is that if you want to move ahead more rapidly, it is important to learn the tongue, the language."

Some Latino immigrants perceive Latino identity as resting on shared physical traits and appearances. As an Ecuadoran woman from New Jersey put it, "Well, I identify them more in terms of the physical." Likewise, an Ecuadoran man in New Jersey told us that "their faces, their faces give them away." Another New Jersey–based migrant, a Mexican male, agreed, insisting that "we look alike—Mexicans, whatever kind of Latino, we all have color." When asked to elaborate, he underscored the importance of skin color in the context of the United States:

RESPONDENT: Color is very important because we are dark. They look at us and say, "Oh, you are a Mexican." Yes, I am Mexican, and I am going to make it, so you can't say otherwise.

INTERVIEWER: So it's like Latino are more mixed and in this way they can be identified?

RESPONDENT: Yes. One identifies them quite easily.

INTERVIEWER: Well, tell me, and this is very important, why not language first, or something else?

RESPONDENT: Yes, because when you go on the street, or you arrive at a new restaurant, right away they identify you as Mexican—shorter, lower in stature, a little fatter at times, darker.

Of course, physical appearance is not a foolproof indicator of origins. Indeed, the Ecuadoran woman quoted earlier admitted that "at times I get it wrong, because there are people that seem like they're Latino, from other countries in Latin America, for example, and they are not." Despite occasional misidentifications, she nonetheless insisted, "I still think there is a common identity." Another respondent, a Salvadoran man in New Jersey, was more cautious, pointing out that the diversity of racial-ethnic origins and the frequency of racial and ethnic mixing in Latin America could make identification on the basis of appearance problematic:

> Look, it is rather difficult, because among Latinos we have a little of every-thing, understand? Look, I am, I am, well, in my country my skin is white, right? You in my country would be white. But there are also people who are swarthy, black, dark in an Indian way, white but Indian-colored, even redhead. . . . So, among Latinos, we have the dark Indian—the dark Indian is, well, a dark person like, shall we say, my brother-in-law, or maybe even a little darker in terms of skin color. And in the white person, like you, for example, you have white skin, but it is a white that is very white, as we would say here, like a piece of paper. Then we have the bronze or olive-skinned person. So here is the thing. Well, like I said, when you see a person and you think that he or she is Latino and you speak in Spanish and they answer, "I don't speak Spanish," well, look, there is the contro-versy. Because sometimes you have to speak English.

A number of respondents saw Latino identity in terms of shared val-ues, customs, and sensibilities, what one Ecuadoran man from New Jer-sey called "the way of being" and another labeled "the way we con-nect." For a young Dominican man in New York, Latino identity came from the fact that "customs are a little similar—the language as well, but the customs are something similar that always are going to make me feel comfortable." Similarly, an Ecuadoran man from New York at-tributed Latino identity to a common way of "going about life . . . basi-cally the same tastes," whereas a Dominican woman in Philadelphia said that Latinos shared an identity "because of our spontaneity." A Co-lombian man in New York asserted that "wherever you go, there are always Latinos, and always they are doing something active—they're never quiet." For one Mexican man in New Jersey, the "one thing that identifies us . . . is our happiness. This is important, our joy. With every-thing, everything that is Latin America, we are happy. At times we take some of the saddest things and turn them into a belly laugh. We may be suffering something very sorrowful, like that, and at the same time we can have joy." For a Nicaraguan woman from New Jersey, an essential trait was "having an open mind, not using egotism, having goodwill for everyone."

Some of our respondents argued that a shared Latino identity arose from the common grounding of migration in economic necessity. As a Mexican man in New York told us, "For one thing, everyone comes here out of necessity, out of monetary necessity . . . even though here they have to work more here, they can live better than in their countries of origin." When we asked how migrating out of economic need produced a common identity he replied:

> In identity, well, maybe it's like when you have the same interest about something. Maybe when you have united with another person who has the same religion as you, you are able to make your own group because something identifies you as equal. . . . Yes, experience, of, well, having lived or having the experience of lacking money and having to move from your country of origin to relocate here to the United States to have a better level of life. This is an identity that you can share with others.

In this opinion this respondent concurred with a Dominican man in New York who told us, "Yes, there is an identity," because, "like the great majority, we left our countries and came here in search of a better future, a better tomorrow for our families and our children, and . . . this makes us identify with one another. . . . We all came for the same reason."

For other migrants, however, identity is less rooted in necessity than in a common desire to succeed and move forward. As a Honduran woman from New York pointed out, "We all came with the same goal of getting ahead," and a Dominican woman from New Jersey noted that "the great majority came here from other countries looking for opportunity, a better life, and for that reason they identify with each other." According to a Brazilian man from Philadelphia, "The fact of being a migrant is itself an identity—it confers similar experiences that one lives, like the sentiment of leaving behind, not necessarily your homeland, but your friends and family. It is an experience common to all of us." When pushed, he admitted that this experience was common to all immigrants, but insisted that it nonetheless was the basis for a shared Latino identity because Latin Americans tended to interact with one another in the same neighborhoods:

> I think that you're more likely to see this in neighborhoods that are a little more, oh, I don't know, that are more clearly the definition of this—the ties of the Chinese, of our countrymen, of Latinos. I think, for example, that in North Philly there are places where the neighborhood is Latino, with Puerto Ricans and Dominicans and people like that, and I think that these are the places where cultural identities form, because it is a more expansive setting.

In addition to common motivations and the shared experience of leaving behind friends and family, immigrants also experience similar challenges and difficulties once they arrive in the United States, providing yet another basis for solidarity and identity. One Mexican woman in Philadelphia told us that, "with all the bad things that happen to us, you are always going to see something." For a Mexican man in New Jersey, this "something" was "the work," as it was for a young Dominican woman who noted that Latino immigrants "obviously look for jobs that pay low, you know, so they are most likely to . . . I don't know, maybe do car washes and stuff like that, you know." She also pointed out that shared identities emerge in response to common experiences of discrimination: "There's a lot of discrimination against Mexicans too, especially the kids. . . . There's some discrimination . . . in society."

Another basis for common identity among immigrants is illegal status, which yields a shared sense of marginalization. When we asked what accounted for the emergence of a common identity among Latin American immigrants in the United States, a Mexican man in New York responded, "Well, maybe you see that we are illegal immigrants." When we asked whether undocumented status was indeed a basis for identity, he confirmed that "that *is* the identity." Another source of marginalization experienced by many immigrants is being unable to read and understand English; with no English-language skills, it is difficult to shop, among other things. A Puerto Rican man in New York explained to us why he shopped at Latino-owned shops: "You can go to where José and where Rafaelito have a Cuban store, and they sell to you on credit and give you Latino portions. And you go to the Hispanic supermarket, and the lady there says, 'Look, Guillermo, here are the specials.' Understand? Because we don't know how to read the Sunday newspaper and clip the coupons." He also told us that "when I arrived in this country I saw American restaurants, and I said, 'There I could never enter,' because I didn't see other Latinos."

This sense of marginalization was also evident in the words of a Mexican man in New Jersey who told us that he felt like part of a Latino community "because I think that we are by ourselves," noting that: "In this sense we are a community, yes. . . . I feel like, feel toward people as if we were a solitary community. We are from different countries, yes, but the good thing is that, well, I feel that we are equal and that we have neither more nor less in the way of value. I think that we are all the same—Cubans, Dominicans, Puerto Ricans."

A young Dominican male in New York who had just finished high school and started work told us that "in secondary school—I was talking about how mixed it was—at times the Latinos that were there did not fit in well . . . but when I began to work, there were people that were—one of the things that I like and doesn't matter where they are from—Argentine, Panamanian, I joined with them, and I talked with them a lot, and things like that." An Ecuadoran female in New Jersey confessed to us that "with Americans you never know what's going on with them, maybe with their customs . . . but with Latinos one knows what they are thinking, what they like, how to treat this person."

One respondent saw a common identity among Latinos emerging through a long-term process of intermarriage: "I think that ten or twenty years from now you're not going to see so many Dominicans, Puerto Ricans, Venezuelans, and Colombians. They are just going to say, 'I am Latino,' because today many people are mixing nationalities. You can see a girl with both Puerto Rican and Dominican parents, a boy with a Venezuelan father and a Colombian mother. So I think that in ten to twenty years we will identify ourselves as Latino and that's it."

Not all respondents who perceived a common Latino identity were able to offer a coherent explanation, as the following exchange with a young Ecuadoran man from New Jersey indicates. When asked whether he perceived a common identity among Latin American migrants in the United States, he said:

RESPONDENT: Naturally.

INTERVIEWER: Yes? From which places?

RESPONDENT: From all over the world.

INTERVIEWER: All of the world?

RESPONDENT: Mexicans, Guatemalans . . .

INTERVIEWER: And you understand one another even though you're from different countries?

RESPONDENT: Yes.

INTERVIEWER: Yes? And what is it that makes you understand one another so well?

RESPONDENT: I don't know.

Although they constituted a distinct minority of the immigrants we spoke to, a few respondents said that they did not perceive a shared identity among Latin Americans. One Puerto Rican man in New York vented his frustrations about the lack of solidarity he perceived in certain national-origin groups. "What gives me a pain also is this—that I have gone to places and sometimes the Brazilians, Portuguese, and Argentines are very remote. . . . The rest help us out." He then complained about those Latinos who sought to assimilate and turn their backs on their fellow immigrants: "Some Latinos reach a certain level [and] they want their children to move to Long Island and marry whites and nothing more."

A similar sentiment was expressed by an Ecuadoran woman from New Jersey who noted that Latin American immigrants at times "lose their identity here and make, well, they forget their countries, forget where they came from. Their traits here say it all, and their voices here sound like they are trying to be someone else, but they don't yet have a well-formed identity. . . . Many of them forget their roots and try to imitate the Americans who live here or pretend that they are Americans."

Class differences seemed to prevent a few better-educated, higher-status migrants from perceiving a shared fate with others from Latin America, as with a Venezuelan man from New Jersey:

RESPONDENT: There are many Latinos of low class who come here and others from a higher level, understand? There are some who come to study, but the great majority are purely illegal immigrants. I don't have anything against them, because they come here to look for a better future as well, but . . .

INTERVIEWER: You don't identify with them?

RESPONDENT: No, because even though they are Latino, they are not at the same level, we are not at the same level, understand? I never could talk in a restaurant or a pizzeria in a nice conversation with one of these people because they couldn't understand the words, even if they wanted to. It is that, that you are speaking to them, no? They talk about the baby, or hearing the Tigres del Norte play. They don't know anything about jazz or classical music. None of that. They live in another world, another thing that I grasp and feel my privilege, thank God. I was well situated in my country, college paid. I had this preparation.

INTERVIEWER: Sure, at another level.

RESPONDENT: Or perhaps another class. No, these people who come are in the large majority lower-class.

Several respondents rejected the notion of a common Latino identity entirely, without much in the way of explanation, such as the Mexican man from Philadelphia who responded to our question by answering simply, "No—we are very unintegrated," or the Dominican woman from New York who pointed out that "there are definitely divisions." When we asked whether she was sure there was no common identity, she bluntly told us: "Among Latinos that come here, for example? One identity? I don't think so. No. At least I don't see it." The response of a young second-generation Mexican female in New Jersey was even more terse:

> INTERVIEWER: Do you perceive a common identity among Latino immigrants in the United States?
>
> RESPONDENT: No.
>
> INTERVIEWER: No? When you get together with other young Latinos, you have nothing in common?
>
> RESPONDENT: No.

A Mexican male from Philadelphia was more verbose, but equally adamant about the lack of a common identity: "I have thought about this, and really, I think that among Mexican migrants there is one, among Puerto Rican migrants there is one, among Cuban migrants, and among other groups. But a global identity? I don't think that it exists, because from one group to another there are various differences, as much in terms of personality as political activity or political leanings or cultural tendencies."

As indicated by table 7.1, however, these contrary voices were well outside of the majority of respondents who did indeed perceive a common identity among Latin American immigrants. One respondent went so far as to argue that even though there were many disputes between immigrants of different nationalities, it was this very fractiousness that somehow united them. In his view, Latinos shared a common identity, "even if we fight a lot":

> That is what unites us—we fight and then afterward we are together, drunk. Like we say, "No! What an Inca you are!" And then, "Says who, gaucho?" And then, "Fishmonger!" And so on, whatever, you know? Things like that. We fight among ourselves when things get hot, and this delights me because we are all South Americans. There are also disputes between countries, but I like how we know how to control it. We know how to say, "No, we are not going to talk about that, but about this." Understand? Because with Mexicans, this one, that is our group. There is a new guy that my friend brought, and you know, we are very tight-knit and don't just accept anyone. We are quite closed—nice people but very reserved. And the new guy, this Mexican, for example, he came out with us drinking, getting drunk.

Apparently, for this respondent cross-national differences were eminently soluble in alcohol, and Latino identity emerged from good-natured badinage between groups.

The Content of Latino Identity

The words of our respondents clearly suggest that a Latino identity that cuts across national origins could emerge in the United States. Indeed, although a few people questioned whether a common Latino identity in fact existed, everyone identified themselves as Latino. When asked to explain the basis for a common identification, roughly one-quarter (24 percent) referred in some fashion to race or ethnicity or mentioned some aspect of their physical appearance. Another 19 percent referred to a particular cultural attribute, such as food, music, art, or style; 18 percent mentioned values; 15 percent referred to Spanish as a unifying factor; and 10 percent talked about common emotions.

What is perhaps most impressive in these data about constructing an identity in the United States is the salience of race and ethnicity, which are featured in nearly one-quarter of the rationalizations given. Racial and ethnic justifications were generally offered in the context of group pride or feelings of exclusion from American society. One prideful Puerto Rican woman in Philadelphia told us that even though "I am American because I was born here and have citizenship," she nonetheless felt "100 percent Latino because I support my race. I am Latino." A Mexican woman in New Jersey likewise emphatically identified herself as Latino "because, in the first place, I was born down there and I am 100 percent rooted there, the roots and the upbringing that, for example, my parents gave me." Mixed with this woman's expression of pride, however, was a certain anxiety about rejection in the United States: "In the second place, because if I were to identify myself as American, then I would not be defending my origins. I couldn't do it. Nor would the Americans accept me, nor would my own Latino race. The Americans are always going to see me as Latino even if I were to speak in perfect English."

A Dominican woman from New Jersey expressed a similar combination of pride instilled by her parents and wariness about her reception in American society. In terms of pride, she forthrightly stated that: "I identify myself as Latino. I think that my parents have always inculcated in me my roots, even though I arrived here very young. I always remember wherever I may go that I am Dominican. I am Dominican, and that is something that I make others understand." At the same time, however, she expressed clear hesitation and concern about how she might be treated in U.S. society: "I think as a woman, a Latina, if I am not sure of myself, not sure of my, my base, from where I come from, then I am going to encounter people who will use this against me. I think that one has to be proud of where one comes from."

A similar kind of hesitation was articulated by a Mexican woman in New Jersey:

I feel Latino, and they recognize this and know that I am Latino, and sometimes when I speak with them, I try to talk as if I was one of them, but the real truth is, what happens is that, when one speaks, when I speak with an American . . . how can I put it? It's like it's mixed, the Mexican and the Hispanic, so that at times I think, as I was telling you, it's difficult to explain because at times I would like to be like them, free and everything, sometimes like. . . . Here, for Hispanics, it's difficult to get a driver's license, and sometimes I see a young guy here, and he already has a car, and I say, oh, look, if I could just get a license, I could do this, that, and the other thing.

A number of respondents mentioned language in voicing identity, such as the Dominican woman in New York who told us: "What happens is that at times the Latino comes out more—like when you are speaking to different people. Like, in general, if you see me on the street and I am speaking with a Latino, even though he may be Jewish, Latino comes first." A Colombian man from Philadelphia identified himself as Latino because he did not think he could pass as American because of his accent: "When I was speaking English, my Latino accent came out. I got frustrated that someone might say that I seemed Latino. It seemed a terrible thing to me." He ended up embracing his Latino identity somewhat reluctantly because he was loath to link himself to immigrants with lower-class accents. Referring to himself as a "classist" because "in my city they put a lot on how you speak," he explained that, "if I arrive somewhere and I am working with this person who is Mexican, who has no education, doesn't have that, and I arrive and find myself someplace where, I don't know, I am in this restaurant or whatever, with someone not of the same educational level as me, right? Probably I won't even acknowledge him or anything."

For other migrants, the basis of identity lay not in race, class, or language, but in culture. One Honduran man in Philadelphia expressed his identification in terms of the cultural value of mutual support among Latinos, because "they should support me." A young Dominican man in New York put it more succinctly: "I feel completely Latino because I think that it is my culture, even though I may have adopted part of the American culture." A Dominican woman in New York told us that she felt "Latino-American, a combination," because "it's the same thing, you know—I have always grown up in this culture." Likewise, a Puerto Rican woman in Philadelphia said that she identified with both because "I was raised here. I was born here, but then again, like, my parents are from over there, so, like, both." She did note, however, that encountering recently arrived migrants made her feel more American: "Like, I have neighbors, and they just moved from Puerto Rico. They're up the street, and they're, like, totally different. The way they speak and, like, they're so loud. And, like, the way they dress is different. They still dress like they are in Puerto Rico."

A Dominican woman from New York seemed to compartmentalize herself into separate American and Latino identities: "In personal issues and in professional issues, I think I'm, like, more American," but speaking Spanish triggered more of a Latino identity:

> I guess in many ways, when I'm with them, the fact that we speak a language other than what Americans speak, English, babbling in another language at home, or that you can fall into it, all of the sudden someone is speaking Spanish and my Spanish gets better, and I love the . . . I don't know, I guess coming back to that work passion. I love the sense of enthusiasm, and when I get to express that, I feel more Latino.

Perhaps it is not surprising that the most problematic relations with Latino identity were expressed by Brazilians. One man in Philadelphia flatly said that, "No, I don't feel like I fall under the label Latino." He then complained about how much trouble he had negotiating identity in American society: "Ah, no. No. Because you have no idea. It's not just that people think that I am Brazilian or Latino. It is more. They already confuse me a lot—as an Italian or many times as a Greek. Everyone, or at least many people, have told me that I look Greek. So I say that I am Brazilian, but hardly ever Latino. South American, yes." He was particularly critical of middle-class Americans, who generally know "very, very little" about Brazil, "even people of a certain level of culture, who went to the university and have a better education and know something about Brazil, they know just a little more, but . . . middle-class people are limited." He was also resentful toward immigrants from Spanish-speaking countries, such as the coworker who pestered him with leading questions like, "Why is it that Brazil is the only country that speaks Portuguese? Everyone else speaks Spanish!"

Another Brazilian from Philadelphia outlined the complications of being Brazilian in Latin America as well as the United States: "It's more like I identify myself a little as a Brazilian, not necessarily from a continental viewpoint. I don't think that I have the concept of a Latino identity, let's put it that way. . . . You have to see that Brazil is a bit isolated from Latin America . . . because of language and culture. . . . It's a different thing. We don't have salsa. We don't have merengue."

The Feeling of Being Latino

Although interesting insights came in response to our question about the basis for Latino identity, richer information emerged in response to a follow-up question we posed on what it was that made our respondents *feel* Latino. As before, race figures prominently in the answers provided. A Dominican woman in New Jersey stated that "it's because I live in the United States and I don't have to change my identity as a Latino—I have to represent the Latino race." A Puerto Rican female from Philadelphia simply told us, "Well, I am 100 percent Latino. I am Puerto Rican."

To illustrate why they felt Latino in racial-ethnic terms, several respondents mentioned their physical features and appearance, such as the young Colombian man from New Jersey who, when asked what made him feel Latino, answered, "That I have black hair and dark eyes," or the Honduran man in Philadelphia who said that Latinos identify themselves "in the hair, the face, in the color of the skin, you know, many things." A Honduran man in New Jersey saw Latino identity in "my way of being, the color of my skin." For a young Ecuadoran man in New York, first and foremost among the reasons he felt Latino was the darkness of his skin, which to him was more important than speaking Spanish: "First, the color of my skin. Second, that I speak Spanish. Anyone can speak Spanish, but the blood that I have is Latino, and all my life it will be until I die."

Several other respondents also referred to "blood" when explaining the source of their Latino identity, such as the young Dominican man in New York who told us, "Blood . . . that is life itself, because blood is everything, it is the roots of oneself, and of course, one doesn't hide it," or the Dominican woman from New Jersey who said that a Latino identity is "something that you carry in your blood . . . something that comes from the soul, something from inside." Another respondent, a Mexican woman from New Jersey, spoke not in terms of blood but in terms of birth as well as appearance, explaining that she was Latino "because I am from another country. The land where I was born is the land where I come from. Just that. Me in America and my homeland down there. It's my homeland, and I can't change it. I can't just say, I'm American. I am something else because, first, I don't speak the language of this place, and second, I don't look like them."

Although most respondents conceptualized race in terms of birth, blood, or appearance, a young Ecuadoran man from New Jersey broadened his definition of race to incorporate attitudes and personality:

INTERVIEWER: What makes you feel Latino?

RESPONDENT: Umm, my race.

INTERVIEWER: How's that? Tell me.

RESPONDENT: It's my attitude. We have a different attitude than the North Americans. The main thing is my attitude.

INTERVIEWER: I know, but your opinion is important. It's for this reason we are taping. Besides your attitude, what else?

RESPONDENT: The personality.

Beyond race, culture, conceived in a variety of different ways, also loomed large for respondents trying to explain what made them feel Latino. For one Colombian woman in New York, culture meant "things related to the family, holidays, and the ways, for instance, at Christmas time, the preparations for Christmas. I guess it's sort of religious." When we asked a Dominican man in Philadelphia what made him feel Latino, he answered, "The accent," and at first we thought he was referring to language, but it turned out that he was using the term metaphorically to refer to certain dimensions of Latino culture, such as "the way of perceiving things, [being] more flexible. The American is more rigid. The Latino always has more, always puts a little more spice into things. Like, if things don't work and you can't do it this way, then you try by that way. You invent something."

A Mexican man in New Jersey also appeared to be referring to the Spanish language when he said that he felt Latino because "communication is easier," but when we probed it turned out that he was thinking of something deeper: "Because, I guess, we are all Latino and we carry inside ourselves, I don't know, but between Latinos, like an expression that is easier, more open, not only because of the language but also by the way of thinking that we have." For a Venezuelan woman in New York, what made her feel Latino was "the richness of Latino culture more than anything . . . my culture is Latino, a big, rich culture." For a Dominican man in New York, "what makes me feel Latino is the variety in our culture." He elaborated on what he meant by variety:

> You can go to Argentina and see people who are very white; you can go to Panama and see people who are very black; and you can go to Venezuela where it could be white or black or Indian; and we all speak Spanish, even though we have different accents and we use different words for different things. Our music. Our food is very delicious. The women from our countries are very pretty. I like just about everything having to do with Latino culture. Yes, Latin culture is very happy and willing to stand up and fight for itself. I feel very proud of being Latino and of speaking Spanish.

Pride was often mentioned by respondents in explaining why they felt culturally Latino. For example, an Ecuadoran woman in New Jersey told us that she felt Latino because of "where I was born, our culture. I am proud of the language, of what we speak, of our traditions, of our way of living, of looking at life. It's everything, not one thing, a whole set of things that makes me feel proud to feel Latino." Similarly, a Honduran man we spoke to in Philadelphia asserted that what made him feel Latino was "pride . . . the pride of being Latino"; when we asked him to elaborate, he spoke of "the manner of being, the culture that we carry."

A Peruvian man in New York became quite emotional about his cultural pride, telling us:

> I am very attached to my culture. I love my culture. Where I go, I always show my face proudly and don't care what is said behind my back. It does not matter what they say, that you are South American and that you don't speak Spanish like in Spain. Neither do they speak that Spanish in Mexico or Central America. Like I say, apart from being Peruvian, Argentine, Chilean, Venezuelan, you are South American inside yourself. It's my way of speaking, my accent, my customs.

When we asked this respondent what kind of customs he was talking about, he quickly answered, "The food," which was also mentioned by a Mexican woman in New York who recited a whole list of cultural elements that made her feel Latino, including "the customs," "the music," "respect for others," and, "above all, the food." Music and food were also mentioned by a Mexican man in New York who initially emphasized music in his response, but when he remembered that he and many of his friends also listened to music in English, he switched to an emphasis on food, noting that "Mexican food is the best," a sentiment echoed by another male Mexican New Yorker who told us that he felt Latino because of "my family and the food I eat every day."

Other respondents mentioned music and food but emphasized the music, such as the Dominican woman in New York who told us that it was "the music, the food," that made her feel Latino, but then added that "more than anything" it was the music, because "your country is something that comes from within." A young Mexican woman in New Jersey also emphasized music as a source of identity, in her case "Latin hip-hop." In contrast, a Puerto Rican man in Philadelphia singled out "salsa and merengue," noting that "you wake up with music and go to sleep with music. You have that rhythm. I think we, we just have that spice where you can go anywhere and you'll still stand out even if there are beautiful people around you. You'll still stand out because you have that spice or you have that culture."

Closely related to culture in expressions of Latino identity are values; one Venezuelan woman in New York told us that what made her feel Latino was, "above all, the values." One of the most important values cited by respondents was the emphasis on family. When we asked a

Puerto Rican adolescent in New Jersey what made him feel Latino, for example, he answered in two simple words: "My family." Similarly, a Puerto Rican man in Philadelphia responded by saying, "I'm very family-oriented," and emphasized that "family is something big," as did a young Dominican woman in New York who affirmed that "the family is really important." She said that close family relations were not limited to Dominicans but were common to all Latin Americans, noting that "they're all Spanish, and we come from Spanish-speaking countries, but, you know, I guess family is really important." Another Dominican woman from New York wholeheartedly agreed, pointing out that "in the home the grandmother is there, the aunt is there, the family is nearer to you. There is always the family there to help you and all that."

When we asked a Colombian man in Philadelphia what made him feel Latino, he answered, "Undoubtedly the values and customs," and then offered a treatise on what is wrong with the American family:

We might say there is something that I think differentiates us, and that is how we conceive of the family. And this also enters into the earlier answer about fears. Something that worries me about making a family here in the United States is that the concept of the family they have here is a little different. It seems to me at times that family ties are much tighter in our countries. Parents in some ways are more overprotective of their children, but here not so much. It is not clear, or shall we say it is not so clear, that there are such strong ties here. They are ties that are much weaker, we can say. I do not share with North American society the idea that children leave home at such an early age, shall we say. In fact, I see it as a serious problem, serious for society.

Beyond family values, some respondents emphasized a concern for others as a cultural ideal among Latinos. Thus, a Dominican woman in New York told us that "what makes me feel Latino is when I can help someone, that we are united mainly, that we don't have hunger anywhere, that if someone needs something, one has to give what one can." In contrast, she saw the United States as a place where "every person here has his own thing, understand? Here everyone has someone at their back." In her view, "at least the Latinos that arrive here get a helping hand if they need it." She felt that Americans could not be counted on for this kind of help because "here everyone is afraid of everyone else. Better to go to an Hispanic. You come and at least he'll offer something. We Latinos live in a country of one."

Another person, an Ecuadoran man in New Jersey, saw Latino identity not in terms of family values or concern for others but in terms of "the value that we place on work. We have a lot of desire to work. . . . We like to, we love to work." While emphasizing work, he also saw Latinos as more sociable and romantic than Americans: "Romantics we are, very romantic, more friendly, more sociable, more attached to our spouses." For a Mexican woman in New Jersey, the key value was ambition. In her words, "What makes me feel Latino is the way of thinking, I would say. . . . I tell you, all Hispanics come here in order to get ahead, more than anything, and that is the only thing that I like—that all Hispanics come here to realize their goal of advancing themselves."

For many respondents, the issue of culture was intimately tied to the Spanish language, as with the Dominican woman in New York who said that for her, Latino identity came from "the language and the culture. That's it mainly. What makes me feel Latino is that I can speak Spanish." Similarly, when we asked an Ecuadoran man in New Jersey what made him feel Latino, he said, "Ah, I don't know. How can I explain it? That which feels Latino? I don't know. The language, I think." A Dominican woman in Philadelphia answered, "Mostly by speaking Spanish, right?" This response was similar to that of a Mexican man in New York who noted, "Well, Latinos always speak in Spanish, right? I think it's really nothing more than this."

Related to culture, values, and language are emotions, and many respondents noted a large gulf between Latinos and Americans in the expression of feelings and sentiments. A Venezuelan man in New Jersey told us that, in contrast to the American, "the Latino is like, more sentimental—feelings first and money later. In this country it is very . . . well, you know. I'm always doing something else when it should be love first." A Puerto Rican man in Philadelphia expressed the belief that "the Latino always looks for another Latino—one feels more comfortable finding a Latino friendship." Although he admitted that Americans also look out for each other, he felt that Latinos do so with "more warmth." Likewise, a Dominican woman in New York opined that "my culture is better than any other sentiment, any other culture. Yes, that totally makes me Latino. That I have not lost the sentiment of being Hispanic. I don't have to feel weighed down for having lived here for so long."

A Colombian woman in Philadelphia saw herself and other Latinos as "very giving. If I can help you, I help you, and I try to all the time. Really, this is what happens. All the time I am trying to give advice to others if they are Latinos. Yes, yes. If I see that they need something and will accept it I give it. . . . If I see that I can help you in something, I help." In contrast, she told us, "I don't think this happens with the Americans—even among themselves it doesn't happen," because "it's like they're solitary." A Mexican man in New York similarly saw a difference between Latinos and Americans in "the way we connect with each other," pointing out that "we are more effusive, or maybe more expressive, [and] I think that it is easier for us to establish friendships among ourselves and with others compared with other groups."

According to a Guatemalan man in New Jersey, Latinos "can normally talk and share. We talk a lot in my country. We know this territory and can maintain a conversation." For an Ecuadoran woman in New Jersey, being Latino was "a way of being that is more open, a form that is more spontaneous, the fact that a Latino will greet you with a kiss and an embrace," and for a Dominican woman from Philadelphia, Latino identity came from the fact that "you feel good when you run into someone from your neighborhood. . . . You feel good, good, to speak with another Latino, even though that person may be from another country. . . . Among Latinos, it is easier, it is easier. There is very little of this, very little among Americans, be they white or black, even after you get to know them. It is the way of speaking, the trust that one has with Latinos."

A Dominican female in New York explained that what made her feel Latino was "how we connect . . . I think [we] are more open." Indeed, in her weekly book club, "we talk about anything, I mean, as if we were sisters. We talk about everything. I've known these people for some time, and they also work with me, though they aren't my old friends from high school. But since we have known one another, we have talked about everything, from start to finish. I don't know how I could feel more at home." Another Dominican woman in New York felt that Latino identity came from "the way of dealing with people, for example. This affection that one feels for a person. For example, where I live now, there, I knew two Hispanic women. In reality, these two people are friends of my daughter, and we also became good friends. We are very friendly and affectionate with them—different than with other people—because they are Hispanic."

A Colombian woman in New York noted the lack of physical interaction and expressions of affection among Americans relative to Latinos:

> I definitely think that there's more physical interaction. You can see two women in communities, either in my neighborhood or around, whatever. It's all very Latino in its base. Certain areas, even in Long Island, two women can walk on and on, and it's not a problem. Two Latin American women may hold hands and walk down the street. There's a little bit more affection shared between the couple than you tend to see in an American couple. There is, you know, a certain relaxed atmosphere, I think. Here in the United States, meeting the parents or meeting the families is always, like, they don't look forward to it.

An Ecuadoran woman from New Jersey echoed this perception, pointing out that, "here, an American only offers a 'hello' or a 'hi' and that's it. It's very rare that people here embrace you, at least not until you get to know them better. But in our country, when you meet someone for the first time, you give them a kiss and an embrace."

As the foregoing passages suggest, our respondents generally saw American culture as cold, less personal, more competitive, and more rational and calculating. According to a young Dominican woman in New York, "We Latinos are more explosive, maybe more out there. The relation between them is colder—colder, more distant, something like that." A Venezuelan man from New Jersey stressed "the spontaneity and affection" of Latinos and their proclivity to "get into mischief" by "thinking of doing things a different way, not according to the book, to find ways around things." Compared to Americans, he saw in Latinos "a lack of punctuality, if you will, a lack of planning ahead."

A Mexican man from New Jersey viewed Latinos as "more playful, we play with words. All Latinos play with words, especially Mexicans." He asserted that Latinos are also "a little dreamier. Aha. Whatever it is that makes me feel Latino, well, more than anything it is the way of expressing ourselves, the way of feeling. We feel, at least in my case, we feel life differently." The idea that Latinos feel things differently was also expressed by a Mexican man in Philadelphia, who told us, "What makes me feel Latino is the fact that Latinos know how to feel, know how to express their sentiments, to have a sense of the aesthetic. They have a certain love of life and family, and this desire is always connected with people." This view was also articulated by a Mexican man in New York who explained: "I am more open than the people here . . . I like to talk, I like to get along, to mix with the best. We Latinos are happier. We like to party, maybe, and to be jokers. There are many things, I tell you, that I identify with in terms of personality."

For a Venezuelan woman in New Jersey, being Latino meant "smiling constantly. To be disposed to speak to you and to look at you, not eye to eye, as they say, but as the human being that you are." She took special umbrage at the stereotypes that Americans have about Latinos, especially about Latin women as sexy bombshells—"that they paint their mouths red and all that"—because "in reality they don't know what she is." When we asked her what womanhood meant in Latino culture, she replied: "She is a well-prepared woman, full of values, a very human woman, very caring, hardworking woman who gives her all. You just can't imagine for whom besides you. I declare and emphasize that we are very, very human. That we always think not only of ourselves but of others, and from there comes so much warmth."

The contrast between the warmth of Latinos and the coldness of Americans was a common theme in discussions of identity. According to a Mexican woman in New Jersey, the difference boiled down to the fact that "a Latino has more charisma and more spice." A Dominican man in New York saw Latinos as distinctive in

the friendly way we generally behave with others, because, well, for example, the workers here, we are Colombians, Dominicans, and other nationalities, and we treat each other as if we were all the same people, you know, ummm . . . [*Like brothers?*] Brothers, exactly, which I don't feel especially with the Anglos. Anglo Americans feel to me very different, very different. . . . Many of them are very nice, very friendly, but there are others who are cold and vain, not very friendly, and I have seen that they are very . . . well, at times they discriminate. [*They're discriminatory?*] Yes, discriminatory, exactly, and at times I think that they think, you know, that they are the greatest thing God created on this earth.

A Colombian woman in New York argued that, while Latinos and Americans both have passion, it is directed toward very different ends:

I don't mean to sound like Americans don't have passion. They are pretty driven. They are more driven. Maybe that's the difference. They are more goal-oriented, and their passion [is] to find a lot of success, or the passion is to achieve a certain image. It is more goal-oriented. I think when I speak of passion, between either a Latino upbringing or a Greek or Italian upbringing, that's the sense of the word "passion." It's more the journey. I mean, that's the difference.

When asked what made them feel Latino, a few respondents basically said, "Everything." A Dominican woman in New York replied: "My roots, my black roots, my white roots, all my roots. My history, my atmosphere, my people, my music, my drums. Those things make me feel Latino." A Mexican man in Philadelphia listed language, values, customs, music, and dancing as the things that made him feel Latino. A Puerto Rican woman in Philadelphia was more explicit, telling us that what made her feel Latino was "everything, everything. My appearance, my language, my parents, the atmosphere, where I work, yeah, everything." A similar view was voiced by a Mexican man in New Jersey who also responded with the word "everything." When pressed to elaborate, he said, "I don't know. The spicy flavor with which life is lived, no? I'm not sure. I have never thought of being anything but Latino. It enchants me. I wouldn't change for anything."

Choosing Identities: American Versus Latino

As many of these comments suggest, our respondents tended to define Latino culture and identity in sharp contrast to the American way of life. One Puerto Rican man in New York went so far as to describe American culture as "a Mickey Mouse mentality" built on political lies; even as a child, he said, "I didn't believe everything that they told me politically." Seeing his values as "different, very different," he listed them as "respect, the care of my grandmother and grandfather, the respect of my mother, the greeting when one enters a room, good salted cod with real fried ripe bananas, girls writing you poems, taking them to a picnic."

Given widespread perceptions of American society as cold, calculating, and competitive and Latino culture as warm, nurturing, and communal, it is perhaps not surprising that most Latin American immigrants rejected American identity categorically. The bottom panel of table 7.1 presents how subjects responded when asked about their personal self-identification. First we asked whether they self-identified as Latino, and then we asked whether they identified with Americans. Since the two questions were asked separately, respondents could, if they wished, easily identify themselves as both Latino and American, or as one and not the other.

The large majority of respondents (62 percent) picked Latino identity by itself and explicitly rejected an American identity. Only 22 percent claimed an unalloyed American identity, and 13 percent said that they were attached to both identities. The tendency to claim both identities was considerably stronger among documented migrants (26 percent) than among the undocumented (6 percent), but in both cases a singular Latino identity was the majority position (58 percent among the former and 66 percent among the latter). Overall, then, three-quarters of all respondents expressed a Latino identity alone or in combination with an American identity (62 percent plus 13 percent equals 75 percent), whereas nearly two-thirds (62 percent) categorically rejected an American identity.

Even those who identified as American were typically guarded and hesitant in their expression of American identity and were quite selective about the aspects of American identity they embraced. For example, when we asked a Honduran man in Philadelphia whether he identified as American, his reply indicated considerable ambivalence: "Well, I've now been here for twelve years, so I guess so, but I continue being Hispanic because that's what I am, just one who has Americanized." Similarly, an Ecuadoran man in New York admitted to identifying with Americans only "a little bit," and that was simply because he had American friends whom he perceived as "funny and amiable." A young Honduran woman in Philadelphia said that she identified as American only "up to a certain point" because she was aghast at the disrespect that American children showed to elders and how they talked back to parents:

And this is something that got me to thinking deep inside, that I would never dare to do this with my mother. My mother has inculcated in me a respect that I could never overlook. I have never spoken to my mother in that tone of voice or with that kind of attitude, because I would never dare to say a bad word to her. Never has it occurred to me to raise a hand against her. . . . There are limits, and I see that Americans don't have them.

A Puerto Rican man in Philadelphia admitted to identifying as an American only

> because I was born here and have lived here all of my life, and for these reasons I identify. What I know is here. Maybe I feel American because of my nationality, being born here, even though I don't feel it. I speak the language with them, but I eat Puerto Rican food, and the music I listen to is Latino. Even though I was born here, I have never been much involved in American music, and I don't listen to it very much.

Several other respondents also said that they identified as American only because they spoke English, such as the Puerto Rican woman in Philadelphia who said that she felt American mainly because of "the language, the way I live I guess," or the young Colombian man in New Jersey who told us, "Well, I live here, I speak English, and I am a person who is civilized with American people, but my blood is Latino, so it's like I'm in between." A Mexican man in Philadelphia admitted that his "social identity is American" because "I understand American institutions. I understand the language. I understand the rules of being a citizen here, but my personal identity is Mexican, properly speaking." This emphasis on the connection between language and identity was emphasized by a young Peruvian woman in Philadelphia who, when asked whether she identified as an American, responded:

RESPONDENT: Yes, because of the language.

INTERVIEWER: Not the customs?

RESPONDENT: No.

INTERVIEWER: So it's just the language that gives you a certain identification with Americans?

RESPONDENT: Yes. When I speak English.

In our interviews, it became increasingly clear that whereas Latino identity tended to be a constant, permanent feature of respondents' makeup, American identity was more fleeting and situational. A Dominican woman in New York reported that "sometimes I feel American and sometimes I feel Latino. It depends. I mean, it depends on the circumstances." A Mexican woman in New York felt that "I am American because when I am out, I do American things, and then when I come home with my mother and her Mexican dishes and her religion and the Virgin of Guadalupe, I feel both." A young Dominican woman from New York told us that "around certain Latin people I would consider myself more American. Because of the way I was brought up in my house, I think I'm more American. But then, around Americans, I consider myself more Latino because I am a mixture and I'm kind of unique." A Mexican male university student in Philadelphia identified only with those Americans who "have read and studied the same things. But with the typical American I really have little in common. . . . If I have a strong connection, it is with those groups of people who have a certain level of education or who have studied at some university, I identify with them. But not with Americans in general."

A number of respondents said they identified as American only to the extent that they were attracted to certain specific features of American life, such as the Mexican man in New York who said that he only identified "in some things . . . in their likes, their pleasures," especially baseball, "and basketball too." For a Mexican woman in Philadelphia, it was politics, not sports, that attracted her; she told us that she identified with Americans "in many political things. We talk a lot about world conflicts like the Palestinians against the Israelis, the problem of Iraq, North Korea, things like that." What a Guatemalan woman in New Jersey identified with was that "Americans are normally open to talking with you. They begin by asking you where you're from, how you came, and other things, and that gives you the opportunity to tell them a little about how [your] life has been."

Several respondents told us that they identified with Americans only in the arena of work and employment. A Venezuelan woman in New Jersey told us: "I identify myself with them in the sense of work, because I am a really good worker," but apart from that she felt little identification because she saw the United States as a society "where there is a big lack of love, an absence of communication, and this creates prohibitions against so many things, as well as pressures toward many things." Likewise, a Columbian woman in New York said that she identified with Americans "maybe more so with work, but when it comes to attitudes about family and everything else, I definitely identify with Latino."

In general, it proved quite difficult to get respondents to offer an unqualified endorsement of American identity. The closest we came was in two conversations in which each respondent said that they identified as Americans on the basis of principle rather than any specific feature of American culture they liked or admired. One of them, a Mexican man in New York, said that he identified with Americans because "every human being is the same. We have the same nature and do the same things. I don't mean in terms of color or things like that, but inside I think we are all the same." The other, a Mexican man in Philadelphia, said that, yes, he did identify with Americans, because "we're all human beings." One of the most positive endorsements came from a young Dominican woman in New York who said, "I think I consider myself mostly an American," but even she was quick to add that "anything that I can do to help the background of my culture, I would."

Rather than expressing enthusiastic acceptance or guarded embrace of certain features of American culture, far more common among respondents was the categorical rejection of American identity in any way, shape, or form. A young Dominican man in Philadelphia told us that "I always feel Latino, always. I never would say I am American because nobody would believe me." A Puerto Rican man in Philadelphia rejected American identity by saying, "No, in truth, no—you may think I'm American, but I'm not, and moreover, I don't want to be. I don't change my culture for anyone." A Dominican man in New York was equally adamant, telling us, "No. . . . Because I don't feel like an American. At least, given that I'm a U.S. citizen, I have the same rights as anyone who was born here, except for being president—I don't have that right because I wasn't born here—but I don't identify as an American citizen because I don't feel proud of the American citizenship I have." A Dominican woman in New York said simply that "I identify myself with my Latino community, but not with the Americans."

Several respondents claimed an American identity because of their birth in South or Central America but rejected identification with U.S. Americans. A Dominican man in New York admitted that, "well, yes, I am American, because I'm from Latin America," and then quickly added, "But 'American' American, no, I can't say I identify that way." A Dominican woman in New York said, "I feel American because I am from the American continent, but I don't feel like a U.S. American. Not me, maybe because I have not had a deep relationship with them." Although she admitted that life was good in the United States, she still found Americans off-putting, noting that "it is very easy to live like they live—everyone would like to live like they live—but I still don't identify with them."

A Mexican man in Philadelphia bluntly rejected American identity and seemed rather ashamed of having succumbed earlier to an infatuation with American consumer culture because of peer pressure: "No. . . . When I was sixteen, yes, because then it was all about McDonald's, Nike sneakers, basketball, Michael Jordan, everything that was from America. I took it all in, you know? And if I didn't accept it all, they would all say to me, 'What are you—some kind of Indian?'"

Several respondents mentioned specific features of American culture or society that they disliked in justifying their rejection of an American identity, such as the Colombian woman in Philadelphia who said that "we're more emotional in Colombia than here. But we all have to eat—well, then again, Americans don't eat very well. (*Laughs*.) . . . They are total disasters when it comes to food." A Mexican man in New York abjured American identity "because we have a very different manner, a different way of looking at life, of perceiving things. They are much colder, much more ambitious in monetary terms, not ambitious about wanting to achieve goals in life, more materialistic. They value different things than I value." When asked whether he identified with Americans, a Dominican man in Philadelphia responded: "No way, because we are different, we are distinct. They have one way of thinking and us another—we are different. They think of themselves, you know, they think of nothing but themselves . . . of the individual, and us, we think of the group. Because for us, if we move upward, the whole family advances, and if they move up, no one moves with them."

Several people explained their reluctance to embrace American identity in terms of the racism, exclusion, and discrimination they had encountered. We interviewed a man from El Salvador in New Jersey who told us that, "when I don't see any racism, I am fine. Because that is my point. In so many words, I am antiracist. In other words, I won't tolerate it." A Mexican man in New Jersey also reported that, "if I see Americans who are racist, I don't have anything to do with them, understand? I see the good and get rid of the bad." In speaking about Americans, a Honduran man in Philadelphia noted that, "although not everyone is accepting, most people are. They look at you as if you were any other person, one of them, and they don't say anything to you." But when we asked him whether he felt able to integrate into American society, he responded, "Well, it depends on the circle . . . you wish to come into—if they want you to integrate, [then] they accept you. If yes, then I could do it." A Mexican woman in New Jersey alluded to her exclusion when she said that she "would like to feel American, but it's not possible." A young Dominican woman in New York spoke more directly about the stereotyping and prejudice she has had to overcome:

> Well, I see, with Dominicans and Puerto Ricans, many people don't think they're educated and can overcome, you know, the way they live and how to live. Because I've seen many family members that are like that, I mean, not in school or my family here, because we're an exception. We pretty much moved up from that. But I know of other family members, you know, who live that way and friends in school that live that lifestyle. But, you know, we have to work harder to overcome that image—of the way people, especially whites, see us. And blacks see us as ghetto and not working and then, you know, not having good jobs—it's horrible. . . . It's harder for me because I have to prove that I'm educated, and I have to do all that I can so I can get a good job and go into a good college.

Since the large majority of respondents subscribed to a Latino identity, there was not a great deal of variation to explain, and our efforts to estimate models predicting Latino identity, either by itself or in multinomial specification relative to an American identity, yielded little in the way of interesting findings. The more interesting issue was why 35 percent of the sample embraced an American identity. Classical assimilation theory generally predicts an emergent American identity: with more time spent in the United States and more contact with its people and institutions, immigrants gradually come to see themselves as members of U.S. society and self-identify as Americans. In contrast, theorists such as Portes and Rumbaut (2001) envision the possibility of a reactive rejection of American identity as a "product of confrontation with an adverse native mainstream" (284). This formulation turns classical assimilation theory on its head: the more time people spend in the United States and the more they come to know the realities of prejudice, discrimination, and exclusion, the more likely they are to reject American identity.

To test whether American identity is embraced emergently or rejected reactively we estimated a logistic regression to predict whether or not respondents identified themselves in any way as Americans, either alone or in combination with a Latino identity. This outcome was expressed as a function of the respondent's U.S. job situation, class background, human capital characteristics, perceptions about the United States, motivations for migration, intentions to return, and transnational behaviors, while controlling for racial-ethnic roots, region of origin, demographic background, and immigrant status. As shown in table 7.2, the model is highly significant and accounts for about 58 percent of the observed variance in ethnic identification, with two variables standing out for the size and statistical power of their effects: time in the United States and discrimination.

Contrary to the predictions of classical assimilation theory, adopting an American identity becomes progressive *less likely* the more time a migrant spends in the United States, and consistent with the hypothesis of reactive ethnicity, those who experience discrimination in the United States are far more likely to refuse to label themselves as Americans. In addition, the likelihood of self-identifying as American is negatively related to hours of work, presumably because the more time a person spends in the workplace, the more knowledge he or she gains about exploitive conditions in the secondary labor market. Interestingly, once one holds constant the actual experience of discrimination, African and indigenous roots are associated with a higher likelihood of identifying as American. Not surprisingly, those who are motivated to migrate by attractions in the United States are more likely to embrace an American identity.

Equally salient in the equation is a consideration of which factors are *not* related to the likelihood of taking on an American identity. This tendency is not affected by age, education, gender, class background, English-language ability, skin tone, documentation, or region of origin (with the exception of the Caribbean, whose immigrants are marginally less likely to express an American identity). Our earlier conclusion that trans-

Table 7.2   Logistic Regression Predicting Identification as American Versus Latino Among Latin American Immigrants to the United States

	Identified as American		
Predictors	Regression Coefficient	Standard Error	P-Value
Transnational behavior			
Sends remittances	3.174*	1.518	0.036
U.S. job situation			
Current wage	−0.009	0.018	0.609
Current occupational status	0.047+	0.026	0.079
Current hours worked per week	−0.037+	0.020	0.072
Class background			
Parental occupational status	0.047	0.047	9.313
Human capital			
Years of schooling	−0.040	0.056	0.474
Good English	−1.677	1.284	0.192
Perceptions of United States			
More opportunity	0.800	1.878	0.670
More inequality	2.372*	1.191	0.046
Experienced discrimination	−5.134**	2.047	0.011
Motivation for migration			
Origin conditions	3.873	2.455	0.115
U.S. conditions	6.301*	2.970	0.034
Family or network	1.708	1.295	0.187
Other	—	—	—
Intentions			
Intends to return	−1.886	1.284	0.142
Racial-ethnic roots			
African	3.776*	1.743	0.030
Indigenous	4.758*	2.065	0.021
Dark-skinned	0.579	1.266	0.648
Region of origin			
Mexico	—	—	—
Caribbean	−4.023+	2.146	0.061
Central America	0.441	2.540	0.862
South America	−2.874	1.818	0.114
Demographics			
Age	−0.116	0.110	0.293
Male	1.402	1.192	0.240
Immigrant status			
Documented	2.054	1.770	0.246
Years in United States	−0.060**	0.024	0.012
Intercept	−0.380	4.912	0.938
Likelihood ratio X^2	67.130***		
Pseudo-R-squared	0.582***		
Sample size (N)	142		

Source: Immigrant Identity Project (Office of Population Research 2009).
+p < .10; *p < .05; **p < .01; ***p < .001

nationalism is sui generis—part and parcel of the immigrant experience, not a reaction to discrimination or blocked opportunities in the United States—is confirmed here by the fact that the likelihood of identifying as American is unrelated to the intention to return or to motivations for migration emanating from the origin country, as well as by the fact that the sending of remittances *positively* predicts adherence to an American identity.

Immigrant Identity in Anti-Immigrant Times

The data presented in this chapter clearly indicate widespread adherence to a common Latino identity among immigrants from Latin America living in the urban Northeast. More than 80 percent perceived the existence of such an identity, and more than three-quarters personally identified as Latino. Whereas most people did not identify as Latinos in their homelands, in the United States the speaking of a common language, the sharing of cultural likes and dislikes, the perception of similar values and sentiments, and the common experience of difficulties and challenges in a new land provided a strong basis for an emergent ethnicity.

Once identification as Latino occurs, moreover, it seems to become a fundamental and intrinsic component of immigrant character, relatively constant in its expression and not highly dependent on circumstances or situations. The universal character of Latino identity was confirmed when we attempted to estimate multivariate models predicting whether respondents perceived a common identity among Latin American immigrants. In all cases, no matter how many variables, or which combination of variables, we included in the equation, the predictive power of the model was nil, the coefficients for all variables were insignificant, and the goodness of fit was no better than what would be expected by chance. Among Latin American immigrants in the United States, in other words, the perception of a Latino identity seems to be a global reality that is unrelated to individual perceptions, motivations, or characteristics.

In contrast, almost two-thirds of the Latin American immigrants in our sample explicitly rejected an American identity, and among those who did identify as American, the expression of identity was contingent and selective. The contrast between the enthusiastic and unreserved endorsement of Latino identity and the hesitant endorsement of American identity reflects a fundamental divergence in the meaning and content of the two identities in the minds of respondents. Whereas Latinos were seen as warm, accepting, and caring, Americans were perceived as cold, competitive, and calculating. American society may be efficient, well organized, and wealthy, but to migrants these benefits come at the cost of interpersonal warmth and human interconnection, and most of them end up opposed to it.

Given a hostile context of reception and a highly segmented labor market, the stage is set for the formation of a reactive ethnicity that categorically rejects an American identity. During a time of rising anti-immigrant sentiment, repressive immigration and border enforcement, and the public portrayal of Latino immigrants as criminals, invaders, and terrorists, intergroup boundaries brighten rather than blur, and crossing becomes more difficult. The more time immigrants spend in the United States, the more contact they have with Americans and American society, the more aware they become of the harsh realities of prejudice and discrimination, and the more they come to experience the rampant inequalities of the secondary labor market. Rather than ideologically assimilating, therefore, immigrants become progressively less likely to self-identify as American and reactively reject the label.

Our analysis thus suggests that the greatest threat to the ideological assimilation of immigrants comes not from foreign involvements or transnational loyalties. Indeed, transnational involvement through remitting *positively* predicts adherence to an American identity. Instead, rejection of an American identity stems from the exclusion and discrimination that immigrants experience the more time they spend in the United States. Paradoxically, resistance to an American identity is something "made in the USA" through the accumulation of negative experience with U.S. people and institutions. Rather than berating immigrants for a lack of assimilative zeal and comparing them invidiously with immigrants of the past, American citizens would do better to look closely at the impact of their own attitudes and behavior toward immigrants on the proclivity of newcomers to seek acceptance as Americans.

=Chapter 8=

Visualizing Identity

The last chapter concluded an extended analysis of the narratives offered by immigrants in response to questions we put to them about their hopes, expectations, and experiences in the United States. Our purpose was to give voice to immigrants' side of the identity issue, allowing them to speak for themselves in articulating the complex process of identity formation in the United States. Despite our efforts to peer directly into the immigrant mind through guided, in-depth conversations, however, the resulting textual data are inevitably filtered. It is the interviewer who asks the questions and decides in which direction to steer the conversation, and it is the researchers who select segments of the conversation to include in tables and feature in quotes and assign codes to specific passages.

These various subjectivities embedded in the process of qualitative data collection offer many opportunities for investigators to impose, wittingly or not, their own views and interpretations on the resulting data. We therefore sought to include in our process of data collection a second, confirmatory methodology that would offer respondents another, independent opportunity to show us what the world really looked like to them. Specifically, we offered immigrants a chance to visualize identity and to transmit their visualizations directly to us. We accomplished this goal by giving disposable cameras to a random subset of respondents and asking them to take pictures of the people, situations, and objects in their daily environment that, to them, seemed "American" and those people, situations, and objects that seemed "Latino." We developed and analyzed the resulting photographic images to discover the content and meaning of the two identities as seen through immigrant eyes.

Identity Through Immigrant Eyes

To set in motion our visualizing methodology, we chose a 10 percent systematic sample of the qualitative interviews by giving two disposable cameras to every tenth person on our list. A total of sixteen respondents

Table 8.1   Characteristics of Sample for Study of Visual Representations
of Latino and American Identity

Characteristics	Photographer Sample	Total Ethnographic Sample
Generation		
First	40.0%	69.4
Second	60.0	30.6
National origin		
Mexican	60.0	34.4
Caribbean	0.0	24.4
Central or South American	40.0	41.3
Gender		
Male	50.0	41.9
Female	50.0	58.1
Place		
New York	20.0	29.4
New Jersey	40.0	36.3
Philadelphia	40.0	34.4
Sample size (N)	10	160

Source: Immigrant Identity Project (Office of Population Research 2009).

were given the two cameras, each of which contained twenty-seven exposures. One of the cameras had LATINO written on it, and the other was
labeled AMERICAN. Respondents were asked to take pictures of whatever they saw in their daily lives that, to them, seemed to be "Latino" or
"American." They were told to take as many pictures as they wished, up
to the maximum number of exposures on the camera. No further instruc-
tions were issued.

Of the sixteen respondents selected to participate in the photographic
study, ten returned cameras to us, for a response rate of 62.5 percent.
Table 8.1 shows selected characteristics of the final sample of ten photographers compared with the full ethnographic sample of 159 respondents.
Compared with respondents on the sampling frame, those in the photographic subsample were disproportionately of the second generation (60
percent versus 31 percent), and Caribbean respondents were entirely ab-
sent, with their share being made up by Mexicans. Females were slightly
overrepresented (58 percent compared with 40 percent on the sampling
frame), but the distribution of photographers by place roughly paral-
leled that on the frame (allowing for minor departures owing to small
numbers). What the resulting photographs yield, therefore, are the visualized perceptions of a small sample of first- and second-generation
Mexicans and Central and South Americans living in the New York–to–
Philadelphia urban corridor.

Whereas ten respondents returned the Latino camera, only seven turned in American cameras, suggesting that respondents found it more difficult to conceptualize an American than a Latino identity. The three people who did not return American cameras included a second-generation Colombian from New York, a second-generation Mexican from New Jersey, and a first-generation Ecuadoran from New Jersey. Only one respondent used all of the exposures available, and even this person wasted several shots that could not be used because of over- or underexposure or blurriness. In total, the ten Latino cameras provided 134 usable, unique images, and the seven American cameras provided 115 such images.

The photographs were scanned, digitized, and shrunk to a size that enabled each photographer's American or Latino photographs to fit on a single page for easy viewing and comparison, although the photos of the one photographer who shot out both rolls had to be displayed on two pages. Looking over the pictures, it quickly became apparent that a salient feature of their composition was the extent to which they focused on people versus things. We therefore went through the images systematically and coded them according to whether, in our judgment, the primary subject of the photo was a person or people. Thus, a street scene that contains people but does not focus on any particular person or identifiable individuals was coded as focusing on the place rather than on people. However, we did code for which images contain any people versus no people whatsoever.

We also carefully examined the Latino and American images separately to discern key themes and salient motifs. Prominent among the Latino images were pictures of Latin American businesses, places of work, homes, and cars, with some references to gang symbols, Latin cultural products, and schools. The leading categories of content that emerged from the American images were marriage to a white American, monumental architecture, street scenes, cars, and American icons, with less frequent references to schools, commercial displays, and waste or abandonment.

After carrying out our content analysis, as a final step we returned to the photographers to interview them about the content of the pictures they had taken and to ask them to explain why they had picked specific images, locations, or themes. Given that ten to eleven months elapsed between when the cameras were turned in and when we sought the re-interviews, we were unable to locate many of the original respondents. In the end, we successfully located and re-interviewed five of the ten original photographers: a second-generation Mexican female and a second-generation Peruvian female from Philadelphia; a first-generation Ecuadoran male and a second-generation Mexican male from New Jersey; and a second-generation Colombian male from New York.

Table 8.2   Components of Latino Identity Coded from "Latino" Pictures Taken by Ten Respondents in the Photographer Sample

Content Categories	Number	Percentage
Primary subject		
People	83	61.9
Facial close-up	10	7.5
Places or objects	51	38.1
No people at all	41	30.6
Prominent themes		
Interior of Latin business	35	26.1
Places of work	31	23.1
People at work	8	6.0
Latin store front	19	14.2
Interior of home	10	7.5
Display of gang symbols	8	6.0
Latin products	6	4.5
Contains cars	27	20.1
Taken from cars	5	3.7
School settings	7	5.2
Total number of images	134	100.0

Source: Authors' content analysis of photographs taken by photographer sample.

Picturing Latino Identity

Table 8.2 offers a content analysis of Latino identity discerned from our systematic inspection of the 134 Latino images in the data set. The top panel shows the breakdown of images by whether the subject of the photo is a person or people versus places or objects. In conceptualizing Latino identity, our photographers were clearly more people-focused: 62 percent of the images have people as their primary subject matter. Latino identity thus appears to be viewed as constructed through interrelationships with people. The fact that 7.5 percent of the images consist of a facial close-up suggests that the interpersonal construction of identity is often personal and intimate. Only 38 percent of the images focus on places or objects, most of which (31 percent) contain no discernible person anywhere in the photo.

To gain additional insight into the importance of social elements in the perception of Latino identity, we asked the photographers to explain why people, faces, and close-ups appear so frequently in their pictures. In response, one of them, a second-generation Peruvian, said: "Well, I think it is because it's our identity, our . . . as we see ourselves, we Hispanics have our differences from the Americans—we are of different colors, of different faces, different this and that . . . but this is how we see ourselves."

Another one of the photographers, a second-generation Mexican from New Jersey, had strong opinions on the subject of why there were so many people in his pictures:

RESPONDENT: Oh, one could think of many reasons. Perhaps because Hispanics or Latinos are there to see. Wherever you look, there are Hispanics, I would say. In other words, the photo reflects the Latino community a lot. Americans . . . are busy in offices, here or there, and the photo very much....

INTERVIEWER: Maybe for Latinos it's just easier to take photographs of each other.

RESPONDENT: Yes, because they [the Americans] are also going places, whereas Latinos . . . wherever you go, there they are. Wherever you go to take a photo, there is one, two, or three Latinos. . . . Or wherever you see something written in Spanish, you always encounter some Latinos. Yes, because, well, Latinos like being where other Latinos are. Photo or no photo . . . whatever, whenever you see one, you see another. . . . Latinos here are very open. If you say "I want to take your picture," they say, "Okay."

INTERVIEWER: Right away . . .

RESPONDENT: But Americans ask, "What for?" And they make questions: "What is this?" "Am I going to be in a book?" They ask questions because they watch themselves a lot—their identities—they watch themselves.

INTERVIEWER: Yes.

RESPONDENT: But Hispanics, what do they do? They say, "Okay, taking the photo is fine." Without giving it a thought, because that is how Latinos are. They are . . . they give . . . they offer, well, whatever they have.

When asked specifically about close-ups, this is what another photographer, a first-generation Ecuadoran from New Jersey, had to say:

Well, in reality, all the photos are of faces. What happens is that Hispanics have a spark of happiness, no? A smile, right? This is the difference between Hispanics and Americans. For example, if you take a photo of a Latino, he smiles, but he doesn't smile with a feigned smile, or a passing smile . . . it's different. I imagine it's because of . . . their way of life. I don't

know. Because we have different lives. They live one way, we live another.

When we posed the question about the prevalence of people in the
Latino pictures to the Mexican photographer from Philadelphia, we got
a similar response:

> Okay, for sure life here in the United States is very different from what we
> experienced in Mexico and, I imagine, other Latin American countries.
> There, family relations are very strong, from infancy until old age, one
> could say. The family is very united and experiences a lot of closeness.
> Families at times have many members, um, and live in rather close quar-
> ters for a family of eight or nine members. And this has a psychological
> effect that makes us more sociable, more spontaneous, and more open to
> communication. Perhaps for this reason, therefore, we wish to take pic-
> tures of people to demonstrate Latin American identity.

Besides people, another image that frequently appears in the Latino
photos (26 percent of the total) is the interior of a business oriented toward Latin American consumers or products, such as a store specializing in Latin music, a supermarket selling Latin American food products,
or a Mexican restaurant. Indeed, one photographer took all of his Latino
pictures in the Ecuadoran restaurant where he worked, and another shot
many pictures inside the Latin music store where he was employed.

Two examples of this genre are shown in figure 8.1. In the top photo,
a group of high school cheerleaders, all apparently Latino, pose in an
Ecuadoran restaurant while waiting for their food. (Their drinks, notably all Coca-Colas, have already been served.) In the bottom photo, four
Latinos pose inside a Camden, New Jersey, store specializing in Mexican
cultural products. (Note the sombreros, cowboy boots, and piñata in the
background.) These images suggest that food constitutes a salient characteristic of Latino identity, an emphasis that was indeed highlighted by
our interviewees in the last chapter.

Another, somewhat overlapping category of photographs focus on
places of work in the United States, including a parking garage, a market, and various stores and restaurants. This content category constituted 23 percent of the images, with 6 percent focusing on a specific person working or posing at his or her job. The top photo in figure 8.2, for
example, shows the interior of a parking garage in Manhattan where one
respondent worked as a valet, and the bottom shows a Latin American
female migrant working as a dishwasher in a New Jersey restaurant.

Work-related images emerged as one of the most important and significant themes in our ethnographic interviews as well. As we noted in
the last chapter, work is a principal attraction for Latin American mi-

Figure 8.1   Two Latino Images of Businesses Oriented Toward Latin
American Consumers

Source: Photos taken by photographer sample.

Figure 8.2   Two Latino Images of Workplaces in the United States

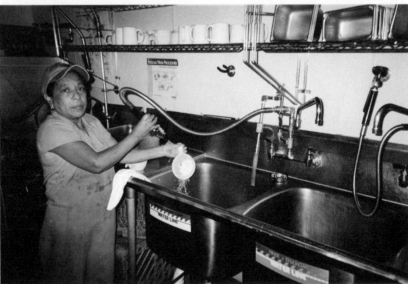

Source: Photos taken by photographer sample.

grants, and getting ahead economically thus appears to be a core feature of Latino identity in the United States. This view was confirmed by the photographers themselves when they were asked to comment on the salience of work sites in their pictures. According to a young male Mexican photographer from New Jersey:

RESPONDENT: Yes, it's true the Latino community is closely associated with work.

INTERVIEWER: And the photos that you took, what do you think of them? What is it that the photos, for you, show about Latino identity?

RESPONDENT: Well, the first thing that occurs to me is that we like to work hard. It doesn't matter if you wash glassware or if it's a task where you hardly use English. Um, in this photo, which is one of the ones I like best because the woman in the photo, who I know very well, has worked at this place since it opened, from when the bread counter was first opened, and now she's been here four, five years and . . .

INTERVIEWER: And she still washes glassware?

RESPONDENT: She's still washing glassware. She is very, the woman is . . . I tell you there aren't many opportunities for those who don't speak much English. Then they have to do . . . this, like I'll tell you.

INTERVIEWER: The problem . . .

RESPONDENT: No, the problem is the English. But they value their work. It doesn't matter what work, because here, without work, one does not get ahead. There's no money. And if there's no money, there's nothing for rent or for bills. Therefore, here, in these photos, it clearly shows that it's not important if they don't know English—but never, never do they stop working . . .

INTERVIEWER: Working.

RESPONDENT: . . . Because this country is pure work. It goes on and on here. Until this very moment, it goes on and on.

This sentiment was consistent with the views of another photographer, a second-generation Colombian male from New York who, when asked about the prevalence of work in his pictures, said:

Well, you know, like, more than anything, as you yourself said, it is [the] way people are, especially in this place. You know, like Latinos, you know, we are seeking ways of, of moving forward. More than anything through

work. Here [in work] is much, you know, that is Latino, or at least something Latino that tries to accommodate, you understand, as best one can
. . . and more than anything in work. Understand?

A related category, making up 14 percent of the total number of images, is Latin American storefronts: pictures taken from the street or
sidewalk in front of businesses that advertise Latin American products
or contain signs marketing to Spanish speakers. Nearly all of the Latino
photos taken by one respondent were of this type. A good example is
shown in the top of figure 8.3. It depicts a store recently opened in South
Philadelphia's Italian Market called La Tienda Mexicana Lupita (Lupita's Mexican Market) and features a replica of the Mexican flag in the
top-right corner. The bottom image shows the offices of an income tax
office whose signs are all in English, suggesting a predominantly Anglo
clientele, but a prominent yellow sign on the front reading HISPANIC
YELLOW PAGES can also be seen, suggesting some effort at marketing to
Latinos.

Cars frequently appear in the Latino pictures (in some 20 percent),
though mostly they are in the background of posed shots or they are in-
cidental objects (parked or moving) within larger landscapes. With one
exception (a photo of his own car taken by one respondent), they do not
appear to be the focus of attention. Very few pictures (just 4 percent)
were taken from the window of a car, a shot that, as we shall see, was
common among the American photos. A relatively small number of photos were taken in school settings, and just a few show Latin American
cultural objects or products, such as Goya-brand canned goods lined up
on a market shelf, plantains sitting in a bin, a Peruvian embroidery de-
picting a llama, and a man playing a Spanish guitar.

In addition to these images of Latino identity affirming the importance of family, work, and cultural icons, some of the photographs contain references to youth gangs. For example, eight of the Latino photos (6
percent of the total) contain gang images, in the form of either hand signals or graffiti. Thus, the top image of figure 8.4 shows the younger
brother of one respondent flashing gang signs to the photographer, a
person who himself was a former member of a gang known as the Latin
Kings. The bottom panel shows gang tags spray-painted onto the side of
a building as graffiti.

Although they make up a small minority of the images that our respondents perceived as Latino, the mere presence of gang symbols suggests that an "oppositional" identity is within the realm of possible
selves for the children of immigrants seeking to make sense of the United
States. Significantly, all the images of gang symbols were taken by members of the second generation. Nonetheless, respondents who referred to
gang imagery in pictures or interviews were usually full-time students

Figure 8.3   Two Latino Images of Latin American Storefronts

Source: Photos taken by photographer sample.

Figure 8.4   Two Latino Images of Gang Symbols

or workers, not delinquents, suggesting that gangs function less as an oppositional identity than as a source of social support and identity, what Portes and Rumbaut (2001) would call a reactive identity.

Consider, for example, the following interview conducted with a member of the Latin Kings, who was a second-generation Colombian from New York:

INTERVIEWER: Do you want to tell me a little about the Latin Kings?

RESPONDENT: Yes, for example, it is a gang that here, only in Queens, has around six thousand members.

INTERVIEWER: And they are of all ages?

RESPONDENT: Of all ages, of all ages. There are little kids of eleven or twelve years. Ten years old, but you see ten-year-olds with people who, you know, don't look like kids, who look older and, like, live on the street. Well, there are at least six thousand or seven thousand members in Queens, without counting the Bronx and Manhattan, who get together every two, like I told you, every two months on the fourteenth to see, you know, about problems with different gangs and all that.

INTERVIEWER: Hmmm.

RESPONDENT: Nowadays, for example, to be a Latin King you need to be working or studying.

INTERVIEWER: Aha!

RESPONDENT: And when they are minors, they have to be studying, you know. But not only that. Always if you go to an older gang leader, the leader always asks you with the psychology of an older boss why you want to join the Latin Kings, what attracts you, and if you say you want to join to meet more women and know more people, you won't be admitted. There has to be a reason like to feel protected, to feel backed up, to help ourselves as Latinos. Well, this is the only option for us, that we help and support one another to be all we are.

INTERVIEWER: And now tell me something: is there a way or a sign, you might say, that, for example, helps you find jobs for one another? Is there such a thing?

RESPONDENT: Yes, that's it. We help each other, yes, yes, to look for work and more than anything to make contacts to get ahead, you understand me. Not, as I tell you, not everyone is like this, but the majority, we help each other, though there are a few who are into drugs or doing bad things. But as I already said, that depends on you. If you want to progress and advance, you go to your contacts or friends and you get ahead.

This view of gangs as a social support system and a source of identity within the United States was consistent with the views of the photographers themselves. When asked to explain the pose of the gangster or rapper shown in figure 8.4, the photographer put it this way:

RESPONDENT: Like I told you before, you know, I like it that Latinos understand what's going on here, you know, with the friendships and everything.

INTERVIEWER: Hmmm . . .

RESPONDENT: With my brother . . .

INTERVIEWER: Hmmm . . .

RESPONDENT: . . . It might be that we just dress ourselves like that, you understand? You know, we make up ourselves, not really to demonstrate that, you know, we are gangsta or anything that, but in the sense that, you know, that we like the music more than anything else. Because apart from this . . .

INTERVIEWER: Hmmm . . .

RESPONDENT: . . . That my brother, you know the one in the photo you selected . . .

INTERVIEWER: Aha.

RESPONDENT: More than that, he is my brother. He is, you know, he wants to be a musician, understand.

INTERVIEWER: Ah, okay.

RESPONDENT: For this reason, I took this photo to, you know, inspire him, you know, to come out like posing with his hairdo and all. Understand?

Nonetheless, other respondents in the broader qualitative sample recognized the downside and dangers of gangs and the "gangsta" lifestyle. As a second-generation Mexican from New York reported:

One year I stayed in the street. I was fifteen. Started out at thirteen. Finished. Got out of gangs by the age of sixteen. Yes. I know how it is, I think that each child, each young person, passes through a phase where he wants to know what it is to be popular, what it is to be around a bunch of people, you know, not knowing their intentions until you actually go with them. And now I realize, you know, I think I exceeded the statistics for my age, and for my . . . for my kind. For my kind, specifically speaking, and those statistics for another state, the state of California in Los Angeles primarily, kids my age, most likely have been arrested, are fathers, have kids, have bad influences . . . or are dead.

The use of slang also appears to be an important element of self-identification for second-generation Latino youth. According to one second-generation Mexican from New Jersey who has relatives on the West Coast:

Yeah, a lot of it is different languages—not different languages, but different slang. Like, we have a difference like "este." I have a cousin, and he'll be coming over here, and we'd be fighting 'cause "este" not fighting, but like "hablando asi," we talk different [using slang]. We talk different, like saying "cool" to them is like saying "bad" for us, is like, "Yeah, let's . . . let's go ganging."

In addition to slang, second-generation Latinos like to cultivate a certain look. As one of the photographers from New York put it:

RESPONDENT: Um, you know, the posturing, like I told you, is a form of expressing yourself, understand? You know, um . . . here, in my neighborhood, um, the truth is that, as they say, we Latinos have a look. And more than this, a way of thinking and everything . . .

INTERVIEWER: Yeah.

RESPONDENT: . . . A way of expressing oneself with signs and hand signals, understand?

INTERVIEWER: Hmmm. Or like, it's a style that predominates among young people, basically?

RESPONDENT: Yes, more than anything, yeah, young people it might be.

INTERVIEWER: Okay, and in the way you placed your fingers, does this have a precise meaning or is it simply a style like any other?

RESPONDENT: Um, more than anything, for example, when one has a group, a group of, of, like I said, the group in which we are members, which is the Latin Kings.

INTERVIEWER: Ah, you told me about the Latin Kings....

RESPONDENT: Uh huh.

INTERVIEWER: . . . And that maybe the hand signals is a little of this, a code of the Latin Kings.

RESPONDENT: Uh huh, yeah. It's the "Crown of Kings." When the fingers are positioned in that way, it is, more than anything, to identify oneself to everyone else as a member of the group.

Picturing American Identity

Table 8.3 presents a content analysis of the "American" photos. In contrast to the Latino images, more than two-thirds (70 percent) of the American photos focus on places or objects. Whereas 62 percent of the Latino images have people as the primary subject, only half as many (30 percent) of the American images do so. Moreover, whereas ten of the Latino images consist of a facial close-up, none of the American images provide a close-up shot of a face. Just as we saw from the interviews, compared to the intimate and rather personalized basis for the construction of Latino identity, immigrants seem to perceive American identity as rather impersonal and distant. Indeed, almost half of the American images (48 percent) are entirely bereft of human beings, and around 9 percent are anonymous, empty street scenes. As a second-generation male Mexican photographer from New Jersey said when asked why his scenes all included objects but no people: "Those objects are something, for example, you see something American, say, and fix on a skyscraper, a building, a sports car . . . because that is what identifies an American. He has goods. He has money."

Two examples of the impersonal nature of the imagery submitted as emblematic of American identity are shown in figure 8.5. The top image shows a collection of newspaper boxes on an empty street corner in the center of Philadelphia, and the bottom one shows an empty walkway near a high-rise apartment complex within an affluent neighborhood of the city. The image of the newspaper boxes sitting together symbolizes technology and the individualized, impersonal way in which news is delivered in the United States, in contrast to the plethora of newsboys and kiosks on the streets of Latin American cities. As Manuel Castells (2004) has pointed out, a characteristic of the information age is the rise of individualism in all its manifestations, a trend that is less a cultural phenomenon than it is an outcome of the material conditions of work in a post-industrial economy.

When we asked the photographer—a second-generation Mexican—to explain his choice of the newspaper boxes as his subject matter, he replied in this way:

Table 8.3   Components of American Identity Coded from "American" Pictures Taken by Seven Respondents in the Photographer Sample

Content Categories	Number	Percentage
Primary subject		
People	35	30.4%
Facial close-up	0	0.0
Places or objects	80	69.6
No people at all	55	47.8
Prominent themes		
Marriage to American	23	20.0
Monumental architecture	19	16.5
Anonymous street scenes	10	8.7
Contains cars	37	32.2
Taken from car	14	12.2
City or highway traffic	12	10.4
American symbol or icon	14	12.2
Commercial displays	10	8.7
Waste or abandonment	8	7.8
School settings	2	1.7
American products	1	0.9
Total number of images	115	100.0

Source: Authors' content analysis of photographs taken by photographer sample.

INTERVIEWER: What do you have to say about this image in which there appear all these newspaper boxes? You know this is supposed to be a perception of American identity.

RESPONDENT: For this very reason. Like I said, the place looked very American to me. More than the building [it] is that, by whatever building, there is always news. Americans keep themselves informed in this way.

INTERVIEWER: How would it be in your country?

RESPONDENT: You would have to go to a kiosk—if you could find one nearby. People are in the streets selling, but in Mexico only older people, those that have a business or who work in an office, are the ones who buy a newspaper to read. For those who ply the streets, for example, as a bricklayer or something, it does not matter if something is happening elsewhere. Their lives never change except at home and at work. Nothing more.

Figure 8.5   Two American Images of Emptiness in Public Space

Source: Photos taken by photographer sample.

The most common theme among the American images is the marriage of a Mexican woman to an American man, but the frequency of images associated with this theme is deceptive since one of the seven respondents chose to shoot all of his American pictures at a wedding. He followed the Mexican bride from home, through the ceremony, and into the reception and celebration, and he finished with the cutting of the cake and the toasts. Should we repeat this experiment in the future, we will probably instruct our photographers not to take more than two photos in any one setting so as to build more diversity into the resulting visual data.

Although a relatively large number of the Latino images contain cars, we have already noted that vehicles do not seem to be a particular focus of most of the shots. In contrast, not only are images containing cars more common among the American photos (32 percent), but the cars themselves play a more prominent role. A significant number of shots (12 percent) were taken from the window of a car, typically while it was in motion. Also relatively common (at 10 percent) are pictures of traffic in busy intersections or on highways.

The top of figure 8.6 shows an example of a within-car shot of traffic on a freeway, and the bottom shows a stationary shot of traffic crowded into a busy intersection. The prevailing sense one takes from these images and from the other car-related shots is of movement and motion. For Latin American immigrants, a predominant impression of the United States seems to be that it is a society on the move, one in which people rush around, on crowded streets and busy highways, and that much of life in the United States is seen through the window of a moving car. For our respondents, a key feature of American identity thus appears to be motion and speed, rather than time or living.

Whereas motion suggests spatial impermanence—Americans never staying too long in one place and life being a constant blur—another impression gleaned from the American photos is the sheer size and scale—the bigness—of American society. Some 17 percent of the American images focus on an example of monumental architecture, such as skyscrapers, the urban canyons formed by tall buildings, a Center City skyline, and a large neoclassical public building. Four examples of monumental American architecture are shown in figure 8.7. In these images, clearly the individual is reduced to insignificance in comparison to the object under scrutiny; the human scale is minimal in contrast to the monumental scale of the constructed environment. The photographers appear not to have seen themselves as users of the space. The huge edifices are monuments to observe, not buildings with functions to be utilized.

Around 12 percent of the images take as their subject a distinctly American symbol or icon, such as the American flag, a jack-o-lantern, a jar of peanut butter, or an image of a famous celebrity. Figure 8.8 presents two images from this category. The top one shows a private porch in front of a Philadelphia row house containing an Uncle Sam figure hold-

Figure 8.6   Two American Images of Cars and Traffic

Source: Photos taken by photographer sample.

Figure 8.7   Four American Images of Monumental Architecture in the United States.

Source: Photos taken by photographer sample.

ing the American flag. The bottom picture shows a sidewalk display of mannequins in front of a store, featuring the young Elvis Presley. It is hard to conceive of two more American icons than the flag and Elvis. As the photographer of the icon pictures said: "The people of the United States have heroes. They like to have heroes; they like to adore them and to have symbols, up to the point where they are manipulated by the media using these heroes. Many or most times, these heroes are part of the economy, part of the social system, and through them a large number of people can be controlled or managed, as with Elvis."

The last two themes that emerged from the American images were those of commerce or enterprise (9 percent) and waste or abandonment (8 percent). Several of the pictures (around 9 percent) contain a visible manifestation of commercial spirit. As shown in figure 8.9, two of our photographers independently selected dollar discount stores as emblematically American subject matter. The flip side of a market economy, of course, is "creative destruction"—the abandonment of old products and structures and their displacement with new and improved products offered by the market. Eight of the images, two of which are shown in figure 8.10, focus on some aspect of waste or abandonment. The top image shows an abandoned building that is partly collapsed, and the bottom one shows unwanted consumer products left curbside for pickup on garbage collection day. The discarded products include a personal computer, a turntable, a tape deck, an amplifier-receiver, a kitchen cabinet, and a blue cooler. The juxtaposition of these two sets of images suggests that immigrants perceive Americans as competitive, high-level consumers, but also as wasteful people.

When asked about the dollar store picture, the photographer, a first-generation Mexican, responded:

RESPONDENT: Well, a dollar an item, that's ridiculous. As you can see, many times it couldn't pay for the materials the thing is made of, in other countries or here. If you want to produce some product for sale at a dollar, not even here in America can you pay for the material they're made from if you sell it for a dollar. The time . . . how much time are you going to use in making a tool, such as a hammer? The material, the metal, the transportation, the selling in the store. I don't know how this kind of store manages to sell it for a dollar.

INTERVIEWER: Then, from your point of view, a dollar does not represent the total value of the work?

RESPONDENT: No! It is a product of exploitation in other countries like China or India or some Latin American country that has created some kind of, you know, system of slave labor.

Figure 8.8   Two American Images of American Symbols or Icons

Source: Photos taken by photographer sample.

Figure 8.9   Two American Images of Commerce in the United States

Source: Photos taken by photographer sample.

Figure 8.10   Two American Images of Waste or Abandonment

Source: Photos taken by photographer sample.

When the same photographer was asked about the garbage picture , he said:

> Well, in this case everything would be used in Mexico. I mean, there everything has a great second use up to the point where it can no longer be used at all. But here, no. Here you find on the street or in trash cans all kinds of castoffs, which in truth do not deserve to be in the garbage. Rather, we call them castoffs because they are presently in the garbage, but they are things that still can function, or which still have much useful life ahead of them, be it furniture or real estate.

Contrasting Visions

Our experimental effort to determine how Latino and American identities are visualized by first- and second-generation immigrants to the United States yields visions of two very different kinds of identity. Our respondents apparently viewed American identity as having to do with bigness and power, as reflected by the phallic imagery of skyscrapers and other monumental buildings. Moreover, the images of cars and those taken from moving cars suggest that Americans are in constant motion and in a hurry; the photos of commercial symbols suggest that they are competitive and commercial; and the predominance of photos centered on places or objects rather than people, the shots of empty streets and walkways, and the lack of a single facial close-up suggests that they are cold, distant, and impersonal. Although these components of American identity may produce a wealthy and powerful society, they also yield much waste, as indicated by the photos of abandoned consumer goods and buildings, and impersonality, if the absence of people in the photos is any indicator.

In contrast, respondents viewed Latino identity as focused on people—who appear in a majority of the shots taken—and composed of intimate social relationships, as indicated by the frequency of facial close-ups among their photos and the relative absence of shots devoid of people. The building blocks of Latino identity in the United States, according to our respondents, appear to be work (the subject of nearly one-quarter of the photos), home (the shots taken in family settings), and Latin American cultural products (the many photos of businesses selling Latin American records, foods, and cultural products).

The generally warm and positive picture of a family- and culture-centered Latino identity is offset, however, by an awareness of a gang identity as an alternative way to be "Latino" in the United States. Two second-generation respondents included multiple shots of gang imagery in their photos, such as graffiti tags and hand signals. These images, however, made up a very small share of all those assembled, and gang identification seemed to be more of a reactive ethnicity undertaken for purposes of mutual support and solidarity than an oppositional identity geared toward criminal activity.

In general, the photographic images offered by our respondents suggest the construction of Latino identity through social links and interpersonal networks experienced predominantly through face-to-face interactions with other immigrants. In contrast, they see American identity in terms of abstract symbols and material objects and view U.S. society as focused on the individual and personal aspirations rather than on the group and social bonds of solidarity. These conclusions generally coincide with the broader literature on Latino identity, which views its construction as an affirmative response to the labels imposed by an increasingly hostile Anglo society (Gutiérrez 1995; Oboler 1995; Chavez 2008).

=Chapter 9=

Identity, Integration, and the Future

In this book, we have analyzed how immigrants living in the urban Northeast of the United States negotiate the social categories and manage the associated meanings that they encounter as they make their way through American society. We conceptualized assimilation and identity formation as a process of boundary-brokering and focused on how immigrants perceive and react to the boundaries that separate them from others in American life. To the extent possible, we have endeavored to let the immigrants speak for themselves, drawing on their own words and images to reveal how integration, adaptation, and identity appear to them. By learning how our respondents perceive American society and conceptualize their place within it, we have sought to open a window into the complex process of identity formation, allowing readers to gain a greater understanding of what the categories "Latino" and "American" mean to immigrants in the United States today. As social scientists, we hope our analyses will yield insights into how identity is constructed and elaborated by immigrants. As U.S. citizens, we hope that our work will help Americans appreciate the extent to which they themselves, through their own actions and inactions, place needless obstacles in the path of immigrant integration, with counterproductive results.

Constructing Immigrant Identity

Our analysis indicates that immigrant identity is actively "made in the USA" and not derived from an ancient set of values, sentiments, and practices imported from abroad or inherited from some mythical past. We argue that identities are constructed on an ongoing basis through the everyday interactions that unfold within the United States. These interactions reveal and over time define the categorical boundaries that define social groups such as "immigrants" and "natives." The processes that delineate boundaries and define identities are both psychological and social, and they may function either to blur or to brighten categorical divisions to make boundary-crossing easier or harder.

Psychologically, all human beings employ framing strategies that either reify or relax boundaries between social groups, and in so doing they either emphasize or obscure differences in the attributes assigned to group members. Socially, people undertake boundary work by engaging in practices that either promote contact and equal access to resources between groups or inhibit contact and skew access, once again serving to brighten or blur intergroup boundaries. Both immigrants and natives engage in framing and boundary work to advance their individual and group interests, of course, but given the asymmetries of power and wealth that prevail in the United States, the actions of natives generally have more weight in determining socioeconomic outcomes. By living in American society, immigrants discover the categorical boundaries and meanings that are imposed on them by natives and do the best they can to broker those boundaries and meanings in ways that enhance their well-being.

We have conceptualized the process of boundary-brokering as having three basic inputs: the characteristics and motivations of immigrants, the context of reception they encounter, and everyday interactions between immigrants and natives over time in different venues, such as work, school, stores, offices, and streets. After reviewing recent empirical and theoretical work on immigrant identity and assimilation, in the first chapter we introduced our ethnographic sample—159 first- and second-generation immigrants from fifteen nations in Central America, South America, and the Caribbean, from a variety of racial and ethnic origins, and running the gamut of skin tones from very light to very dark.

Contrary to the impression often given by the media, our respondents were generally not the poorest of the poor. They were not fleeing desperate circumstances at home, but came from the middle ranges of the class distribution in their origin countries. Most were gainfully employed when they left for the United States, and a significant share had a substantial education. Although some people were driven abroad by a sudden, acute financial need, most left as part of a deliberate, reasoned calculation that involved other household members. About one-third were induced to migrate by friends or relatives, either to reunify their family or to take advantage of the opportunities made available by network connections. Among those who left for economic reasons, some sought to pursue economic advancement in the United States, while others sought only to work in the United States temporarily to finance mobility at home. A majority of respondents hoped to return eventually and live in their country of origin, though the desire to return waned with increasing time spent in the United States.

Thus, the stereotype of poor Latin Americans desperately seeking to settle permanently in the United States does not hold, and the diversity of our respondents' motives complicates the boundary-brokering they undertake after arrival. The brokering of boundaries is also complicated by the racial diversity of Latino immigrants, both because racial prejudice and discrimination have not disappeared from American life and because race is conceptualized so differently in Latin America than in the United States. In Latin America, race is conceived as a continuum with multiple categories whose boundaries are blurred rather than bright, whereas in the United States race has historically been defined as a dichotomy with a very bright boundary between white and nonwhite.

After reviewing the characteristics and motivations that respondents bring to the brokering of boundaries in the United States, we considered recent economic, social, and political trends to evaluate the context of reception faced by immigrants. We documented the long-term rise in inequality and the stagnation of income for the middle classes, as well as more recent trends leading up to the economic collapse of 2008 to 2009. In addition to stagnating incomes, we detailed the rising debt, falling savings, increased interest payments, and declining insurance coverage that American households have experienced in recent decades, all of which contributed to a surge in bankruptcies. Congress tried to block this trend in 2006 by making it more difficult to file for bankruptcy, but the surge resumed anyway in the wake of the recent economic meltdown. During 2008 and 2009, GDP fell by the largest amount since the Second World War, and consumer confidence reached the lowest levels ever recorded.

These trends place the United States very far away from the non-zero-sum political economy that Alba (2009) posits as a crucial precondition for the large-scale assimilation of immigrants and boundary-crossing. Under current economic conditions, American natives are unlikely to perceive immigrants as complements rather than substitutes in the competition for material resources. Accompanying this deterioration in economic conditions has been an increasing tendency to frame Latinos as a threat to American society in newspapers, magazines, the broadcast media, the Internet, and academia. Policymakers have responded to the rising tide of economic insecurity and xenophobia by passing some of the most draconian anti-immigrant legislation in U.S. history and unleashing a wave of repressive police actions directed at foreigners. The United States is now arresting, detaining, and deporting more foreigners than ever before, and even legal immigrants have been systematically stripped of basic social and civil rights.

These trends add up to an extremely hostile context of reception in which immigrants must broker boundaries and advance their interests in the United States. To protect themselves from new penalties directed against noncitizens, documented Latin Americans are naturalizing in record numbers, even as undocumented immigrants continue to languish in supremely vulnerable and exploitable circumstances. The pressure on the undocumented is particularly relevant for Latin Americans, given their high rates of unauthorized status. Overall, 40 percent of Latin Americans in the United States are undocumented, but the figure exceeds 50 percent for Mexicans, Guatemalans, Hondurans, Salvadorans, and Brazilians. Never before have so many Latin American immigrants lacked legal protections in the United States.

This vulnerability quickly became evident in the stories that respondents told us about their experiences in the U.S. labor market. Most people worked in the lower end of the urban service economy in jobs characterized by long hours, low pay, no overtime, few benefits, and little opportunity for advancement in occupational status or earnings. The most common mobility outcome was stasis. A few people with documents and education were able to attain well-paid positions in the primary labor sector, and a few others were able to advance as ethnic entrepreneurs, but the large majority remained mired in a seemingly endless cycle of dead-end jobs in the secondary labor market. Our models have revealed few returns to education, experience, or English-language ability in terms of either wages or occupational status. Those respondents without documents, in particular, experienced significantly lower gains in occupational status in comparison to legal immigrants.

Our respondents' relative lack of progress in the U.S. economy is ironic given that most came to the United States with a firm belief in the American Dream of equal opportunity and individual advancement. As they gained more experience in the United States, however, they came personally to know discrimination and exclusion and began to appreciate the significant barriers to mobility they actually faced. Most respondents saw as much or more inequality in the United States as in their country of origin, and the large majority reported personal experiences of racial harassment and ethnic discrimination. Other things being equal, undocumented respondents perceived significantly less mobility in the United States than those with documents, and dark-skinned respondents were significantly more likely to perceive the United States as unequal.

Although transnational involvements were pervasive among our respondents, we found little evidence to suggest that they were a reaction to blocked opportunities in the United States. As predicted by Castells (2004), the large majority of our respondents remained in direct and frequent contact with friends and family members in their social networks, mostly via telephone but increasingly via the Internet as well. A majority of those we spoke to regularly sent back remittances to friends and relatives at home, even into the second generation. But in contrast to what one might expect from Castells (2004), transnationalism did not seem to be a resistance identity, but rather sui generis and independent of what happened to immigrants in the United States—behaviors that were intrinsic to the immigrant experience itself and unrelated to individual motivations, intentions, or perceptions. Remittances appear to be part of a socially binding implicit contract connecting migrants in the United States with their social relations at home, with few implications for patterns of integration, assimilation, or identity formation north of the border.

Instead, the construction of identity in the United States had more to do with what happened to respondents after they arrived in the country. We found that respondents from throughout Latin America quickly and readily embraced an emergent Latino identity. Coming from a region with common linguistic and cultural roots, and sharing the common fate of arriving in a foreign land and experiencing the hardships of survival in the secondary labor market, more than 80 percent of respondents said that they perceived the existence of a common Latino identity—a perception shared even by Portuguese-speaking Brazilians—and around 75 percent personally identified as Latino.

Whereas three-quarters of our respondents self-identified as Latino, only around one-third said they self-identified as American, either alone or in combination with a Latino identity. In addition, self-identification as Latino was unrelated either to experiences in the United States or to the characteristics of the interviewees themselves. It was an identity that naturally emerged across all respondents rather quickly after entry into the United States. In contrast, the expression of an American identity was highly contingent and strongly affected by personal circumstances and experiences in the United States. In contrast to the predictions of assimilation theory, the more time our respondents spent in the country as immigrants, the less likely they were to self-identify as American. Likewise, adherence to an American identity was negatively predicted by experiencing discrimination in the United States and by spending more hours in the labor market; this finding suggests that the rejection of American identity was a reactive response to experiences of prejudice and blocked mobility.

Thus, Latino identity seemed to arise emergently as people of diverse national origins but common roots naturally came together in response to shared experiences as immigrants. In contrast, American identity was rejected reactively in response to a difficult and hostile context of reception in the United States. This interpretation is consistent with the descriptions of the content of the labels "Latino" and "American" offered by respondents, who talked at great length about what these terms meant to them. In their verbal reports, respondents described Latinos as warm, lively, supportive, caring people who like to have a good time in one another's company; enjoy music, food, and dance; display intense loyalty to family and friends; and offer one another mutual support and solidarity. Americans were seen as the polar opposite: as cold, calculating, humorless, competitive, mercenary, exploitive, and prejudiced people who do not know how to enjoy food, music, dance, conversation, company, or life in its diversity.

The stark contrast our interviewees perceived between American and Latino identities was confirmed by our experiment in visual sociology. Randomly selected respondents were given disposable cameras labeled "Latino" and "American" and instructed to take pictures of people, objects, and situations in their daily lives that seemed to them to be Latino or American; the photographs that resulted echoed the contrasts emerging from the interviews. The images developed from the "Latino" cameras focused on work, home, food, music, and crafts, and most of the shots included people, who were typically smiling and apparently happy, with a significant number of facial close-ups. Numerous pictures were taken in ethnic restaurants, and there were also shots of storefronts of businesses catering to Latino clients. The close, person-oriented focus of these photos reflects the strong emphasis in Latino identity on people and social relations, and the shots of Latino businesses, restaurants, and cultural products emphasize the joy of experiencing these things in the company of others.

In contrast, the images developed from the "American" cameras focus on places rather than people. Numerous shots of skyscrapers and other monumental buildings suggest that our photographers viewed American identity as bound up in size and power; the proliferation of shots taken of and from moving cars suggests a people constantly in motion; and the images of commercial symbols suggest a society that is mercenary and competitive. The images of consumer goods left on the curb as garbage and of crumbled, abandoned buildings suggest a society seen as profligate and wasteful. The impersonal nature of American life is suggested by the numerous photos of empty streets, lonely corners, and walkways devoid of a human presence.

Two Scenarios for the Future

The United States stands at a historical crossroads with respect to Latin American immigration. Since 1965, we have made it increasingly difficult for Latin Americans to enter the United States as legal residents, even as we have promoted closer economic integration with our southern neighbors, especially Mexico under the North American Free Trade

Agreement (NAFTA) and with other countries more recently under the Central American Free Trade Agreement (CAFTA). Since 1986, we have militarized the Mexico-U.S. border in an effort to block unauthorized migration, but this effort reduced the outflow of migrants more than it lowered the inflow, and undocumented population growth actually accelerated. In 1996, the United States began to direct repressive police actions against immigrants living within the United States, and after 2001, arrests, detentions, and deportations of foreigners rose exponentially to reach record levels, even as the resources devoted to border enforcement also continued to expand at an unprecedented pace.

The economic collapse of 2008 thus occurred against a backdrop of four decades of increasing anti-immigrant and border enforcement, and the combination of rising joblessness and unprecedented official repression by 2008 finally brought undocumented migration to a halt. Although entries by undocumented migrants, both new and experienced, have ceased, those already present in the country without authorization are not departing. Indeed, rates of return movement by undocumented migrants stand at record low levels, yielding an undocumented population currently frozen at around 12 million persons, some 80 percent of whom are from Latin America.

A new presidential administration came to power in the United States in early 2009 with an explicit commitment to immigration reform and overwhelming support from Hispanic voters. In the face of widespread job losses and implacable opposition from nativist groups, however, the Barack Obama administration has not moved significantly toward immigration reform. Indeed, it has continued the Bush administration's hard line of strict internal and border enforcement while promising eventually to pursue broader reforms. For many years, opponents of immigration reform have insisted on the need to get the border "under control" before discussing options such as legalization, expanded quotas, and temporary worker programs. By 2008 we seemed finally to have reached that moment as new undocumented entries dropped to zero. Although the border for the present is "under control," what the future portends is not at all clear. What is clear is that we stand at a critical juncture in which American policy decisions—to maintain the status quo or to pursue substantive immigration reform—will push the United States along one of two very different pathways.

Maintaining the status quo would involve the increasing use of force against Latin American immigrants, both at the border and within the United States, and the continued restriction of legal avenues for entry. We already know where these policies lead: to the creation of a large underground population that remains detached from the mainstream of U.S. society, has few prospects for socioeconomic mobility, and is supremely vulnerable to exploitation. With no legal rights and under constant risk of deportation at a moment's notice, undocumented migrants are in no position to take action when employers violate fair labor standards, ignore occupational safety regulations, fail to observe tax-withholding requirements, break minimum wage laws, or subvert occupational health standards. They can neither complain when they suffer discrimination in housing markets, at places of business, or in public spaces nor seek justice when they are victimized by criminals who prey on their illegal status.

In a very real way, therefore, undocumented migrants and the people to whom they are related are at significant risk of becoming a new American underclass; this possibility has far-reaching implications not only for the immigrants themselves but for native American citizens. All U.S. citizens suffer when the existence of a vulnerable, exploitable population in U.S. markets puts downward pressure on wages and working conditions for all market participants and when the detachment of this population from health and human services promotes the spread of communicable diseases and the progression of medical conditions to acute stages that might otherwise have been easily and less expensively treated, thereby increasing the ultimate burden on taxpayers.

Perhaps the most vulnerable U.S. citizens are those who reside in households that contain one or more undocumented migrants. As already noted, around 12 million undocumented migrants currently reside in the United States, but more than 15 million persons live in undocumented families once we take into account the roughly 3 million children living in these households who are U.S.-born citizens. To the extent that the parents and older siblings of these newest citizens are detached from society and suffer discrimination and exclusion, these children also suffer from associated economic, social, and medical depredations.

In addition, among the 12 million undocumented migrants are at least 3 million people who entered the country as minors and are guilty of no sin except obeying their parents. Many arrived as babies, toddlers, or young children and know no country other than the United States. The overwhelming majority speak English, have graduated from high school or are on their way to doing so, and have no criminal history aside from immigration violations. Until the stigma of illegality is removed from their shoulders, however, they have nowhere to go in American society and no realistic possibility of mobility out of the secondary labor market, no matter what their ambitions and talents.

Thus, the potential size of the immigrant underclass is much greater than the 12 million people who are currently out of status; it includes not only their U.S.-born children but also the children of their foreign-born children who have come of age in the United States. The potential for future conflict is suggested by the reaction against constructing an

American identity the more time Latino immigrants spend in the United States. To date, this reactive anti-American identity does not seem to be paired with a transnational or Latino identity of resistance, as defined by Castells (2004). Although Latin American immigrants quickly subscribe to a Latino identity after arrival in the United States and make use of modern telecommunications to construct social networks and maintain contact with friends and family abroad, these activities are not pursued in reaction to negative experiences in the United States. Although the visualization of Latino identity did hint at the oppositional formation of gang identities, these were not widely represented or strongly rooted and appeared to be more social and stylistic than criminal in nature.

In other words, although the Latino immigrants we spoke to seemed to be well advanced in a process of identity formation that rejected the label "American" and thus positioned them categorically as outside the mainstream of U.S. society, they were not yet drawing on Latino or transnational identities as tools of resistance or points of mobilization to achieve political or programmatic ends in the United States. A Latino underclass has not yet formed, but this situation cannot be expected to last forever, and if an underclass scenario is to be avoided, U.S. policymakers need to implement several concrete policy changes very soon.

The most pressing need is for the creation of a path to legalization for undocumented migrants already present in the United States, many of whom by now have deep roots in American society. The systematic deportation of 12 million people is hardly realistic, much less humane, and the longer such a large population is allowed to languish outside the bounds of legal protection without civil, social, or economic rights, the deeper and more intransigent the problems the country will face. As already noted, of those presently unauthorized, at least 3 million entered the country as minors and thus cannot legitimately be held responsible for violating U.S. immigration laws. In the absence of a criminal record, therefore, undocumented migrants who entered as juveniles should be offered an immediate and unconditional amnesty so that they can get on with their lives in the only country they really know. The longer this action is put off, the worse off all concerned will be.

For those who became undocumented migrants as adults, the obvious solution is an earned legalization program. Whatever one's beliefs about the morality of an amnesty for people who knowingly broke the law, this is the only politically viable and practical option. An earned legalization would offer undocumented migrants a chance to register for temporary legal status, confer on them economic rights in the United States, and set forth a pathway by which they could earn permanent legal residence over a specified period of time. Points would be awarded for socially desirable behaviors or circumstances legitimately linking people to the United States, such as being gainfully employed, paying taxes, owning a home or business, having U.S.-born children, learning English, taking civics classes, doing volunteer work in the community, or whatever other action or outcome policymakers might deem worthy. After meeting some minimum threshold of points, migrants would become eligible for legal permanent residence and then, after paying a monetary fine to make amends for breaking the law, would be duly adjusted to legal status, having paid their debt to society.

Such a two-pronged legalization program would solve the immediate problem of regularizing a large undocumented population that is at risk of becoming a permanent underclass, but it probably would not solve the problem moving forward. Although undocumented migration to the United States may have ceased for the moment, at some point the U.S. economy will revive, the demand for immigrant workers will return, and one way or another the baby boomers will exit the labor force in large numbers. Now is the time, therefore, to build provisions into U.S. immigration law to enable the legal entry of Latin Americans at realistic levels, and nowhere is the need more acute than for Mexico.

Among all the nations that send immigrants to the United States, Mexico is clearly unique. It is the only developing nation to share a land border with the United States, and its history of migration to the United States is longer than any other nation's, extending back to the early twentieth century and occurring continuously since then except for a short break during the 1930s. Mexico has repeatedly been the target of labor recruitment from the United States, both official and unofficial, and it is currently linked to us by a well-established free trade agreement that has dramatically lowered the barriers to cross-border movements of all sorts, including goods, capital, commodities, information, services, and many kinds of people (investors, exchange visitors, corporate employees, business owners). Since NAFTA took effect, exchange visitors to the United States from Mexico have increased 2.2 times, business visitors 2.3 times, total trade 4.5 times, corporate visitors 5.5 times, and treaty investors 87 times (Massey 2010). Despite the high and growing degree of economic integration and Mexico's unique geographic and historical position with respect to the United States, that country receives the same number of legal permanent resident visas as any other nation. What is urgently needed is an increase in the number of legal immigrant visas accessible to Mexicans to something well above the 20,000 visas allocated to other countries each year—say, to 100,000 visas per year or more. This policy could also be applied to Canada.

Although legitimate demands for residence visas are inevitably created in the course of economic integration and free trade, most immigrants do not wish to settle permanently in the United States, at least initially. Most of the people we interviewed migrated to solve an economic problem at home and aspired to return to their sending community. For this reason, a large share of the demand for immigrant workers historically was met by making temporary work visas available to Mexicans. Such was officially the case from 1917 to 1929 and from 1942 to 1964, periods when the U.S. government itself sponsored guest worker programs. Rather than militarizing the border, therefore, a better strategy would be to accompany an expanded quota for legal immigrants with a generous temporary worker program that encourages circularity, thereby minimizing the social and economic costs to the United States while maximizing the social and economic benefits to Mexico. The current strategy of border militarization and internal repression has perversely had the effect of restricting rather than encouraging circularity.

Some observers see great potential for the future integration of immigrants in the aging of the baby boomers, which in theory should open many positions throughout the occupational structure to create new avenues of social mobility (Myers 2007; Alba 2009). Although the emergence of such a non-zero-sum economy may seem a distant hope given the current context of economic recession, financial crisis, and double-digit unemployment, it is nonetheless inevitable that the huge cohorts of workers born between 1947 and 1964 who flooded labor markets in the 1960s and 1970s will exit the labor market in growing numbers after 2015, through either retirement or mortality. If the unique generational opportunities offered by the aging of the baby boomers are to be realized, however, immigration reforms must soon be enacted, for the dividends will be difficult if not impossible to realize if millions of immigrants remain in the shadows, languishing in the no-man's-land of undocumented status.

Assimilation as a Two-Way Street

A long-standing debate among immigration researchers and the public has focused on whether assimilation constitutes a one-way movement of immigrants toward the host society or whether it involves shifts by natives as well as immigrants to create a common mainstream. We believe the evidence is clear that assimilation is a two-way street and, moreover, that American natives play a critical role in determining the direction and pace of immigrant adaptation, integration, and assimilation. Assimilation occurs and identities are constructed through an ongoing process of boundary-brokering in which immigrants arrive with their individual motivations, social expectations, and psychological framings and encounter natives, who have their own motivations, expectations, and framings, through a series of daily interactions that unfold over time. In the course of these interactions, intergroup boundaries are brokered and the content of categories negotiated in ways that either blur the boundaries between immigrants and natives to promote contact and exchange or brighten them in ways that make assimilation less likely.

Our results call into question older conceptualizations of assimilation as inevitable and linear. Clearly integration is contingent on the actions and beliefs of both immigrants and natives, but especially the latter because of their greater power and influence in determining the context of reception and the structural conditions that channel immigrant identification in a reactive or integrative direction. Our findings underscore the important role played by natives in shifting immigrant trajectories upward or downward, toward or away from the American mainstream. If Americans expect assimilation to occur and the United States to evolve as an integrated and coherent society, then U.S. citizens must be prepared to accept and indeed facilitate, through their individual actions and collective policies, the blurring of categorical boundaries between immigrants and natives.

Unfortunately, trends in public discourse and political action over the past two decades have worked, we believe, in the opposite direction, serving to brighten intergroup boundaries, heighten categorical divisions, and discourage the crossing of the social and psychological lines separating immigrants and natives. Our analysis here suggests that this anti-immigrant framing and boundary work have been counterproductive, yielding a reactive rejection of American identity by immigrants who otherwise would be disposed to believe and follow the American Dream. A majority of the immigrants we interviewed could describe one or more specific instances of discrimination or exclusion they had witnessed or experienced in the United States, and these people were especially likely to reject American identity.

The fact that a large share of immigrants experience discrimination and perceive the United States as biased and unfair and that these people are very likely to reject American identity suggests the potential for oppositional identity formation and segmented assimilation among immigrants today. Segmented assimilation is by no means a foregone conclusion, however, for in addition to the rejection of American identity and the perception of American society as cold, competitive, and calculating, we found ample evidence that Latin American immigrants are actively embracing an emergent Latino identity grounded in warmth, compassion, and mutual support.

The emergence of a Latino identity in the United States and a vibrant transnationalism in no way preclude the positive acceptance of American identity, and some respondents did indeed find a way to embrace both identities. The reluctance of these immigrants to self-identify as Americans had less to do with attachments to other Latinos or to ongoing connections with friends and relatives at home and more to do with their experiences in United States. It is really up to Americans to provide a welcoming context of reception as a basic precondition for successful integration and assimilation, a task at which we have unfortunately fallen short in recent decades as economic conditions have deteriorated, especially in the wake of the events of September 11, 2001.

The ongoing demonization of immigrants is paradoxically occurring during a time when globalization and transnationalism are ever more apparent. Although transnational attitudes and behaviors were common in the first era of globalization before 1914, today's transportation and communication technologies make transnationalism more ubiquitous and more dynamic than in the past. As we have seen, the vast majority of immigrants are in constant contact with friends and relatives abroad via telephone and increasingly via the Internet, and most also regularly remit money and send goods back as well.

What Americans need to understand is that these transnational actions and orientations in no way threaten American identity. Indeed, we found that those who regularly remitted funds abroad were *more*, not less, likely to adopt an American identity. Ironically, the greatest threat to the creation of a strong, vibrant, forward-looking American identity among immigrants comes not from immigrants but from American citizens themselves, who by embracing nativist ideas and promoting anti-immigrant policies harden the categorical boundaries that define immigrants and make integration more difficult and assimilation less likely. Immigrants inevitably must bear most of the burden in brokering boundaries within the United States, but we do not have to make it so difficult for them.

= Appendix A =
Sampling, Interviewing, Coding, and Data Analysis

Immigrant identity and assimilation have long been of core interest to social scientists, especially in the field of sociology. Indeed, within American sociology the systematic study of immigration goes back to the discipline's founding in 1892, with the creation of the nation's first department of sociology at the University of Chicago. Seminal figures in the emergent "Chicago School," such as Ernest Burgess, Robert Park, and Louis Wirth, were fascinated with the social and spatial assimilation of immigrants in industrial cities (Park 1928; Park, Miller, and Thompson 1921; Park and Burgess 1925; Wirth 1928, 1938). Their studies were self-consciously multi-method, drawing on qualitative data compiled from ethnographic fieldwork, archival sources, immigrant newspapers, and letters between immigrants and their families, as well as quantitative data compiled from the U.S. census, early social surveys, and other statistical sources.

After the Second World War, this multi-method approach continued to be used, except that sociologists focused less on immigrants and more on their children and grandchildren, studying their interactions, adaptations, and identity in urban America by using ethnographic methods (Whyte 1943; Gans 1962), quantitative analyses (Duncan and Lieberson 1959; Duncan and Duncan 1968; Lieberson 1963), and combinations of the two (Warner and Srole 1945; Glazer and Moynihan 1963; Gordon 1964). With the advent of high-speed computers, statistical sampling theory, and modern survey methods, however, the weight of research on immigration shifted in a quantitative direction during the 1970s (Massey 2001).

The result was a host of well-controlled studies of assimilation with respect to quantitative outcomes such as education, occupational status, income, English-language ability, residential integration, family structure, and fertility (for reviews of this voluminous literature, see Massey 1985; Waters and Jiménez 2005). It was mostly this body of work that led Richard Alba and Victor Nee (2003) to conclude that, despite challenges made by Nathan Glazer and Daniel Patrick Moynihan (1963), Michael Novak (1972), and others, massive assimilation on the part of third-generation European Americans was indeed a social and demographic reality.

Researchers also endeavored to use survey data and statistical methods to study the structure and determinants of immigrant identity (see Tienda and Ortiz 1986; Bean and Tienda 1987; Denton and Massey 1989; Waters 1990; Portes and Rumbaut 1990; Massey and Denton 1992). Whereas variables such as education, occupation, and income are straightforwardly measured using censuses and surveys (though not, of course, without error), identity is subjective, not readily observable, and therefore more difficult to analyze quantitatively. As a result, statistical studies of immigrant identity focused mainly on self-identification using various group labels and examined how labeling varied by generation, family circumstances, socioeconomic status, and residential location (Waters and Lieberson 1988; Waters 1990). Although quantitative studies of identity contributed importantly to the consensus that European assimilation was indeed widespread by showing that these labels were being combined in ever more complex and highly contingent ways, the data available from standard surveys offered little information on the actual content of the identities behind the labels.

To get at the subjective elements of assimilation and identity, during the 1990s social scientists returned to their roots in the Chicago School and began to draw more heavily on data from ethnographic fieldwork and qualitative interviews to produce a new generation of multi-method studies of the burgeoning communities of new immigrants from Asia, Latin America, and the Caribbean (Hondagneu-Sotelo 1994; Waters 1999; Portes and Rumbaut 2001; Rumbaut and Portes 2001; Kasinitz, Mollenkopf, and Waters 2004; Lee 2004; Smith 2006; Kasinitz et al. 2008). The present study seeks to build on this record of multi-method research by analyzing qualitative data gathered through in-depth ethnographic interviews to describe the construction of immigrant identity during a time of anti-immigrant mobilization.

Sampling

Our study was organized as a subproject of two larger, ongoing research projects: the Mexican Migration Project (see Durand and Massey 2004) and the Latin American Migration Project (see Donato et al. 2010), both of which were self-consciously designed to blend ethnographic and survey methods (see Massey 1987a; Massey and Zenteno 2000; Massey and Capoferro 2004). Initially developed by Douglas Massey and his colleagues (1987), the "ethnosurvey" approach combines intensive fieldwork in strategically chosen migrant-sending communities with representative sampling designs and semistructured interview methods to produce reliable, high-quality data on the patterns and processes of documented and undocumented migration to the United States.

The data emanating from these studies are freely available from the project websites (see http://mmp.opr.princeton.edu/ for the Mexican Migration Project and http://lamp.opr.princeton.edu/ for the Latin American Migration Project). Both data sets have supported numerous studies of immigrant departure, adaptation, and return, both quantitative (Massey et al. 1987; Massey, Durand, and Malone 2002; Durand and Massey 2004) and qualitative (Durand 1994, 1996, 2002; Durand and Arias 2000, 2005; Durand and Massey 1990, 1995). They have also been used extensively to study assimilation with respect to objective outcomes such as earnings (Massey 1987b; Donato, Durand, and Massey 1992; Donato and Massey 1993; Phillips and Massey 1999; Aguilera and Massey 2004; Aguilera 2005; Chiquiar and Hanson 2005; Livingston 2006; Gang and Yun 2008), labor force participation (Aguilera 2002, 2003), English-language ability (Espinosa and Massey 1997; McConnell and Leclere 2002; Gang, Bauer, and Epstein 2005), remittances (Massey and Basem 1992; Massey and Parrado 1994; Roberts and Morris 2004; Sana and Massey 2005; Amuedo-Dorantes and Pozo 2007; Amuedo-Dorantes, Bansak, and Pozo 2005; Quinn 2008), and residential location (Gang, Bauer, and Epstein 2007; McConnell 2008).

To this point, however, neither the MMP data nor the LAMP data have been used to study subjective dimensions of immigrant adaptation and integration such as identity. One reason for this gap is that ethnographic work in both projects has focused more on sending than receiving communities, yielding relatively little in-depth qualitative data about Latino immigrants living in the United States. Although teams of interviewers affiliated with each project did enter destination communities in the United States to gather data among settled immigrants, the duration of fieldwork was short and the emphasis was on the compilation of quantitative data. The current project on immigrant identity sought to redress the lack of in-depth information on immigrants residing in the United States.

Our original plan was to study whether the construction of immigrant identity conforms to the postulates of classic assimilation theory, segmented assimilation theory, or transnational theory. The plan was conceived in late 2000 and first proposed for funding in early 2001, well before the events of September 11 and the hardening of public policies and attitudes against immigrants. After several revisions, the project was finally funded in 2002, and the bulk of the fieldwork was done in 2003, with fieldwork ending in January 2004. By then, the tenor of the times had changed, and the focus of inquiry became the brokering of categorical boundaries in anti-immigrant times.

The project design called for recruiting a quota sample of first- and second-generation immigrants in the urban corridor that stretches from New York City through New Jersey to Philadelphia. Although New York and its suburbs in northern New Jersey are traditional immigrant gateways of long standing, Philadelphia and its suburbs in southern New Jersey also began to receive significant migration from Mexico, Central, and South America during the 1980s, and there had been a relatively small flow of Puerto Ricans into the area during the 1950s and 1960s. Our sampling quotas were defined by the cross-classification of location (Philadelphia, New Jersey, and New York), origin (Caribbean, Mexican, Central American, South American), and generation (first or second), yielding a 3×4×2 social space of twenty-four cells. Within each cell, we sought to compile ten interviews roughly balanced between males and females, for a target of 240 interviews. We tried to recruit mostly young immigrants, between the ages of thirteen and thirty-five, though we did not exclude those who fell outside these bounds.

Owing to funding limitations and a shortage of field interviewers, in the end we were able to conduct interviews with only 159 first- and second-generation immigrants, about two-thirds of the original target. In New Jersey we focused our recruitment activities on the towns and cities lying along the dense urban axis that stretches between New York and Philadelphia. Fieldwork began in Philadelphia and then moved northward through New Jersey to progressively incorporate Camden, Trenton, Princeton, New Brunswick, Newark, Kearney, and finally New York City.

Within each of the two anchor cities, we recruited widely, incorporating respondents from four of New York's five boroughs (Manhattan, Queens, Brooklyn, and the Bronx) and all of Philadelphia's traditional residential areas (North Philly, South Philly, West Philly, Center City, and the Northeast). For our purposes, we labeled as second-generation those who were born abroad but who arrived before age thirteen and grew up in the United States, a class of people whom Rubén Rumbaut (1991) has labeled the 1.5 generation.

Interviewing

The fieldwork was directed by Magaly Sánchez, who supervised the compilation of the sample and conducted interviews along with two bilingual assistants, one a native of Venezuela and the other a native of Mexico. Sánchez, who is herself Venezuelan, speaks Portuguese in addition to Spanish and English, and that enabled us to include several Brazilians in the sample.

The dynamics of fieldwork proceeded in four basic phases:

1. *The contact phase.* The first phase was the contact phase. Field investigators went to neighborhoods that displayed a visible Latino presence, as indicated by the dress and bearing of the people on the streets, the presence of Latino-oriented businesses, the display of Spanish-language signs, and other symbols of Latin American settlement.

Within such settings, contacts were established in two ways. *Street contacts* were established in public spaces by exchanging glances, engaging in friendly conversations, and making a sympathetic and inviting self-presentation. *Institutional contacts* were established in various contexts away from public streets, including restaurants, stores, and cafés that catered to a Latino clientele, public conveyances such as buses and subways, and various nongovernmental organizations such as health clinics, Latino cultural centers, and neighborhood schools. Institutional contacts proved to be essential in reaching members of the second generation, whereas most first-generation contacts were made on the street or at workplaces such as restaurants and shops.

In our initial encounters with immigrants, we discovered that the Spanish word for research—*investigación*—carried menacing connotations for many of them and generated the mistaken impression that we were working with U.S. immigration authorities on an official "investigation." Therefore, we reformulated our approach to say simply that we were gathering information to write a book about Latino identity in the United States and that we defined the term "identity" as how people feel or identify themselves as Latino in the United States, in their home country, and in moving back and forth between the two places.

All of the first-generation adults were over the age of eighteen, and we arranged interviews directly with them. Although most of those in the second generation were also adults, some were still under eighteen at the time of the interview, and for these interviews we obtained parental permission. As with our adult interviewees, we explained the purpose and nature of the interview to the parents of these minors and gave them an information sheet (discussed later). Our youngest respondent was thirteen years old. Although we gained parental permission to conduct interviews with minors, we did ask the parents not to be present during the interview so as not to influence their children's responses. Separating young people from their parents gave these second-generation respondents greater latitude to express themselves freely and to opine candidly on the various topics covered in the questionnaire.

2. *The ingratiation phase.* After the initial contact came the second phase of recruitment, the ingratiation phase. In this phase, field-workers sought to build trust and cultivate relationships with prospective respondents. We offered letters of introduction and identification to con-

firm both our identities and our institutional affiliation. We also described the project and its goals and emphasized the importance of each and every person's views on the subjects of interest to us. Appendix B shows the English and Spanish versions of the information sheet that we gave and explained to each prospective respondent. As can be seen, the sheet briefly described the purpose and nature of the study, named the institutional sponsor, assured each respondent of confidentiality, and provided information on how to contact project investigators with questions or concerns.

3. *The interview phase.* Occasionally contact, ingratiation, and interviewing followed in close succession because a respondent expressed a desire to go on to the third phase immediately and be interviewed then and there. When this happened, we made every effort to accommodate the respondent; the main logistical problem was locating a quiet corner in which to converse at length. Sometimes a table in a café served the purpose, and at other times we sought out a bench in a quiet corner of a public park or square. In most cases, however, the ingratiation phase ended with the exchange of contact information such as telephone numbers and e-mail addresses and an agreement to make arrangements for a later interview.

4. *The networking phase.* In the final phase of recruitment, the networking phase, field-workers gathered contact information for other potential interviewees by identifying eligible people in the respondent's social network. We then sought out and approached these people, once again launching the cycle of contact, ingratiation, interviewing, and networking.

The project was presented to potential respondents as a study of Latino identity that was based at the University of Pennsylvania (the authors' home institution at the time) and designed to learn the opinions of Latin Americans living in the United States so as to derive an accurate picture of the circumstances under which they lived. We emphasized that we were interested in the views of second- as well as first-generation immigrants and that the study was focused on urban areas in the northeastern United States. Naturally, upon first approach, many respondents were somewhat suspicious, especially if they lacked legal documents, but once we succeeded in communicating who we were and the purpose of the project, the doubts usually gave way to a smile and we were allowed to proceed. The biggest problem was locating a block of time to do the interview given that most respondents, especially those in the first generation, were burdened with a heavy workload seven days a week. Despite the time constraints and other logistical difficulties, we experienced only three refusals once initial contact was established.

Each interview was taped, with the permission of the respondent, using an unobtrusive digital micro-recorder. The conversations followed one of two semistructured interview guides tailored either to first- or second-generation immigrants. Most of the interviews were conducted in Spanish, but a few were done in English or Portuguese. Appendix C contains the interview guide in Spanish and English for first-generation immigrants, which begins with an abbreviated life history and then moves on sequentially to discuss respondents' motivations for coming to the United States, their use of social networks in making the move, their perceptions about identity and belonging, the nature of their work and experiences on the job, their participation in transnational activities, their values and aspirations in the United States, and their perceptions about discrimination and inequality in the United States. Appendix D shows the interview guide in Spanish and English for second-generation immigrants, which covers the same basic set of topics but frames the questions differently to take account of the fact that the respondents grew up in the United States.

The content of both questionnaires was mostly set before the surge of anti-immigrant sentiment after September 11. The interview items were designed to address issues of identity in ways that might shed light on various theoretical issues related to immigrant identity and assimilation, not to elicit complaints about life in the United States. By the time we were doing our fieldwork, however, government policies and public attitudes toward immigrants had hardened and the economy had substantially deteriorated; over and over, the interviews began to highlight the struggles that immigrants were facing and the exclusion and hostility they perceived in the United States. The focus of this book on the construction of immigrant identity in anti-immigrant times thus emerged from the data itself, not from a preconceived ideological or theoretical view.

We did not consider interviews to be a one-way exchange in which immigrants passively provided us with information, but rather as an opportunity for an exchange of information between investigators and subjects. Although we did not pay respondents for their time, following the precepts of action research (Barbier 1996; Stringer 1999) we did offer to provide links to respondents that might prove useful for people in their circumstances, such as information about access to English-language instruction, free education centers, health clinics, city housing offices, labor rights offices, and various immigrant advocacy groups. In our experience, when respondents are paid, they tend to see the interview in instrumental terms as a commercial transaction rather than as a mutually beneficial exchange of information. Doing the interview for money rather than out of personal interest, curiosity, or generosity undermines the conversation as a give-and-take exchange between social equals and generally impedes honesty and the free flow of information.

Respondents generally enjoyed the opportunity to pause for a few moments in their busy lives to reflect on their status as first- or second-generation immigrants and to situate their experiences in a broader context. At the end of each interview, we asked respondents how they felt while doing the interview and whether they had anything to suggest. The responses suggested that most people saw the encounter as a valuable opportunity for the exchange of information and social interaction—a chance to engage a sympathetic listener on an equal-status basis.

We kept track of the progress of the interviews by creating a master interview reference table in Microsoft Excel. Every time we located an eligible contact who agreed to be interviewed, we added this person to the spreadsheet and assigned him or her an identification number, which then served as the primary means of identification. Although first names were used in field notes to keep track of the respondents while we extracted information, the assignment of an ID number allowed us to keep each participant's identity confidential as the project moved forward. It became the key link in all the files developed from the project.

The master file also recorded the date of initial contact, the place of the interview, the country of origin, generation, age, education, and gender, along with contact information such as telephone numbers, e-mail addresses, home addresses, and work locations. This contact information was necessary for scheduling the interview but was not retained in the files once the interview was completed. In general, we sought to minimize the time between the initial contact and the interview date. The master file also contained a data field for comments in which interviewers could provide additional information about the respondent, such as how he or she was originally contacted, the respondent's relationship to other study respondents, his or her situation at work, and other noteworthy features of the respondent or the interviewer.

We also maintained another spreadsheet in which we listed all of the people with whom we made contact in the course of the investigation, even if we did not formally interview them. Some of these contacts did not meet our criteria for inclusion, being in the third generation or of mixed Latino-Anglo ancestry. Others fell into a quota category (for example, Mexican males in New York) that was already substantially filled. We nonetheless made contact with these individuals as the study progressed. Often they were useful in opening doors and making introductions to locate respondents from scarce categories. We also interviewed them off the record to solicit their views on Latino identity and generate background information, even though we did not include their responses in the final qualitative database. Each interview was transcribed from the recordings we made to create a narrative database of 159 interviews. The texts were stripped of identifying information and are publicly available to investigators through the link on the LAMP website (http://opr.princeton.edu/archive.iip).

Data Processing

Besides the master file that we used to keep track of contacts and interviews as they were completed, we developed two additional machine-readable files. First, we entered the interview text itself into a database using NVivo software. We began by transcribing all interviews in their original language. After reviewing the transcriptions for clarity and accuracy, we converted them into rich text format and then read them into the NVivo program. NVivo allows each interview to be identified separately by one or more respondent attributes that are of interest to the researcher. These attributes can be used for retrieval, organization, and cross-tabulation of qualitative data. In the NVivo database we constructed, we classified each case according to four basic characteristics: generation, location of interview, region of origin, and country of origin.

In addition to identifying each case by these attributes, we used NVivo to assign content codes, known as nodes, to specific passages of text. In the program, text associated with a particular topical node is highlighted with a color assigned to that node, a feature that allows the researcher to read through the interviews and quickly locate passages on those topics. The various nodes can be organized logically into "trees" through subdivision into specific subtopics. To develop our coding scheme, we began by reading each interview transcript to form a basic impression about its different patterns and meanings concerning immigrant adaptation, integration, and identity. After this initial reading, we used NVivo to assign specific codes and subcodes to particular passages that touched on various theoretically specified dimensions of interest. We also coded new topics that emerged inductively in the course of reading itself.

As shown in table A.1, in the course of coding the transcribed texts we developed eleven basic nodes that contained two to twelve subnodes, yielding ninety discrete topical categories. Each of the separate main nodes and subnodes constitutes a classification tree that identifies passages of text according to topic and meaning. The *life history* tree includes six separate nodes corresponding to age, geographic origin, U.S. occupation and employment, family-of-origin characteristics, sibling characteristics, and family-of-destination characteristics; a seventh node for second-generation migrants only corresponds to the circumstances of parental arrival. A tree corresponding to *formation at origin* includes eight nodes: quality of origin dwelling, skills learned or acquired at origin,

Table A.1 Summary of Topical Trees and Nodes of Meaning Used in Coding Transcriptions of Interviews

Principal Nodes for Tree	Number of Subcodes	Number of Passages Coded with Subcode
Life history	6	165, 394, 275, 244, 152, 85
Origin formation	7	307, 125, 168, 315, 185, 105, 69
Migrant motivations	4	166, 243, 243, 127
Social networks	6	161, 297, 52, 212, 152, 297
Documents	2	202, 149
Work	11	176, 210, 197, 128, 126, 129, 116, 105, 323, 110, 101
Destination formation	10	183, 90, 75, 139, 126, 147, 150, 49, 88, 49
Transnational links	9	175, 155, 127, 87, 136, 156, 131, 159, 162
Values and aspirations	12	189, 177, 115, 130, 114, 109, 170, 140, 166, 154, 131
Perceptions of inequality	11	169, 196, 254, 149, 65, 184, 178, 149, 87, 176, 152
Facets of identity	12	189, 199, 173, 136, 105, 197, 177, 44, 58, 107, 36

Source: Authors' compilation based on qualitative interviews from the Immigrant Identity Project (Office of Population Research 2009).

quality of origin neighborhood, experiences of violence at origin, formal education at origin, occupation and employment at origin, ideals held before migration, and quality of current dwelling. The tree corresponding to *migrant motivations* has four nodes: reasons for migrating, reasons for selecting the United States as a destination, reasons for choosing the northeastern United States as a destination, and place of entry. The *social networks* tree has six nodes: the social organization of departure, networks of support and assistance, knowledge of destination, family and friendship connections, social links to housing and employment, and the social organization of border crossing. The *documents* tree includes just two nodes corresponding to information about documents from the country of origin and those from the United States.

The remaining sets of nodes and subnodes we created are larger and more complex. The *work* tree includes eleven distinct nodes corresponding to the nature and timing of the initial U.S. job, current U.S. occupation and employment, current U.S. earnings, current hours worked per day, current days worked per week, form of payment, deduction of taxes, other jobs held, presence of paisanos at work, presence of Latinos at work, and overtime. The tree corresponding to *formation at destination* includes ten nodes: English-language ability, aspirations to learning, school attendance in the United States, U.S. educational attainment, educational requirements at work, Spanish-language ability, Spanish use at home, Spanish use at work, Spanish use on street, and bilingual abilities. The *transnational links* tree has nine nodes: whether the respondent was in contact with family or friends, the kind of communication, whether money was sent home, the quantity and frequency of financial remittances, financial remittances as a proportion of earnings, how money was sent, the possession of bank accounts, the cost of remitting, and whether gifts were sent. The *values and aspirations* tree includes eleven nodes covering what the respondent likes about the origin country, what he or she likes about the United States, preferences about staying or returning, preferences about family formation, interactions with Americans, interactions with Latinos, whether U.S. expectations have been met, feelings of deception, goals for U.S. achievement, immediate expectations of achievement, and return intentions. The tree for *perceptions of inequality* includes eleven nodes: perceptions about opportunities, perceptions about inequalities, perceptions of discrimination, experiences in the neighborhood, experiences at work, freedom to express opinions, with whom opinions are expressed, political participation in the United States, desire to become a U.S. citizen, desire to vote in the United States, fears in the United States, and dislikes in the United States. Finally, the *facets of identity* tree includes eleven nodes: respondent's identification as American, respondent's identification as Latino, what makes respondent feel Latino, the nature of the respondent's interaction and communication with Latinos and others, whether Latino immigrants share a common identity, with which Latino groups the respondent interacts, interactions at church, interactions through sports, interactions at restaurants, interactions through gangs, and support for Latino identity.

Undertaking qualitative analysis with NVivo involved creating references in the text to the foregoing nodes, known as coding passages, which were then extracted, arrayed for analysis, tabulated relative to each other, and cross-classified by respondent attributes to discern patterns of meaning. Using NVivo, we found it easy to select segments of each interview corresponding to the eleven principal nodes and the ninety subnodes for presentation as data. We placed coded passages in tables and then quoted from these tables to present and illustrate the meanings attributed by the immigrants themselves to different facets of adaptation and integration.

Based on the nodes, subnodes, and attributes coded in NVivo, we developed a second, quantitative database that assigned numerical values to each of the codes for each respondent to create a rectangular data file in which rows corresponded to respondents and columns to specific variables. The variables include objective factors such as generation, place of interview, age, gender, nationality, education, English ability, ethnic-racial origin, skin color, documentation, intergroup associations, years in the United States, first and current U.S. occupation, parental occupation, wages and hours worked, contact with home country, amount of remittances, use of remittances, U.S. and foreign bank accounts, and means of communication with home country, as well as codes for subjective factors such as motivation for migration, return intentions, perceptions of inequality and discrimination, American versus Latino identity, and the reasons for identifying as a Latino. The variables were entered into Excel spreadsheets that were then consolidated into a single file that was converted into Stata for tabulation and statistical analysis. This data set is also publicly accessible via links on the LAMP website (http://opr .princeton.edu/archive/iip).

══ Appendix B ══
Information Sheet Presented to
Potential Respondents

A Quien Pueda Interesar: Información para el Entrevistado
Trabajamos en el Departamento de Sociología y en el Centro de Estudios de Población de la Universidad de Pennsylvania, y estamos realizando una investigación científica sobre "La Identidad Transnacional y Comportamiento: Comparación Etnográfica entre la Primera y Segunda Generación de Inmigrantes Latinos."

Nuestro proyecto busca conocer sobre la Identidad Latina Transnacional, cómo se construye y se expresa, cómo se mantiene o no a través de la Primera y Segunda generación de Latinos. Nuestro trabajo abarca los centros urbanos de Filadelfia, New Jersey, y Nueva York. La opinión de las personas que contactamos la registramos a través de entrevistas abiertas, dirigidas a jóvenes mujeres y hombres (entre los 13 y 35 años de edad) que residen en la actualidad en cualquiera de las ciudades mencionadas, que hayan nacido o que tengan padres que nacieron en cualquier país de América Latina.

La información es totalmente confidencial. Su identidad queda registrada con un número y código correspondiente a su generación y al país de origen que le identifica. Si usted desea, puede usar un apodo o solamente darnos su primer nombre. Cualquier información personal (como nombre, teléfonos, dirección de trabajo, etc.) que se nos da será destruida una vez se ha completado el estudio.

Las opiniones de los participantes podrán ser utilizadas en la publicación de artículos o de un libro sobre la identidad transnacional. Si tiene alguna pregunta, puede llamar a la Dra. Magaly Sánchez al (215) 573-9788. Mucho agradecemos su colaboración y disposición para la realización de la entrevista.

Translation

To Whom It May Concern: Information for Respondents

We work in the Department of Sociology and the Population Studies Center of the University of Pennsylvania, and we are undertaking a scientific investigation on "Transnational Identities and Behavior: An Ethnographic Comparison of First and Second Generation Latino Immigrants."

Our project seeks to learn about transnational Latino identities—how they are constructed and expressed and how they are maintained or not between first and second generation Latinos. Our work encompasses urban areas located around Philadelphia, New Jersey, and New York. We will register the opinions of people we contact through open interviews directed to young men and women between the ages of 13 and 35 years of age who live in the aforementioned urban areas, who were born or have parents who were born in some country of Latin America.

The information is completely confidential. Your identity will be represented only by an identification number and codes indicating your generation and country of origin to identify you. If you wish, you may use a nickname or only give us your first name. Any personal information that you give us (such as name, telephone number, work address, etc.) will be destroyed once the study has been completed.

The opinions of participants will be used in the publication of articles or a book on transnational identity. If you have any question, you may call Dr. Magaly Sanchez at 215-573-9788. We thank you very much for your collaboration and willingness to undertake the interview.

═ Appendix C ═
Guía de Entrevista: Primera Generación / Interview Guide: First Generation

Historia de Vida/Life History

Nombre/Name:
Edad/Age:
Lugar de Nacimiento/Birthplace:
Lugar de Origen/Place of Origin:
Tamaño de Comunidad de Origin/Size of Origin Community:
    Rancho/Village
    Pueblo/Town
    Ciudad/City
    Zona Metropolitana/Metro Area
    Para Areas Urbanas/For Urban Areas:
        Barrio/Neighborhood
Familia Original/Family of Origin:
Familia Actual/Present Family:
¿Que hacías antes de venir a EEUU?/What did you do before coming to the U.S.?
¿Hasta qué grado o año estudiaste?/How many years of schooling did you complete?
¿Te gustaría seguir estudiando? ?Y porqué?/Would you like to continue studying? Why?

Motivaciones/Motivations

¿Cómo surge el deseo de salir para EEUU?/How did you decide to leave for the U.S.?

¿Porqué se escoje una gran ciudad en el este de EEUU? / Why did you choose a large U.S. city?
Amigos / Friends:
Familiares / Relatives:
Referencias / References:
Rumores / Hearsay:
Conocimiento Previo / Previous Knowledge

Redes Sociales/Social Networks

¿Podrias hablarme un poco más sobre las redes y conexiones de ayuda y solidaridad? / Can you tell me a little more about your social connections for help and assistance?
    ¿Dónde empiezan? / Where do they originate?
    ¿Como se enrriquecen? / How are they extended?
    ¿Hay lugares de encuentro? / Are there meeting places?
        ¿De intercambio? / Places of interchange?
        ¿De entretenimiento? / Places of entertainment?
¿Cómo te enterastes de (Filadelfia, Nueva York, Nueva Jersey)? / How did you learn about (Philadelphia, New York, New Jersey)?
    ?Tienes amigos aqui? / Do you have friends here?
¿Existen conexiones en conseguir vivienda y trabajo? / Are there connections you use to find housing and work?
¿Cómo llegastes acá? / How did you arrive here?
¿Me podrías hablar un poco acerca de el viaje y la entrada en EEUU? / Can you tell me a little about your trip and entry into the U.S.?
    ¿Quienes te ayudaron? / Who helped you?
    ¿Cómo te ayudaron? / How did they help you?
    ¿Cuánto tuviste que pagar? / How much did you have to pay?
    ¿Estás documentado? / Are you documented?
    ¿Qué tipo de papeles tienes? / What kind of papers?
    ¿Tienes pasaporte de tu pais de origen? / Do you have a home country passport?
    ¿Dónde llegastes la primera vez? / Where did you arrive on your first U.S. trip?

Identidad/Identity

¿Qué tipo de identificación tienes? / What type of identification do you have?
¿Parece que existe una identidad entre los inmigrants latinoamericanos en los EEUU? / Do you think there is a common identity among Latin American immigrants in the United States?
¿Te identificas como Latino en los EEUU? / Do you identify yourself as Latino in the U.S.?

¿Te identificas con los Americanos? /Do you identify yourself with Americans?

Trabajo/Work

¿Cuándo y cómo empezaste a trabajar en EEUU? /Where and when did you begin to work in the U.S.?

    ¿En qué? /At what?

    ¿Y dónde? /Where?

    ¿Salario? /Wages?

    ¿Horas al día? /Hours per day?

    ¿Días a la semana? /Days per week?

¿Realizas algún trabajo extra, para ayudarte más con dinero? /Do you take on any additional work to earn more money?

¿Hablas inglés? /Do you speak English?

    ¿Te gustaría aprenderlo? /Would you like to learn it?

    ¿Tienes tiempo para asistir a clases? /Do you have the time to attend classes?

    ¿Te hace falta el ingés para moverte aqui? /Do you need English to get ahead here?

¿Hasta qué nivel educativo llegastes? /Through what grade did you attend school?

    ¿Te gustaría seguir estudiando? /Would you like to continue studying?

    ¿Qué formación o especialidad? /What subject or specialty?

    ¿Porqué?/Why?

¿Aspirarías tener una formación y regresar a tu país? /Do you wish to acquire training before returning home?

Relaciones Transnacionales/ Transnational Relations

¿Mantienes contacto con tu familia y amigos en tu lugar de origen? /Do you stay in contact with family and friends in your place of origin?

¿Has logrado enviar regularmente dinero a tu familia en el lugar de origen? / Have you been able to send money regularly to your family in your place of origin?

    ¿Cuánto y con qué frequencia? /How much and how often?

        ¿Qué proporción de tu sueldo? /What proportion of your earnings?

        ¿Te queda algo para ahoirrar acá? /Anything left for you to save?

    ¿Cómo envías el dinero? /How do you send the money?

        Empresas o bancos /Banks or companies

        Casa de envios /Exchange houses

        Paisanos /Fellow townspeople

        Amigos /Friends

¿Tienes cuenta bancaria? / Do you have a bank account?
 ¿En EEUU? / In the U.S.?
 En tu pais de origen? / In your country of origin?
¿Para qué es el dinero que envías? / For what is the money you send?
 ¿Comida y ropa? / Food and clothing?
 ¿Escuela? / School?
 ¿Construir or mejorar la vivienda? / Build or improve dwelling?
 ¿Un negocio? / A business?
 ¿Deudas? / Debts?
¿Te comunicas regularmente con tu familia o amigos en tu pais de origin? / Do you communicate regularly with family and friends in your country of origin?
 ¿Por teléfono? / By telephone?
 ¿Por correo ordinario? / By regular mail?
 ¿Por correo express? / By express mail?
 ¿Por Internet? / By Internet?
¿Mandas regalos a tu familia allá? / Do you send gifts to your family at home?
 ¿Ropa? / Clothes?
 ¿Zapatos? / Shoes?
 ¿Música? / Music?
 ¿Medicinas? / Medicines?
 ¿Libros? / Books?
 ¿Aparatos electrónicos (TV, estereo, etc.)? / Electrical equipment (TV, stereo, etc.)?
 ¿Algo más? / Anything else?

Valores y Aspiraciones/ Values and Aspirations

¿Podrías decirme qué es lo que mas te gusta de tu pais de origen? / What do you like best about your place of origin?
¿Qué es lo que mas te gusta de acá? / What do you most like about the U.S.?
¿Te gustaría quedarte a trabajar y vivir acá? / Would you like to stay here to live and work?
¿Preferirías regresar? / Or would you prefer to return?
Para solteros / For the unmarried:
 ¿Te gustaría formar una familia? / Would you like to start a family?
 ¿Tienes novia allá? / Do you have a girlfriend (boyfriend) at home?
 ¿Te gustan las chicas americanas? / Do you like American women (men)?
 ¿Te gustaria casarte con una americana? / Would you like to marry an American?
¿Se te ha cumplido tu ideal del norte? / Has the North fulfilled your ideals?

¿Te sientes decepcionado? /Do you feel deceived?

¿Qué es lo que más te gustaría lograr hacer acá en EEUU? /What would you most like to achieve here in the U.S.?

¿Cómo visualizes tu futuro próximo? /How do you see your immediate future?

¿Regresarías para quedarte, o irías y vendrías? /Will you go back to stay or will you come and go?

Percepciones de Desigualdad/ Perceptions of Inequality

¿En términos de oportunidades, percibes más oportunidades acá que allá? /In terms of opportunities, do you see more here or there?

¿Y en términos de desigualdades, percibes más acá que allá? /In terms of inequalities, do you see more here or there?

¿Te has sentido alguna vez discriminado? /Have you ever experienced discrimination?

¿Sientes que puedes opinar acá? /Do you feel you have a right to your opinions here?

¿Con quién lo haces? /With whom do you share your views?

¿Has tenido participación política en tu pais de origen? /Have you been able to participate politically in your country of origin?

¿Has tenido participación política aquí? /Have you been able to participate politically here?

¿Te gustaría votar aquí en los EEUU? /Would you like to vote here in the U.S.?

== Appendix D ==
Guía de Entrevista: Segunda Generacion/Interview Guide: Second Generation

Historia de Vida/Life History

Nombre/Name:

Edad/Age:

Lugar de Nacimiento/Birthplace:

Lugar de Origen en EEUU/Place of Origin in U.S.:

    Ciudad y Estado/City and State:

Familia original/Family of Origin:

    ¿Cuándo llegaron tus padres a EEUU?/When did your parents arrive in the U.S.?

    ¿Vinieron juntos como familia? ?Quién vino primero?/Did you come as a family? Who came first?

    ¿A dónde?/Where?

    ¿En que trabajaban tus padre al venir a EEUU?/What work did your father and mother do when they came to the U.S.?

    ¿En que trabajan ahora?/What work do they do now?

Redes Sociales/Social Networks

¿Podrias hablarme un poco más sobre las redes y conexiones de ayuda y solidaridad?/Can you tell me a little more about who you turn to for help and assistance?

¿Te vinculas con jóvenes latinos?/Are you friends with other Latinos?

¿Quiénes son tus mejores amigos?/Who are your best friends?

¿Cuáles son los lugares de encuentro que frecuentas?/Where do you go to hang out with friends?

¿Opinas que existe comunidad acá en América? / Do you think there is community here in America?

Identidad/Identity

¿Qué tipo de identificación tienes? / What type of identification do you have?

¿Parece que existe una identidad entre los inmigrants latinoamericanos en los EEUU? / Do you think there is a common identity among Latin American immigrants in the United States?

¿Te identificas como Latino en los EEUU? / Do you identify yourself as Latino in the U.S.?

¿Te identificas con los Americanos? / Do you identify yourself with Americans?

Trabajo/Work

¿Cuándo empezaste a trabajar? / When did you begin to work?

    ¿En qué? / At what?

    ¿Y donde? / Where?

    ¿Salario? / Wages?

    ¿Horas al día? / Hours per day?

    ¿Días a la semana? / Days per week?

¿Realizas algún trabajo extra, para ayudarte más con dinero? / Do you take on any additional work to earn more money?

¿Trabajas para ayudarte en tus estudios? / Do you work to help yourself in your studies?

¿Trabajas para auydar a tus padres? / Do you work to help your parents?

¿Cómo hablas el inglés? / How well do you speak English?

¿Hablas el español? / Do you speak Spanish?

    ¿Lo usas con frecuencia? / Do you use it frequently?

    ¿Lo usas en la casa, por ejemplo? / Do you use it at home, for example?

    ¿Lo usas en el trabajo? / Do you use it at work?

    ¿Lo usas en la escuela? / Do you use it at school?

    ¿Tus padres hablan inglés o español contigo? / Do your parents speak English or Spanish with you?

    ¿Te consideras bilingue? / Do you consider yourself to be bilingual?

¿Hasta qué nivel educativo llegastes? / Through what grade did you attend school?

    ¿Te gustaría seguir estudiando? / Would you like to continue studying?

    ¿Qué formación o especialidad? / What subject or specialty?

    ¿Porqué? / Why?

¿Aspirarías tener una formación y regresar al país de tus padres? / Do you wish to acquire training before returning to the country of your parents?

Relaciones Transnacionales/
Transnational Relations

¿Estas en contacto con familiares o amigos en el pais de tus padres? / Are you in contact with family and friends in your parents' country?

¿Has logrado enviar dinero a familiares en el pais de tus padres? / Have you been able to send money home to family members in your parents' country?

    ¿Cuánto y con qué frequencia? / How much and how often?

        ¿Qué proporción de tu sueldo? / What proportion of your earnings?

        ¿Te queda algo para ahoirrar acá? / Anything left for you to save?

    ¿Cómo envías el dinero? / How do you send the money?

        Empresas o bancos / Banks or companies

        Casa de envios / Exchange houses

        Paisanos / Fellow townspeople

        Amigos / Friends

    ¿Tienes cuenta bancaria? / Do you have a bank account?

        ¿En EEUU? / In the U.S.?

        ¿En tu pais de origen? / In your country of origin?

    ¿Para qué es el dinero que envías? / For what is the money you send?

        ¿Comida y ropa? / Food and clothing?

        ¿Escuela? / School?

        ¿Construir or mejorar la vivienda? / Build or improve dwelling?

        ¿Un negocio? / A business?

        ¿Deudas? / Debts?

¿Te comunicas regularmente con to familia o amigos en el pais de tus padres? / Do you communicate regularly with family and friends in your parents' country?

    ¿Por teléfono? / By telephone?

    ¿Por correo ordinario? / By regular mail?

    ¿Por correo express? / By express mail?

    ¿Por Internet? / By Internet?

¿Mandas regalos a familiares allá? / Do you send gifts to family members there?

    ¿Ropa? / Clothes?

    ¿Zapatos? / Shoes?

    ¿Música? / Music?

    ¿Medicinas? / Medicines?

    ¿Libros? / Books?

    ¿Aparatos electrónicos (TV, estereo, etc.)? / Electrical equipment (TV, stereo, etc.)?

    ¿Algo más? / Anything else?

Valores y Aspiraciones/
Values and Aspirations

¿Podrías decirme qué es lo que más te gusta de tu país de origen? / What do you like best about your place of origin?

¿Qué es lo que mas te gusta de acá? / What do you most like about the U.S.?

¿Preferirías regresar al pais originario de tus padres? / Would you like to return to your parents' country?

¿Te gustaría formar una familia? / Would you like to start a family?

¿Tienes novia allá? / Do you have a girlfriend (boyfriend) abroad?

> *¿Te gustan las chicas americanas?* / Do you like American women (men)?
>
> *¿Te gustaría casarte con una americana?* / Would you like to marry an American?
>
> *¿O preferirías una chica latina?* / Or would you prefer a Latina (Latino)?

¿Se te ha cumplido tu ideal acá en el norte? / Have you fulfilled your ideals in the North?

¿Te sientes decepcionado? / Do you feel deceived?

¿Te sientes americano o latino? / Do you feel American or Latino?

¿Te has sentido discriminado alguna vez? / Have you ever felt discriminated against?

¿Qué es lo que más te gustaría lograr hacer acá en EEUU? / What would you most like to achieve here in the U.S.?

¿Cómo visualizes tu futuro próximo? / How do you see your immediate future?

¿Te atrae la idea de ir a vivir en el país de origen de tus padres? / Does the idea of living in your parents' country attract you?

¿Tienes parientes allá? / Do you have relatives there?

> *Abuelos* / Grandparents
>
> *Tios* / Aunts and uncles
>
> *Primos* / Cousins

Percepciones de Desigualdad/
Perceptions of Inequality

¿En téminos de oportunidades, percibes más oportunidades acá que en el pais de tus padres? / In terms of opportunities, do you see more here or in the country of your parents?

¿Y en términos de desigualdades, percibes más acá que allá? / In terms of inequalities, more here or there?

¿Te sientes excluido, empobrecido, o discriminado? / Do you feel excluded, impoverished, or discriminated against?

¿Sientes que puedes opinar acá y que eres oido? / Do you feel you can state your views here and have them heard?

¿Con quién lo haces? / With whom do you share your views?

¿Has tenido participación política en el pais de origen de tus padres? / Have you been able to participate politically in your country of origin?

¿Has tenido participación política aqui? / Have you been able to participate politically here?

¿Te gustaría votar en los EEUU? / Would you like to vote in the U.S.?

¿Qué es lo que más temes en esta sociedad? / What do you most fear in this society?

¿Qué es lo que menos te gusta? / What do you like least?

References

Administrative Office of the U.S. Courts. 2009. "Bankruptcy Statistics." Washington: Administrative Office of the U.S. Courts. Available at: http://www.us courts.gov/bnkrpctystats/bankruptcystats.htm (accessed March 17, 2010).

Aguilera, Michael B. 2002. "The Impact of Social Capital on Labor Force Participation: Evidence from the 2000 Social Capital Benchmark Survey." *Social Science Quarterly* 83(3): 853–74.

———. 2003. "The Impact of the Worker: How Social Capital and Human Capital Influence the Job Tenure of Formerly Undocumented Mexican Immigrants." *Sociological Inquiry* 73(1): 52–83.

———. 2005. "The Impact of Social Capital on the Wages of Puerto Rican Migrants." *Sociological Quarterly* 46(4): 569–92.

Aguilera, Michael B., and Douglas S. Massey. 2004. "Social Capital and the Wages of Mexican Migrants: New Hypotheses and Tests." *Social Forces* 82(2): 671–702.

Alba, Richard D. 1985. *Italian Americans: Into the Twilight of Ethnicity*. Englewood Cliffs, N.J.: Prentice-Hall.

———. 1990. *Ethnic Identity: The Transformation of White America*. New Haven, Conn.: Yale University Press.

———. 2009. *Blurring the Color Line: The New Chance for a More Integrated America*. Cambridge, Mass.: Harvard University Press.

Alba, Richard, and Victor Nee. 2003. *Remaking the American Mainstream: Assimilation and Contemporary Immigration*. Cambridge, Mass.: Harvard University Press.

Allen, Paul A., and Eugene Turner. 1997. *The Ethnic Quilt: Population Diversity in Southern California*. Northridge, Calif.: Center for Geographical Studies.

Alvarado, Steven E., and Douglas S. Massey. Forthcoming. "In Search of Peace: Structural Adjustment, Violence, and International Migration." *Annals of the American Academy of Political and Social Science*.

Amuedo-Dorantes, Catalina, Cynthia Bansak, and Susan Pozo. 2005. "On the Remitting Patterns of Immigrants: Evidence from Mexican Survey Data." *Economic Review* (Federal Reserve Bank of Atlanta) 90(1): 37–58.

Amuedo-Dorantes, Catalina, and Susan Pozo. 2007. "Do Remittances Decay with Emigrants' Foreign Residencies? Evidence from Mexican Migrants." *Bienestar y Política Social* (Well-Being and Social Policy Journal) 2: 31–42.

Andreas, Peter. 2000. *Border Games: Policing the U.S.-Mexico Divide.* Ithaca, N.Y.: Cornell University Press.

Andrews, George R. 2004. *Afro-Latin America, 1800–2000.* New York: Oxford University Press.

Appelbaum, Nancy P., Anne S. Macpherson, and Karin A. Rosemblatt. 2007. *Race and Nation in Modern Latin America.* Chapel Hill: University of North Carolina Press.

Aysa, María, and Douglas S. Massey. 2004. "Wives Left Behind: The Labor Market Behavior of Women in Migrant Communities." In *Crossing the Border: Research from the Mexican Migration Project,* edited by Jorge Durand and Douglas S. Massey. New York: Russell Sage Foundation.

Barbier, René. 1996. *La Recherche-Action.* Paris: Economica.

Barth, Fredrik. 1969. *Ethnic Groups and Boundaries: The Social Organization of Culture Difference.* Boston: Little, Brown.

———. 1981. *Process and Form in Social Life.* London: Routledge and Kegan Paul.

Basch, Linda, Nina Glick-Schiller, and Christina Blanc-Szanton. 1994. *Nations Unbound: Transnational Projects, Postcolonial Predicaments, and Deterritorialized Nation-States.* New York: Routledge.

Bashi, Vilna. 2007. *Survival of the Knitted: Immigrant Social Networks in a Stratified World.* Stanford, Calif.: Stanford University Press.

Baugh, John. 1983. *Black Street Speech: Its History, Structure, and Survival.* Austin: University of Texas Press.

Bean, Frank D., and Marta Tienda. 1987. *The Hispanic Population of the United States.* New York: Russell Sage Foundation.

Bernhardt, Annette, Ruth Milkman, Nick Theodore, Douglas Heckathorn, Mirabai Auer, James De Filippis, Ana Luz Gonzalez, Victor Narro, Jason Perelshteyn, Diana Polson, and Michael Spiller. 2009. "Broken Laws, Unprotected Workers: Violations of Employment and Labor Laws in America's Cities." New York: National Employment Law Project.

Bharat-Ram, Vinay. 1994. *Towards a Theory of Import Substitution, Exchange Rates, and Economic Development.* New York: Oxford University Press.

Borjas, George J. 1998. "To Ghetto or Not to Ghetto: Ethnicity and Residential Segregation." *Journal of Urban Economics* 44(2): 228–53.

Buchanan, Patrick J. 2006. *State of Emergency: The Third World Invasion and Conquest of America.* New York: Thomas Dunne Books.

Capozza, Dora, and Rupert Brown. 2000. "New Trends in Theory and Research." In *Social Identity Processes: Trends in Theory and Research,* edited by Dora Capozza and Rupert Brown. Thousand Oaks, Calif.: Sage Publications.

Castells, Manuel. 2004. *The Power of Identity: The Information Age: Economy, Society, and Culture,* vol. 2, 2d ed. London: Blackwell.

Cerrutti, Marcela, and Douglas S. Massey. 2001. "On the Auspices of Female Migration Between Mexico and the United States." *Demography* 38(2): 187–200.

Chavez, Leo R. 2001. *Covering Immigration: Population Images and the Politics of the Nation.* Berkeley: University of California Press.

———. 2008. *The Latino Threat: Constructing Immigrants, Citizens, and the Nation.* Stanford, Calif.: Stanford University Press.

Chiquiar, Daniel, and Gordon Hanson. 2005. "International Migration, Self-Selection, and the Distribution of Wages: Evidence from Mexico and the United States." *Journal of Political Economy* 113(2): 239–81.

Cohen, Joseph Nathan, and Miguel A. Centeno. 2006. "Neoliberalism and Patterns of Economic Performance 1980–2000." In *Chronicle of a Myth Foretold: The Washington Consensus in Latin America*, edited by Douglas S. Massey, Magaly Sánchez R., and Jere R. Behrman. Thousand Oaks, Calif.: Sage Publications.

Cohen, Robin A., Diane M. Makuc, Amy B. Bernstein, Linda T. Bilheimer, and Eve Powell-Griner. 2009. "Health Insurance Coverage Trends, 1959–2007: Estimates from the National Health Interview Survey." *National Health Statistics Reports* 17(1): 1–28. Washington: U.S. Department of Health and Human Services, Centers for Disease Control and Prevention, National Center for Health Statistics.

Consumer Confidence Board. 2009. "Quarterly Consumer Confidence Index." New York: Consumer Confidence Board.

Cordero-Guzman, Hector, Robert C. Smith, and Ramon Grosfoguel. 2001. *Migration, Transnationalization, and Race in a Changing New York*. Philadelphia: Temple University Press.

Danziger, Sheldon, and Peter Gottschalk. 1995. *America Unequal*. New York: Russell Sage Foundation.

Darity, William A., Jr., and Patrick L. Mason. 1998. "Evidence on Discrimination in Employment: Codes of Color, Codes of Gender." *Journal of Economic Perspectives* 12(2): 63–90.

Denton, Nancy A., and Douglas S. Massey. 1989. "Racial Identity Among Caribbean Hispanics: The Effect of Double Minority Status on Residential Segregation." *American Sociological Review* 54(5): 790–808.

DeVaney, Sharon A., and Sophia T. Chiremba. 2005. "Compensation and Working Conditions: Comparing the Retirement Savings of the Baby Boomers and Other Cohorts." Washington: U.S. Bureau of Labor Statistics. Available at: http://www.bls.gov/opub/cwc/cm20050114ar01p1.htm (accessed March 17, 2010).

DiCarlo, Lisa. 2008. *Migrating to America: Transnational Social Networks and Regional Identity Among Turkish Migrants*. London: I. B. Tauris.

Dickens, William T., and Kevin Lang. 1988. "The Reemergence of Segmented Labor Market Theory." *American Economic Review* 78(2): 129–34.

D'Innocenzo, Michael, and Josef P. Sirefman. 1992. *Immigration and Ethnicity in American Society: "Melting Pot" or "Salad Bowl"?* Westport, Conn.: Greenwood Press.

Dobbs, Lou. 2006. *War on the Middle Class: How the Government, Big Business, and Special Interest Groups Are Waging War on the American Dream and How to Fight Back*. New York: Viking.

Donato, Katharine M., Jorge Durand, and Douglas S. Massey. 1992. "Changing Conditions in the U.S. Labor Market: Effects of the Immigration Reform and Control Act of 1986." *Population Research and Policy Review* 11(2): 93–116.

Donato, Katharine M., John Hiskey, Jorge Durand, and Douglas S. Massey, eds. 2010. *Continental Divides: International Migration in the Americas*. Thousand Oaks, Calif.: Sage Publications.

Donato, Katharine M., and Douglas S. Massey. 1993. "Effect of the Immigration Reform and Control Act on the Wages of Mexican Migrants." *Social Science Quarterly* 74(3): 523–41.

Duncan, Otis D., and Beverly Duncan. 1968. "Minorities and the Process of Stratification." *American Sociological Review* 33(3): 356–64.

Duncan Otis D., and Stanley Lieberson. 1959. "Ethnic Segregation and Assimilation." *American Journal of Sociology* 64(4): 364–74.

Dunn, Timothy J. 1996. *The Militarization of the U.S.-Mexico Border, 1978–1992: Low-Intensity Conflict Doctrine Comes Home.* Austin: University of Texas, Center for Mexican American Studies.

Durand, Jorge. 1994. *Más Allá de la Línea: Patrones Migratorios entre México y Estados Unidos.* México, DF: Consejo Nacional de la Cultura.

———. 1996. *El Norte es Como el Mar: Entrevistas a Trabajadores Migrantes en Estados Unidos.* Guadalajara: Universidad de Guadalajara.

———. 2002. *Rostros y Rastros: Entrevistas a Trabajadores Migrantes en Estados Unidos.* San Luis Potosí: El Colegio de San Luis.

Durand, Jorge, and Patricia Arias. 2000. *La Experiencia Migrante: Iconografía de la Migración México-Estados Unidos.* Guadalajara: Altexto.

———. 2005. *La Vida en el Norte: Historia e Iconografía de la Migración México-Estados Unidos.* Guadalajara: Universidad de Guadalajara y El Colegio de San Luis.

Durand, Jorge, and Douglas S. Massey. 1990. *Doy Gracias: Iconografía de la Emigración México-Estados Unidos.* Guadalajara: Programa de Estudios Jaliscienses, Secretraría de Educación y Cultura, Universidad de Guadalajara.

———. 1995. *Miracles on the Border: Retablos of Mexican Migrants to the United States.* Tucson: University of Arizona Press.

———. 2004. *Crossing the Border: Research from the Mexican Migration Project.* New York: Russell Sage Foundation.

———. Forthcoming. "New World Orders: Continuities and Changes in Latin American Migration." *Annals of the American Academy of Political and Social Science.*

Durand, Jorge, Douglas S. Massey, and Emilio A. Parrado. 1996. "Migradollars and Development: A Reconsideration of the Mexican Case." *International Migration Review* 30(2): 423–44.

Espinosa, Kristin E., and Douglas S. Massey. 1997. "Determinants of English Proficiency Among Mexican Migrants to the United States." *International Migration Review* 31(1): 28–50.

Faist, Thomas. 2000. *The Volume and Dynamics of International Migration and Transnational Social Spaces.* New York: Oxford University Press.

Faist, Thomas, and Eyüp Özveren. 2004. *Transnational Social Spaces: Agents, Networks, and Institutions.* Aldershot, U.K.: Ashgate.

Feagin, Joseph, and Clairece Feagin. 1989. *Racial and Ethnic Relations.* Englewood Cliffs, N.J.: Prentice-Hall.

Federal Bureau of Investigation (FBI). 2009. "Hate Crime Statistics." Washington: FBI. Available at: http://www.fbi.gov/ucr/ucr.htm#hate (accessed March 17, 2010).

Fiscia, August B., and J. L. T. Kovacs. 1994. *Beyond the Lost Decade: Debt and Development in Latin America.* New York: Perseus.

Flores, Juan. 2008. *The Diaspora Strikes Back.* New York: Routledge.

Foner, Eric. 1988. *Reconstruction: America's Unfinished Revolution, 1863–1877.* New York: HarperCollins.

Foner, Nancy. 2000. *From Ellis Island to JFK: New York's Two Great Waves of Immigration.* New Haven, Conn.: Yale University Press.

Fredrickson, George M. 2002. *Racism: A Short History.* Princeton, N.J.: Princeton University Press.

Frey, William H. 1997. "Immigration and Demographic Balkanization: Toward One America or Two?" In *America's Demographic Tapestry: Baseline for the New Millennium*, edited by James W. Hughes and Joseph J. Seneca. New Brunswick, N.J.: Rutgers University Press.

Funkhouser, Edward. 1992. "Migration from Nicaragua: Some Recent Evidence." *World Development* 20(8): 1209–18.

Gang, Ira N., Thomas Bauer, and Gil S. Epstein. 2005. "Enclaves, Language, and the Location Choice of Migrants." *Journal of Population Economics* 18(4): 649–62.

———. 2007. "The Influence of Stocks and Flows on Migrants' Location Choices." *Research in Labor Economics* 26: 199–229.

Gang, Ira N., and Myeong-Su Yun. 2008. "Immigration Amnesty and Immigrants' Earnings." *Research in Labor Economics* 27: 273–309.

Gans, Herbert C. 1962. *The Urban Villagers: Group and Class in the Life of Italian-Americans*. New York: Free Press.

———. 1992. "Comment: Ethnic Invention and Acculturation: A Bumpy-Line Approach." *Journal of American Ethnic History* 12(1): 42–52.

Ganzeboom, Harry B. G., and Donald J. Treiman. 1996. "Internationally Comparable Measures of Occupational Status for the 1988 International Standard Classification of Occupations." *Social Science Research* 25(3): 201–39.

Gieryn, Thomas F. 1983. "Boundary-Work and the Demarcation of Science from Non-science: Strains and Interests in Professional Ideologies of Scientists." *American Sociological Review* 48(6): 781–95.

Glazer, Nathan, and Daniel P. Moynihan. 1963. *Beyond the Melting Pot: The Negroes, Puerto Ricans, Jews, Italians, and Irish of New York City*. Cambridge, Mass.: MIT Press.

Glick-Schiller, Nina, Linda Basch, and Cristina Blanc-Szanton. 1992. *Towards a Transnational Perspective on Migration: Race, Class, Ethnicity, and Nationalism Reconsidered*. New York: New York Academy of Sciences.

Goldin, Claudia. 1994. "The Political Economy of Immigration Restriction in the U.S., 1890 to 1921." In *The Regulated Economy: A Historical Approach to Political Economy*, edited by Claudia Golden and Gary Libecap. Chicago: University of Chicago Press.

Gordon, Milton M. 1964. *Assimilation in American Life: The Role of Race, Religion, and National Origins*. New York: Oxford University Press.

Goza, Franklin. 2004. "An Overview of Brazilian Life in United States in the Year 2000." *Annals of the Brazilian Association of Population Studies* 14: 432–51.

Grasmuck, Sherri, and Patricia R. Pessar. 1991. *Between Two Islands: Dominican International Migration*. Berkeley: University of California Press.

Greeley, Andrew M. 1971. *Why Can't They Be Like Us? America's White Ethnic Groups*. New York: Dutton.

Guarnizo, Luis E., Alejandro Portes, and William Haller. 2003. "Assimilation and Transnationalism: Determinants of Transnational Political Action Among Contemporary Migrants." *American Journal of Sociology* 108(6): 1211–48.

Gutiérrez, David G. 1995. *Walls and Mirrors: Mexican Americans, Mexican Immigrants, and the Politics of Ethnicity*. Berkeley: University of California Press.

Handlin, Oscar. 1951. *The Uprooted: The Epic Story of the Great Migrations That Made the American People*. New York: Grosset & Dunlap.

Hatton, Timothy J., and Jeffrey G. Williamson. 1994. "What Drove the Mass Migrations from Europe in the Late Nineteenth Century?" *Population and Development Review* 20(3): 533–60.

———. 1998. *The Age of Mass Migration: Causes and Economic Impact.* Oxford: Oxford University Press.

Haugan, Steven E. 2009. "Measures of Labor Underutilization from the Current Population Survey." Working paper 424. Washington: U.S. Bureau of Labor Statistics.

Hechter, Michael. 1975. *Internal Colonialism: The Celtic Fringe in British National Development.* New Brunswick, N.J.: Transaction Publishers.

Henry, Sally. 2006. *The New Bankruptcy Code.* Washington: National Bar Association.

Hernández León, Rubén, and Victor Zúñiga. 2005. *New Destinations: Mexican Immigration in the United States.* New York: Russell Sage Foundation.

Herring, Cedric, Verna M. Keith, and Hayward Derrick Horton. 2003. *Skin Deep: How Race and Complexion Matter in the "Color-Blind" Era.* Urbana: University of Illinois Press.

Higginbotham, A. Leon. 1996. *Shades of Freedom: Racial Politics and Presumptions of the American Legal Process.* New York: Oxford University Press.

Higham, John. 1955. *Strangers in the Land: Patterns of American Nativism 1860–1925.* New Brunswick, N.J.: Rutgers University Press.

Hoefer, Michael, Nancy Rytina, and Bryan C. Baker. 2008. *Estimates of the Unauthorized Immigrant Population Residing in the United States: January 2007.* Washington: U.S. Department of Homeland Security, Office of Immigration Statistics.

———. 2009. *Estimates of the Unauthorized Immigrant Population Residing in the United States: January 2007.* Washington: U.S. Department of Homeland Security, Office of Immigration Statistics.

Hondagneu-Sotelo, Pierette. 1994. *Gendered Transitions: Mexican Experiences of Immigration.* Berkeley: University of California Press.

Hopkins, Daniel J. 2008. "Threatening Changes: Explaining Where and When Immigrants Provoke Local Opposition." Working paper. New Haven, Conn.: Yale University, Center for the Study of American Politics.

Hout, Michael. 1988. "More Universalism, Less Structural Mobility: The American Occupational Structure in the 1980s." *American Journal of Sociology* 93(6): 1358–1400.

Huntington, Samuel P. 2004. *Who Are We? The Challenges to America's National Identity.* New York: Simon & Schuster.

Jacobson, Robin Dale. 2008. *The New Nativism: Proposition 187 and the Debate over Immigration.* Minneapolis: University of Minnesota Press.

Jasso, Guillermina, and Mark R. Rosenzweig. 1982. "Estimating the Emigration Rates of Legal Immigrants Using Administrative and Survey Data: The 1971 Cohort of Immigrants to the United States." *Demography* 19(3): 279–90.

Jones, Richard C. 1989. "Causes of Salvadoran Migration to the United States." *Geographical Review* 79(2): 183–94.

Jouët-Pastré, Clemence M., and Leticia J. Braga. 2008. *Becoming Brazuca : Brazilian Immigration to the United States.* Cambridge, Mass.: Harvard University, David Rockefeller Center for Latin American Studies.

Kahneman, Daniel, and Amos Tversky. 2000. *Choices, Values, and Frames.* New York: Cambridge University Press.

Kasinitz, Philip, John H. Mollenkopf, and Mary C. Waters. 2004. *Becoming New Yorkers: Ethnographies of the New Second Generation.* New York: Russell Sage Foundation.

Kasinitz, Philip, John H. Mollenkopf, Mary C. Waters, and Jennifer Holdaway. 2008. *Inheriting the City: The Children of Immigrants Come of Age.* New York: Russell Sage Foundation.

Katznelson, Ira. 2005. *When Affirmative Action Was White: The Untold History of Racial Inequality in Twentieth-Century America.* New York: Norton.

Kennedy School of Government. 2009. "Immigration in America: The NPR/Kaiser/Kennedy School Immigration Survey." Cambridge, Mass.: Harvard University, John F. Kennedy School of Government. Available at: http://www.npr.org/news/specials/polls/2004/immigration (accessed March 17, 2010).

Kivisto, Peter. 2002. *Multiculturalism in Global Society.* New York: Wiley-Blackwell.

Kohut, Andrew, and Roberto Suro. 2006. *America's Immigration Quandary: No Consensus on Immigration Problem or Proposed Fixes.* Washington, D.C.: Pew Research Center for the People and the Press and Pew Hispanic Center.

Krueger, Alan B., and Robert M. Solow. 2002. *The Roaring Nineties: Can Full Employment Be Sustained?* New York: Russell Sage Foundation.

Kyle, David J. 2000. *Transnational Peasants: Migrations, Networks, and Ethnicity in Andean Ecuador.* Baltimore: Johns Hopkins University Press.

Lamont, Michele. 2000. *The Dignity of Working Men: Morality and the Boundaries of Race, Class, and Immigration.* Cambridge, Mass.: Harvard University Press.

Lamont, Michele, and Vireg Molnar. 2002. "The Study of Boundaries in the Social Sciences." *Annual Review of Sociology* 28: 167–95.

Lee, Jennifer. 2004. *Asian American Youth: Culture, Identity, and Ethnicity.* New York: Routledge.

Legomsky, Stephen H. 2000. "Fear and Loathing in Congress and the Courts: Immigration and Judicial Review." *Texas Law Review* 78(7): 1612–20.

Levit, Katherine R., Gary L. Olin, and Suzanne W. Letsch. 1992. "Americans' Health Insurance Coverage." *Health Care Financing Review* 14(1): 31–57.

Levitt, Peggy. 1998. "Social Remittances: Migration Driven Local-Level Forms of Cultural Diffusion." *International Migration Review* 32(4): 926–48.

———. 2001. *The Transnational Villagers.* Berkeley: University of California Press.

Levitt, Peggy, and Nina Glick-Schiller. 2004. "Transnational Perspectives on Migration: Conceptualizing Simultaneity." *International Migration Review* 38(3): 595–629.

Levitt, Peggy, and Nadiya Jaworsky. 2007. "Transnational Migration Studies: Past Developments and Future Trends." *Annual Review of Sociology* 33(1): 129–56.

Levy, Frank. 1998. *The New Dollars and Dreams: American Incomes and Economic Change.* New York: Russell Sage Foundation.

Lie, John. 1995. "From International Migration to Transnational Diaspora." *Contemporary Sociology* 24(4): 303–6.

Lieberson, Stanley. 1963. *Ethnic Patterns in American Cities.* New York: Free Press.

Livingston, Gretchen. 2006. "Gender, Job Searching, and Employment Outcomes Among Mexican Immigrants." *Population Research and Policy Review* 25(1): 43–66.

Lopez, Mark Hugo, and Gretchen Livingston. 2009. "Hispanics and the Criminal Justice System: Low Confidence, High Exposure." *Pew Hispanic Center Report*, April 7. Washington, D.C.: Pew Hispanic Center.

Lopez, Mark Hugo, and Susan Minushkin. 2008. "2008 National Survey of Latinos: Hispanics See Their Situation in U.S. as Deteriorating; Oppose Key Immigration Enforcement Measures." *Pew Hispanic Center Report*, September 18. Washington, D.C.: Pew Hispanic Center.

Lowell, B. Lindsay, Frank D. Bean, and Rodolfo O. de la Garza. 1986. "The Dilemmas of Undocumented Immigration: An Analysis of the 1984 Simpson-Mazzoli Vote." *Social Science Quarterly* 67(1): 118–27.

Lundquist, Jennifer H., and Douglas S. Massey. 2005. "The Contra War and Nicaraguan Migration to the United States." *Journal of Latin American Studies* 37(1): 29–53.

Mahler, Sarah J. 1995. *American Dreaming: Immigrant Life on the Margins*. Princeton, N.J.: Princeton University Press.

Margolis, Maxine L. 1993. *Little Brazil*. Princeton, N.J.: Princeton University Press.

Massey, Douglas S. 1985. "Ethnic Residential Segregation: A Theoretical Synthesis and Empirical Review." *Sociology and Social Research* 69(3): 315–50.

———. 1987a. "The Ethnosurvey in Theory and Practice." *International Migration Review* 21(4): 1498–1522.

———. 1987b. "Do Undocumented Migrants Earn Lower Wages Than Legal Immigrants? New Evidence from Mexico." *International Migration Review* 21(2): 236–74.

———. 1990. "Social Structure, Household Strategies, and the Cumulative Causation of Migration." *Population Index* 56(1): 3–26.

———. 1995. "The New Immigration and the Meaning of Ethnicity in the United States." *Population and Development Review* 21(3): 631–52.

———. 1999. "International Migration at the Dawn of the Twenty-First Century: The Role of the State." *Population and Development Review* 25(2): 303–23.

———. 2001. "The Prodigal Paradigm Returns: Ecology Comes Back to Sociology." In *Does It Take a Village? Community Effects on Children, Adolescents, and Families*, edited by Alan Booth and Ann C. Crouter. Mahwah, N.J.: Lawrence Erlbaum Associates.

———. 2007. *Categorically Unequal: The American Stratification System*. New York: Russell Sage Foundation.

———. 2008. *New Faces in New Places: The Changing Geography of American Immigration*. New York: Russell Sage Foundation.

———. 2010. "The Past and Future of Mexico-U.S. Migration." In *Beyond the Border: The History of Mexico-U.S. Migration*, edited by Mark Overmyer-Velazquez. New York: Oxford University Press.

Massey, Douglas S., Rafael Alarcón, Jorge Durand, and Humberto González. 1987. *Return to Aztlan: The Social Process of International Migration from Western Mexico*. Berkeley: University of California Press.

Massey, Douglas S., Joaquín Arango, Graeme Hugo, Ali Kouaouci, Adela Pellegrino, and J. Edward Taylor. 1994. "An Evaluation of International Migration Theory: The North American Case." *Population and Development Review* 20(4): 699–752.

———. 1998. *Worlds in Motion: International Migration at the End of the Millennium.* Oxford: Oxford University Press.

Massey, Douglas S., and Lawrence Basem. 1992. "Determinants of Savings, Remittances, and Spending Patterns Among Mexican Migrants to the United States." *Sociological Inquiry* 62(2): 186–207.

Massey, Douglas S., and Chiara Capoferro. 2004. "Measuring Undocumented Migration." *International Migration Review* 38(3): 1075–1102.

———. 2006. "'Sálvase Quien Pueda': Structural Adjustment and Emigration from Lima." In *Chronicle of a Myth Foretold: The Washington Consensus in Latin America*, edited by Douglas S. Massey, Magaly Sánchez R., and Jere R. Behrman. Thousand Oaks, Calif.: Sage Publications.

Massey, Douglas S., and Nancy A. Denton. 1992. "Racial Identity and the Segregation of Mexicans in the United States." *Social Science Research* 21(3): 235–60.

———. 1993. *American Apartheid: Segregation and the Making of the Underclass.* Cambridge, Mass.: Harvard University Press.

Massey, Douglas S., Jorge Durand, and Nolan J. Malone. 2002. *Beyond Smoke and Mirrors: Mexican Immigration in an Age of Economic Integration.* New York: Russell Sage Foundation.

Massey, Douglas S., Jorge Durand, and Karen Pren. 2009. "Nuevos Escenarios de la Migración México-Estados Unidos." *Papeles de Población* 61: 101–28..

Massey, Douglas S., Mary J. Fischer, and Chiara Capoferro. 2006. "Gender and Migration in Latin America: A Comparative Analysis." *International Migration* 44(5): 63–91.

Massey, Douglas S., Luin Goldring, and Jorge Durand. 1994. "Continuities in Transnational Migration: An Analysis of Nineteen Mexican Communities." *American Journal of Sociology* 99(6): 1492–1533.

Massey, Douglas S., Frank Kalter, and Karen A. Pren. 2008. "Structural Economic Change and International Migration from Mexico and Poland." *Kölner Zeitschrift für Soziologie und Sozialpsychologie* 60(1): 134–62.

Massey, Douglas S., and William Kandel. 2002. "The Culture of Mexican Migration: A Theoretical and Empirical Analysis." *Social Forces* 80(3): 981–1004.

Massey, Douglas S., and Nolan J. Malone. 2003. "Pathways to Legalization." Population Research and Policy Review 21(6): 473–504.

Massey, Douglas S., and Jennifer A. Martin. 2003. "The New Immigrant Survey Skin Color Scale." Available at: http://nis.princeton.edu/downloads/NIS -Skin-Color-Scale.pdf (accessed March 17, 2010).

Massey, Douglas S., and Emilio A. Parrado. 1994. "Migradollars: The Remittances and Savings of Mexican Migrants to the United States." *Population Research and Policy Review* 13(1): 3–30.

Massey, Douglas S., Magaly Sánchez R., and Jere R. Behrman. 2006. "Of Myths and Markets." In *Chronicle of a Myth Foretold: The Washington Consensus in Latin America*, edited by Douglas S. Massey, Magaly Sánchez R., and Jere R. Behrman. Thousand Oaks, Calif.: Sage Publications.

Massey, Douglas S., and Audrey Singer. 1995. "New Estimates of Undocumented

Mexican Migration and the Probability of Apprehension." *Demography* 32(2): 203–13.

Massey, Douglas S., and J. Edward Taylor. 2004. *International Migration: Prospects and Policies in a Global Market*. Oxford: Oxford University Press.

Massey, Douglas S., and René Zenteno. 1999. "The Dynamics of Mass Migration." *Proceedings of the National Academy of Sciences* 96(8): 5328–35.

———. 2000. "A Validation of the Ethnosurvey: The Case of Mexico-U.S. Migration." *International Migration Review* 34(3): 765–92.

Mauss, Marcel. 1969. *The Gift: The Form and Reason for Exchange in Archaic Societies*. New York: Norton.

McConnell, Eileen Diaz. 2008. "The U.S. Destinations of Contemporary Mexican Immigrants." *International Migration Review* 42(4): 767–802.

McConnell, Eileen Diaz, and Felicia B. Leclere. 2002. "Selection, Context, or Both? The English Fluency of Mexican Immigrants in the American Midwest and Southwest." *Population Research and Policy Review* 21(3): 179–204.

McKeown, Adam. 2001. *Chinese Migrant Networks and Cultural Change: Peru, Chicago, and Hawaii 1900–1936*. Chicago: University of Chicago Press.

Meyers, Eytan. 2004. *International Immigration Policy: A Theoretical and Comparative Analysis*. London: Palgrave Macmillan.

Mintz, Sidney W., and Richard Price. 1992. *The Birth of African-American Culture: An Anthropological Perspective*. Boston: Beacon Press.

Myers, Dowell. 2007. *Immigrants and Boomers: Forging a New Social Contract for the Future of America*. New York: Russell Sage Foundation.

Newton, Lina. 2008. *Illegal, Alien, or Immigrant: The Politics of Immigration Reform*. New York: New York University Press.

Novak, Michael. 1972. *The Rise of the Unmeltable Ethnics: Politics and Culture in the Seventies*. New York: Macmillan.

Nugent, Walter T. K. 1992. *Crossings: The Great Transatlantic Migrations, 1870–1914*. Bloomington: Indiana University Press.

Oboler, Suzanne. 1995. *Ethnic Labels, Latino Lives: Identity and the Politics of Representation in the United States*. Minneapolis: University of Minnesota Press.

Office of Population Research. 2009. Immigrant Identity Project. Available at: http://opr.princeton.edu/archive/iip (accessed March 16, 2010).

Omi, Michael, and Howard Winant. 1986. *Racial Formation in the United States*. New York: Routledge.

Ondrich, Jan, Alex Stricker, and John Yinger. 1998. "Do Real Estate Brokers Choose to Discriminate? Evidence from the 1989 Housing Discrimination Study." *Southern Economic Journal* 64(4): 880–901.

Ong, Aihwa. 1999. *Flexible Citizenship: The Cultural Logics of Transnationality*. Durham, N.C.: Duke University Press.

Packard, Jerrold M. 2002. *American Nightmare: The History of Jim Crow*. New York: St. Martin's Press.

Park, Robert E. 1928. "Human Migration and the Marginal Man." *American Journal of Sociology* 33(6): 881–93.

Park, Robert E., and Ernest W. Burgess. 1925. *The City: Suggestions for the Study of Human Nature in the Urban Environment*. Chicago: University of Chicago Press.

Park, Robert E., Herbert A. Miller, and Kenneth Thompson. 1921. *Old World Traits Transplanted*. New York: Harper.

Passel, Jeffrey. 2005. "Unauthorized Migrants: Numbers and Characteristics." Washington, D.C.: Pew Hispanic Center.

Passel, Jeffrey, and D'Vera Cohn. 2009. "A Portrait of Unauthorized Immigrants in the United States." Washington, D.C.: Pew Hispanic Center.

Perlman, Joel. 2005. *Italians Then, Mexicans Now: Immigrant Origins and Second-Generation Progress, 1890 to 2000*. New York: Russell Sage Foundation.

Pew Hispanic Center. 2007. "The 2007 National Survey of Latinos: As Illegal Immigration Issue Heats Up, Hispanics Feel a Chill." Washington, D.C.: Pew Hispanic Center.

Phillips, Julie, and Douglas S. Massey. 1999. "The New Labor Market: Immigrants and Wages After IRCA." *Demography* 36(2): 233–46.

Piore, Michael J. 1979. *Birds of Passage: Migrant Labor in Industrial Society*. New York: Cambridge University Press.

Piore, Michael J., and Peter B. Doeringer. 1976. *Internal Labor Markets and Manpower*. Boston: D. C. Health.

Portes, Alejandro. 1997. "Neoliberalism and the Sociology of Development." *Population and Development Review* 23(2): 229–59.

———. 1999. "Globalization from Below: The Rise of Transnational Communities." In *The Ends of Globalization: Bringing Society Back In*, edited by Don Kalb, Marco van der Land, and Richard Staring. Boulder, Colo.: Rowman and Littlefield.

Portes, Alejandro, and Robert L. Bach. 1985. *Latin Journey: Cuban and Mexican Immigrants in the United States*. Berkeley: University of California Press.

Portes, Alejandro, Cristina Escobar, and Alexandria Walton Radford. 2007. "Immigrant Transnational Organizations and Development: A Comparative Study." *International Migration Review* 41(1): 242–81.

Portes, Alejandro, and Kelly Hoffman. 2003. "Latin American Class Structures: Their Composition and Change During the Neoliberal Era." *Latin American Research Review* 38(1): 41–82.

Portes, Alejandro, and Robert D. Manning. 1986. "The Immigrant Enclave: Theory and Empirical Examples." In *Competitive Ethnic Relations*, edited by Susan Olzak and Joane Nagel. New York: Academic Press.

Portes, Alejandro, and Rubén G. Rumbaut. 1990. *Immigrant America: A Portrait*. Berkeley: University of California Press.

———. 2001. *Legacies: The Story of the Immigrant Second Generation*. Berkeley: University of California Press.

———. 2006. *Immigrant America: A Portrait*, 3d ed. Berkeley: University of California Press.

Portes, Alejandro, and Alex Stepick. 1993. *City on the Edge: The Transformation of Miami*. Berkeley: University of California Press.

Portes, Alejandro, and Min Zhou. 1993. "The New Second Generation: Segmented Assimilation and Its Variants." *Annals of the American Academy of Political and Social Science* 530(November): 74–96.

Pries, Ludger. 1999. *Migration and Transnational Social Spaces*. Aldershot, U.K.: Ashgate.

Quinn, Michael A. 2008. "Estimating the Impact of Migration and Remittances on Agricultural Technology." *Journal of Developing Areas* 43(1): 91–115.

Ragin, Charles. 1977. "Class, Status, and Reactive Ethnic Cleavages: The Social Bases of Political Regionalism." *American Sociological Review* 42(3): 438–50.

Rivera-Batiz, Francisco L., and Carlos Santiago. 1996. *Island Paradox: Puerto Rico in the 1990s*. New York: Russell Sage Foundation.

Roberts, Kenneth D., and Michael Morris. 2004. "Fortune, Risk, and Remittances: An Application of Option Theory to Participation in Village-Based Migration Networks." *International Migration Review* 37(4): 1252–81.

Rosaldo, Renato. 1997. "Cultural Citizenship, Inequality, and Multiculturalism." In *Latino Cultural Citizenship: Claiming Identity, Space, and Rights*, edited by William V. Flores and Rina Benmayor. Boston: Beacon Press.

Rotella, Sebastian. 1998. *Twilight on the Line: Underworlds and Politics at the U.S.-Mexico Border*. New York: Norton.

Rumbaut, Rubén G. 1991. "The Agony of Exile: A Study of the Migration and Adaptation of Indochinese Refugee Adults and Children." In *Refugee Children: Theory, Research, and Services*, edited by F. L. Ahearn and J. L. Athey. Baltimore: Johns Hopkins University Press.

———. 2008. "The Coming of the Second Generation: Immigration and Ethnic Mobility in Southern California." *Annals of the American Academy of Political and Social Science* 620(1): 196–236.

Rumbaut, Rubén G., and Alejandro Portes. 2001. *Ethnicities: Children of Immigrants in America*. Berkeley: University of California Press.

Sana, Mariano, and Douglas S. Massey. 2005. "Household Composition, Family Migration, and Community Context: Migrant Remittances in Four Countries." *Social Science Quarterly* 86(2): 509–28.

Sánchez R., Magaly. 2006. "Insecurity and Violence as a New Power Relation in Latin America." In *Chronicle of a Myth Foretold: The Washington Consensus in Latin America*, edited by Douglas S. Massey, Magaly Sánchez R., and Jere R. Behrman. Thousand Oaks, Calif.: Sage Publications.

Santa Ana, Otto. 2002. *Brown Tide Rising: Metaphors of Latinos in Contemporary American Public Discourse*. Austin: University of Texas Press.

Sassen, Sakia. 1988. *The Mobility of Labor and Capital: A Study in International Investment and Labor Flow*. Cambridge: Cambridge University Press.

———. 1991. *The Global City: New York, London, Tokyo*. Princeton, N.J.: Princeton University Press.

———. 1996. *Losing Control? Sovereignty in an Age of Globalization*. New York: Columbia University Press.

———. 2007. *A Sociology of Globalization*. New York: Norton.

Schmeidl, Susanne. 1997. "Exploring the Causes of Forced Migration: A Pooled Time-Series Analysis, 1971–1990." *Social Science Quarterly* 78(2): 284–308.

———. 2001. "Conflict and Forced Migration: A Quantitative Review." In *Global Migrants, Global Refugees: Problems and Solutions*, edited by Aristide Zolberg and Peter Benda. New York: Berghahn Books.

Schuman, Howard, Charlotte Steeh, Lawrence D. Bobo, and Maria Krysan. 1998. *Racial Attitudes in America: Trends and Interpretation*. Cambridge, Mass.: Harvard University Press.

Sherkat, Darren E. 2003. "Religious Intermarriage in the United States: Trends, Patterns, and Predictors." *Social Science Research* 33(4): 606–25.

Shughart, William, Robert Tollison, and Mwangi Kimenyi. 1986. "The Political Economy of Immigration Restrictions." *Yale Journal on Regulation* 4(fall): 79–97.

Singer, Audrey, and Douglas S. Massey. 1998. "The Social Process of Undocumented Border Crossing." *International Migration Review* 32(3): 561–92.

Smeeding, Timothy M. 2005. "Public Policy, Economic Inequality, and Poverty: The United States in Comparative Perspective." *Social Science Quarterly* 86(s1): 955–83.

Smith, Michael P., and Luis E. Guarnizo. 1998. *Transnationalism from Below*. New Brunswick, N.J.: Transaction Press.

Smith, Robert C. 1997. "Transnational Migration, Assimilation, and Political Community." In *The City and the World*, edited by Margaret Crahan and Alberto Vourvoulias-Bush. New York: Council on Foreign Relations Press.

———. 2006. *Mexican New York: Transnational Lives of New Immigrants*. Berkeley: University of California Press.

Stiglitz, Joseph E. 2003. *The Roaring Nineties: A New History of the World's Most Prosperous Decade*. New York: Norton.

Stringer, Ernest T. 1999. *Action Research*. Thousand Oaks, Calif.: Sage Publications.

Tajfel, Henri, and John C. Turner. 1979. "An Integrative Theory of Intergroup Conflict." In *The Social Psychology of Intergroup Relations*, edited by William G. Austin and Stephen Worchel. Monterey, Calif.: Brooks-Cole.

———. 1986. "The Social Identity Theory of Intergroup Behavior." In *Psychology of Intergroup Relations*, edited by Stephen Worchel and William G. Austin. Chicago: Nelson-Hall.

Telles, Edward E. 2004. *Race in Another America: The Significance of Skin Color in Brazil*. Princeton, N.J.: Princeton University Press.

Telles, Edward E., and Edward Murguia. 1990. "Phenotypic Discrimination and Income Differences Among Mexican Americans." *Social Science Quarterly* 71: 682–96.

Telles, Edward E., and Vilma Ortiz. 2008. *Generations of Exclusion: Mexican Americans, Assimilation, and Race*. New York: Russell Sage Foundation.

Thomas, William I., and Florian Znaniecki. 1918–1919. *The Polish Peasant in Europe and America*. Chicago: University of Chicago Press.

Tienda, Marta, and Vilma Ortiz. 1986. "Hispanicity and the 1980 Census." *Social Science Quarterly* 67(1): 3–20.

Tilly, Charles. 1998. *Durable Inequality*. Berkeley: University of California Press.

———. 2005. *Identities, Boundaries, and Social Ties*. New York: Paradigm Publishers.

Timmer, Ashley S., and Jeffrey G. Williamson. 1998. "Immigration Policy Prior to the 1930s: Labor Markets, Policy Interactions, and Globalization Backlash." *Population and Development Review* 24(4): 739–72.

Todaro, Michael P., and Lydia Maruszko. 1987. "Illegal Migration and U.S. Immigration Reform: A Conceptual Framework." *Population and Development Review* 13(1): 101–14.

Tolbert, Charles M., Patrick M. Horan, and E. M. Beck. 1980. "The Structure of Economic Segmentation: A Dual Economy Approach." *American Journal of Sociology* 85(5): 1095–1116.

U.S. Bureau of the Census. 2009. "Measures of Household Income Dispersion." Washington: U.S. Bureau of the Census. Available at: http://www.census

.gov/hhes/www/income/histinc/p60no231_tablea3.pdf (accessed March 17, 2010).

U.S. Bureau of Economic Analysis. 2009. "National Income Accounts." Washington: U.S. Bureau of Economic Analysis. Available at: http://www.bea.gov/national/nipaweb/SelectTable.asp?Selected=N#S5 (accessed March 17, 2010).

U.S. Bureau of Labor Statistics. 2009. "Labor Force Statistics from the Current Population Survey: Historical Unemployment Statistics: Employment Status of the Civilian Noninstitutional Population Sixteen Years and Over, Prior Years to Date." Available at: http://www.bls.gov/cps/tables.htm#History_m (accessed March 17, 2010).

U.S. Federal Reserve Board. 2009. "Household Debt Service and Financial Obligations Ratios." Washington: U.S. Federal Reserve. Available at: http://www.federalreserve.gov/releases/housedebt/default.htm (accessed March 17, 2010).

U.S. Office of Immigration Statistics. 2009. *The 2008 Yearbook of Immigration Statistics*. Washington: U.S. Office of Immigration Statistics. Available at: http://www.dhs.gov/files/statistics/publications/yearbook.shtm (accessed March 17, 2010).

Wade, Peter. 1997. *Race and Ethnicity in Latin America*. New York: Pluto Press.

Waldinger, Roger, and Michael Lichter. 2003. *How the Other Half Works: Immigration and the Social Organization of Labor*. Berkeley: University of California Press.

Wallenstein, Peter. 2002. *Tell the Court I Love My Wife: Race, Marriage, and Law— An American History*. New York: Palgrave Macmillan.

Warner, W. Lloyd, and Leo Srole. 1945. *Social Systems of American Groups*. New Haven, Conn.: Yale University Press.

Waters, Mary C. 1990. *Ethnic Options: Choosing Identities in America*. Berkeley: University of California Press.

———. 1999. *Black Identities: West Indian Immigrant Dreams and American Realities*. Cambridge, Mass.: Harvard University Press.

Waters, Mary C., and Tomás Jiménez. 2005. "Assessing Immigrant Assimilation: New Empirical and Theoretical Challenges." *Annual Review of Sociology* 31(1): 105–25.

Waters, Mary C., and Stanley Lieberson. 1988. *From Many Strands: Ethnic and Racial Groups in Contemporary America*. New York: Russell Sage Foundation.

Whitten, Norman E., and Arlene Torres. 1998. *Blackness in Latin America and the Caribbean: Social Dynamics and Cultural Transformations*. Bloomington: Indiana University Press.

Whyte, William F. 1943. *Street Corner Society: The Social Structure of an Italian Slum*. Chicago: University of Chicago Press.

Williamson, John. 1990. "What Washington Means by Policy Reform." In *Latin American Adjustment: How Much Has Happened?* edited by John Williamson. Washington, D.C.: Institute for International Economics.

———. 2000. "What Should the World Bank Think About the Washington Consensus?" *World Bank Research Observer* 15(2): 251–64.

Wilson, Kenneth, and W. Allen Martin. 1982. "Ethnic Enclaves: A Comparison of the Cuban and Black Economies in Miami." *American Journal of Sociology* 88(1): 135–60.

Winant, Howard. 2002. *The World Is a Ghetto: Race and Democracy Since World War II*. New York: Basic Books.

Wirth, Louis. 1928. *The Ghetto*. Chicago: University of Chicago Press.

———. 1938. "Urbanism as a Way of Life." *American Journal of Sociology* 44(1): 1–24.

———. 1941. "Morale and Minority Groups." *American Journal of Sociology* 47(3): 415-33.

Wyman, Mark. 1993. *Round-Trip to America: The Immigrants Return to Europe, 1880–1930*. Ithaca, N.Y.: Cornell University Press.

Yancey, William L., Eugene P. Ericksen, and Richard N. Juliani. 1976. "Emergent Ethnicity: A Review and Reformulation." *American Sociological Review* 41(3): 391–43.

Zelizer, Viviana, and Charles Tilly. 2006. "Relations and Categories." In *The Psychology of Learning and Motivation*, vol. 47, edited by Arthur Markman and Brian Ross. San Diego: Elsevier.

Zolberg, Aristide R. 2006. *A Nation by Design: Immigration Policy in the Fashioning of America*. New York: Russell Sage Foundation.

Zolberg, Aristide R., Astri Suhrke, and Sergio Aguayo. 1989. *Escape from Violence: Conflict and the Refugee Crisis in the Developing World*. New York: Oxford University Press.

= Index =